# DEVELOPMENT TODAY

# Development Today

## A New Look at U.S. Relations with the Poor Countries

EDITED BY

Robert E. Hunter and John E. Rielly

*Published in cooperation with the*
*Overseas Development Council*
*by*

PRAEGER PUBLISHERS
New York • Washington • London

PRAEGER PUBLISHERS
111 Fourth Avenue, New York, N.Y. 10003, U.S.A.
5, Cromwell Place, London SW7 2JL, England

Published in the United States of America in 1972
by Praeger Publishers, Inc.

© 1972 by Praeger Publishers, Inc.

Library of Congress Catalog Card Number: 72–80453

Printed in the United States of America

# Contents

## PART IV:  U.S. VIEWS

# Preface

What does a rich and powerful nation do about the poor countries of the world? Ten years ago, the United States had an easy answer to this question: We would provide economic and military aid, promote trade, and encourage private firms to invest. We would support the World Bank, administer our own bilateral aid programs, and launch an Alliance for Progress in Latin America to re-establish and build upon the "Good Neighbor Policy" of the 1930's. The New Frontier in 1961 had its vision for foreign policy, as well as for domestic change—and the emphasis was on vigorous prosecution of a broad-scale and optimistic program for action. Our goals for development of the poor countries were ambitious and far-reaching. We were confident of success, even though the task would take some time.

Today, we are generally far less confident—whether of our own development as a nation, or of our ability to prescribe directions for others. Some say we are a nation that has lost its way. Others, perhaps more thoughtful, say rather that we are a nation that has gained a certain maturity but in the process has lost some of the enthusiasm that could exist only in the absence of sobering experience. Be that as it may, the whole nature of U.S. relations with the outside world is now in question, and in few areas is there more doubt and uncertainty than in our relations with the poor countries, which contain more than two-thirds of the world's people.

This seems a fitting moment to look again at policies that went unquestioned for many years—and to consider the needs and

demands of a foreign policy toward poor countries in the decade
of the 1970's. The purpose of this book is to take part in the
lengthy debate that has begun about the forging of a foreign
policy toward the poor countries to replace the one that served
us for the different circumstances and perceptions of the 1960's.
We present the major issues that are up for decision—and attempt to project the major trends that will probably dominate
our view of the poor countries and our relations with them for
many years to come.

Our analysis begins with a section of four chapters to set the
scene. The first presents a general overview of the major problems for U.S. foreign policy in the decade, starting with our
central preoccupations with the arms race and security in Europe
and Asia. Second, because it is important to know where we have
been in our policies toward poor countries, there is a chapter
suggesting the criteria we need to bear in mind as we craft a new
set of attitudes and behavior. Third, because it is valuable to
know what else has been said on the subject, there is a review
of the reports and recommendations made by the many commissions and study groups that have beavered away at the different
problems of economic development and the role that rich countries should play in it. Fourth is a chapter on an area historically
of special concern to the United States—the countries of South
America and our immediate neighbor, Mexico. This chapter, the
only one in the book to look at the poor countries on a regional
basis, presents U.S. policy as a coherent whole, rather than as a
sum of disparate parts.

The next section reviews some particular problems facing
developing countries themselves—and what we should do about
them, if anything. Only by looking squarely at these problems
can we arrive at an intelligent appreciation of the specific needs
of poor countries and shape whatever foreign policy we have
toward them to be of some mutual benefit. First is the troubling
question of violence in the developing world: its causes, its
course, and the possible ways of coping with it. Next is an introduction to questions of the environment: Can the world produce
enough food to feed its people, without putting unbearable strains
on the ecosystem? What are the implications of continued popu-

lation growth or even of a rising standard of living over the years for a population stabilized at today's 3.5 billion? Concluding this section of the book is a chapter that takes a look at what poor countries themselves need to do to develop. Economic growth is no longer enough: In particular, new strategies must be devised to meet the critical problem of unemployment, which in poor countries is growing to dimensions that stagger the imaginations of Americans.

The third section contains four chapters that have a central focus of increasing concern to rich countries and poor alike: the relationships of development with international trade and with the so-called multinational corporation that operates simultaneously in many countries at once. It opens with a chapter on international trade—potentially a mighty engine of growth and development in the poor countries but also a potential threat to their ability to help themselves if adverse trade policies prevail. In view of trends towards protectionism in rich countries, and American dilemmas about the entire international trading system, this issue of trade is becoming one of special importance. The next chapter concentrates on the operations of multinational corporations and their potential conflict with development plans and policies of host governments. The third chapter is a discussion of the experience of the multinational corporation in one region of the world —namely, Latin America. The fourth analyzes one of the most disturbing U.S. domestic developments with regard to the growth of the multinational corporation: the growing conflict between preserving jobs at home and creating them in the poor countries —a conflict that has helped lead organized labor in the United States to turn away from its traditional support for free trade. In each of these four chapters, the authors have advanced their own ideas for reconciling the role of international trade and the multinational corporation with the needs of poor countries and other interested parties.

Finally, the book concludes with three chapters on the politics of foreign aid as seen from Washington. One view is from the House of Representatives, by a congressman who has been deeply involved for many years in the fight to increase U.S. contributions to economic development in the poor countries. Another view is from the Senate, by one of the leading critics of the entire U.S. effort in the Third World. His challenge is followed by a rebuttal to provide the reader with both sides in the continuing debate on a subject beset with uncertainties.

Most of these chapters were originally presented as papers at seminars held by the Overseas Development Council (ODC) in 1970–71. Taking part in the seminars were officials of the U.S. Government, senators, congressmen, business leaders, labor leaders, journalists, representatives of the academic community, and officers of nongovernmental organizations. Ideas put forward in these seminars have been further developed for the book. The editors have made no attempt to impose their own views on any of the authors. Rather, diverse and potentially conflicting points of view have been included in the hope that out of thesis and antithesis will come some synthesis of value in reshaping U.S. foreign policy toward the poor countries of the world. Responsibility for views expressed here rests entirely with the individual authors and with the editors, who have also contributed an introductory note to each chapter. If the editors and authors have added something to discussion of a wide range of issues that will command greater attention in the future, the reader may be better able to judge for himself what the United States should do about matters that affect the way in which billions of people now live and will live in years to come, as well as the way international political and economic systems will change.

The editors are indebted to each of the several authors for their patience and understanding, to our colleagues for their suggestions, and to the Overseas Development Council—particularly its President, James P. Grant—for the opportunity to prepare this book. Our thanks go also to Maria Wilhelm, formerly with the ODC; to Valeriana Kallab, ODC editor; to Lois Decker O'Neill of Praeger Publishers; and to all those tireless secretaries who coped with illegible corrections—in particular, Marilyn Weinstein.

ROBERT E. HUNTER
JOHN E. RIELLY

*Washington, D.C.*
*August, 1972*

# PART I

# THE SETTING

# 1

# The United States in the World

## ROBERT E. HUNTER

*Any view of the three-quarters of the people of the world in the poor countries and of our relationship to them must begin with a wider perspective: the U.S. role in the world as a whole during the 1970's. What do we have to do abroad, by nature of our power, past involvements, and shared responsibilities? Can we continue to ignore the poor countries or do we have to take some account of them? This chapter presents a general view of U.S. involvement in the outside world and assesses where the poor countries fit within over-all U.S. interests and policies.*

—THE EDITORS

For the past several years, the American people have been going through a period of profound doubt and questioning about the foreign policy of the United States and, more broadly, about our place in the world. The tragedy of Vietnam was the most immediate cause: After several years of enervating and unsuccessful military conflict, we found that our judgment of American interests in Southeast Asia was badly flawed, and that our military might—and our superior technology—did not serve us well in seeking a solution to political problems on the Asian mainland.

But Vietnam was not alone. We began to be aware that the "American era"—an era in which we have been the pre-eminent

3

power in the West, responsible for underpinning the security and prosperity of millions of people beyond our shores—is nearing its end. The most pressing concerns—the arms race and Western Europe's security against Soviet attack—now present fewer difficulties. Other centers of power, from the European Community to Japan, are coming to rival us in economic and commercial terms as the very success of two decades of our involvement in most of the world—the major exception being Southeast Asia— has decreased the need for others to rely upon our support. Noting all this, we turned away from our interest in the poor countries of the world; no longer necessary to a view of the cold war, they virtually ceased to command our support and concern. At the same time, we began once again to be concerned with the neglected problems of our domestic society and to shift our attention toward them and away from foreign involvements. Then, as we discovered that our ambitions far outran our ability or willingness to cope with our own problems of poverty, urban decay, and economic and racial injustice, our self-preoccupation increased further.

Despite these foreign and domestic factors, the United States cannot again choose the luxury of isolationism. Indeed, the prospects for a "generation of peace" depend very much on the continuation of an active American foreign policy. Many Americans understand this need, at least as it applies to our relations with major military powers or trading nations.

But whether or not our foreign policy of the mid-1970's will include our paying much attention to the poor countries is quite another matter. Indeed, in the order of U.S. foreign policy priorities, the world's poor and their countries today remain far down the list. Nor has the condition of the developing world yet deteriorated to the extent of becoming a dominant factor in world politics—a factor that might compel action on the part of the United States and other rich countries. We are now between a relationship with the developing countries based on morality and the cold war, and one based on cooperation and a greater interdependence among all nations. This new relationship could be a long time in coming. In addition, developing a greater sense in the United States of the potential importance of poor countries must meet a unique problem: For professionals in the field of development, relating the needs of poor countries to the over-all foreign policy of the United States is a rare experience. And for most specialists in foreign policy, used to looking at problems of U.S. relations with great powers, the impact of the United States and the world's poor on one another is also something rarely considered. Both groups, however, have legitimate viewpoints and interests, and each bears instruction by the other.

In terms of what will happen to U.S. foreign policy, it is more important to focus on the part that poor countries will play in U.S. concerns than to assess the imperatives for U.S. action as viewed by the poor. Put simply, there will be little or no response by the United States to the needs of poor countries, unless these countries are seen to fit within a broader range of U.S. interests in the world—interests that will be served better by cooperative efforts than by benign neglect.

Will the United States respond to problems of developing countries and peoples during the 1970's? To answer this question, it is necessary first to take a general look at those issues that traditionally command most interest in U.S. foreign policy.

Most important, the relationship between the United States and the Soviet Union remains the principal cornerstone of our foreign policy, and fundamental to questions of peace and war in many parts of the world. The need to manage these relations effectively means that we must continue to maintain adequate levels of sophisticated nuclear weapons, despite the conclusion of the Strategic Arms Limitation Agreement and some hopefully anticipated general reduction of defense expenditures. This need requires us to continue having military forces in readiness—such as a large, modern fleet—to offset the possible expansion of Soviet power in places like the Middle East and Mediterranean, where the withdrawal of our military or naval presence could have unfortunate consequences for us, for our Allies, and perhaps also for peace between local powers. And we will continue to focus our diplomatic efforts first upon evolving relations with the Soviet Union before concentrating on problems and possibilities elsewhere.

In additon to this central concern with the Soviet Union, the

United States will continue to be faced with challenges and called upon to exercise responsibilities in Europe, in Asia, and in the developing world.

## IN EUROPE

To begin with, the United States will remain directly involved in European security for the foreseeable future, however far the European Community proceeds toward economic and political integration during the next few years. As politics on the Continent gradually turn from confrontation to *détente*, there will be less emphasis on the role of military forces and more on ways of reordering patterns of security, but the U.S. role will be no less important. Prospects for an orderly reduction of forces on both sides in Europe are still remote; and even if negotiations do lead in that direction, or if the United States decides upon some force reductions on its own, our troop commitment to the Continent will remain significant for many years to come. Furthermore, our political role in Europe could actually increase, placing new demands on diplomatic time and attention. Having become the major power in Western Europe, it is not likely that we will abruptly abdicate power and responsibility.

So, too, there will be new difficulties in preserving and broadening the Atlantic Alliance—still our most vital interest besides deterring war with the Soviet Union itself. The Alliance is now entering a new period of tensions and difficulties, as the relative growth of European economic power requires a different distribution of political power and influence. Henceforth, the strength of the Alliance—and with it Atlantic security in the broadest sense—will depend upon the ability of the Allies to solve problems that go beyond military threats and responses. These problems include monetary and trading relations, conflicting commercial practices, competing internal economic needs of the United States and the European Community, and challenges to national sovereignty and independence posed by the multinational corporation. Here, of course, there is some scope for common action on the needs of poor countries, but how much scope is not yet clear.

In approaching these problems of Alliance relations, the United

States can no longer expect to have its own way. We must now learn to practice more of the cooperation that we preached in NATO during the years when we dominated the making of decisions within the Alliance. Indeed, creating and defining a new form of partnership with our European allies will be a major test of our ability to adjust to a new role as "first among equals," rather than as giant among pygmies.

## In Asia

In Asia, meanwhile, we will find that withdrawal from Vietnam does not decrease our interest in what happens in that part of the world. In the past, we overestimated the threat to Southeast Asia from communism as a doctrine or China as a great power and overestimated our ability to meet either threat with direct military involvement. But critical problems remain that cannot be solved simply by pursuing a limited *détente* with Peking, however important that *détente* is in itself. To some extent, U.S. military power will still be required in the search for regional stability, even though our power may be based primarily at sea, and even though Asia does not have the European tradition of a "balance of power."

The United States also faces very difficult problems in its relations with Japan. Indeed, Japan will continue to be the most important indigenous Asian power for at least the rest of the decade, whatever happens with China. But for the United States, this means influencing Japan to shape its involvement abroad in ways that will center on its economic power—with trade, investment, and aid for poor countries—rather than on an increase of military forces. And it means dealing with the Japanese as full partners, despite their limited military strength, not shunning them as we did during 1971 or permitting them to become isolated economically. Such isolation, reminiscent of the 1930's, would be the surest recipe for a rekindling of Japanese nationalism and perhaps even militarism.

There will be no profit for anyone if U.S. military withdrawal is merely matched by Japanese military build-up or, worse, by Japanese acquisition of nuclear weapons. Either event would be unsettling for all countries in Asia, whether or not they have memories of Japanese occupation during World War II. For the United States, this problem of forestalling the growth of Japanese military or nuclear power is as urgent and important as creating a new relationship with China, if not more so—whether we pursue the Peking-Washington relationship for its own sake or in an effort to bring China to bear in future competitions with the Soviet Union.

## INTERNATIONAL COOPERATION

Our future relations with Japan, like those with the European Community, will also depend on another factor of vital concern to the United States during the 1970's: our need to preserve and extend a sense of common responsibility for international problems. At the moment, these problems center on the system of international trade and monetary relations.

Clearly, the practices established at Bretton Woods in the International Monetary Fund (IMF) and at Havana in the General Agreement on Tariffs and Trade (GATT) are no longer adequate to cope with new demands of economic growth and power. This much was demonstrated by the international financial crisis of 1971, leading to the dollar's devaluation, as well as by the growth of nontariff barriers and protectionist sentiment in general.

During the next few years, therefore, we will be challenged to work out better arrangements in international finance and trade. This task will not be easy, especially in view of changed facts of economic power. And the crucial question is one of attitude rather than of substance: Will the United States continue to exercise leadership in this area? It is certainly true that we can no longer lead alone or dominate the processes of decision. Europe and Japan must do their share as well. Yet it is also true that there will be no leadership by anyone if we choose not to play a major role.

Therefore, the most important unsolved problem for U.S. foreign policy during the 1970's is how to retain the attitude of international responsibility that grew out of our involvement in World War II and postwar reconstruction. This attitude—only thirty years old—is now in serious jeopardy, first, because of developments in the United States (including the growth of economic nationalism and domestic economic problems) and, second, because we have confused our need to disengage militarily from overextended positions with an attempt to withdraw psychologically from the rest of the world. Unproductive military adventures have helped to discredit the more important sense of U.S. responsibility for what happens abroad where our vital interests truly are at stake. Yet, if this trend toward losing our attitude of international responsibility persists and grows, we will find the world a less congenial place than it is now. Most immediately, the international monetary and trading system that emerges will bring with it acrimony, more restrictive practices, and declining trade. The result will be a profound threat to the general prosperity of rich nations upon which our own prosperity and security so much depend. The United States must try to avoid this possibility at all costs.

Taken together, these problems present a rather full agenda for the United States in the world during this decade. It is an agenda that will be all the more difficult to carry out because of the trouble we will have in coming to terms with our loss of pre-eminence, with the growth of economic factors in foreign policy, and with our need generally to act in concert with other countries for our own benefit. In effect, the slogans of cooperation and equality that we uttered during the 1950's and 1960's are coming home to roost in ways that we do not find entirely to our own liking.

## What About the Poor Countries?

Given these problems, what place is there for the poor countries of the world in American concerns? Will their future be of limited importance to us now that the cold war competition for "heart and minds" has waned? Or will there be new reasons for us to take seriously the plight of peoples whose chief concern is with development—a concern that in itself hardly seems to threaten our own security or self-interest?

These are difficult questions to answer. To begin with, the rich

countries have to face the prospect that their own efforts to restructure the international monetary and trading system will require the cooperation of poor countries as well. At this time, it
is not clear how much cooperation will be needed—*i.e.*, how
much damage poor countries could do, if they so desired, to the
smooth functioning of the international economic system. There is
already some evidence that they do desire this. In Latin America,
for example, American firms are being nationalized at least in
part because of a sense within these countries that they are being
"left out" of the rising prosperity in rich countries. And in the
Middle East, oil-producing nations have banded together to change
the balance of bargaining power and to gain higher returns for
their precious natural resource. This development is now spreading to other commodities in which the rich have an interest, beginning with copper.

Furthermore, the poor countries are becoming increasingly
eager to play a more active role in deciding how the broader international system of finance and trade will work. The U.N. Conference on Trade and Development (UNCTAD) is focusing ever
more sharply on poor-country claims against the rich, including
demands that trade reform include preferential access for poor
country goods into the developed world.

Clearly, these demands will not have very much impact on
us for some time. But for how long? Even more, there are fundamental questions of international equity that go to the heart of
any restructuring of international economic cooperation. Can the
rich countries keep the fruits of their efforts almost exclusively for
themselves and still make their system work? Or must questions
of equity among the rich be broadened to include *all nations* that
are necessarily part of the total system? (See Chapter 8.) This
question becomes especially important at a time when the IMF
has created a new form of international reserves—the "Special
Drawing Rights" (SDR's)—to supplement monetary gold and the
dollar. The SDR's (often called "paper gold") represent a windfall
for countries getting them because, unlike gold and dollars, they
are provided without cost. Should they be distributed almost
exclusively among the rich as has happened so far? Or should
the poor countries get a major share as well? In strict terms

of voting power in the IMF, the answer to the latter question is no. But, if equity becomes more important as a necessary part of having a workable system at all over the long term, then there will need to be a different answer.

At the same time, there are the longer-term questions of the possible emergence of preferential trading blocs; the structure of exchange rates and the over-all growth of liquidity; the elimination (or control) of nontariff barriers; and the vexed matter of increased international competition in goods. All these questions will affect the poor countries directly, even if their role in solving them is of marginal importance in some cases. In addition, poor countries are affected by the growth of the multinational corporation—an issue that the rich countries have to face, as well. Here, it is clearly of common interest that some means be found both for poor countries to benefit more from the activities of the multinational corporation within their borders (a possibility that is by no means assured) and for the corporations to find a welcome for their investment.

## THREATS TO THE ENVIRONMENT

This search for areas of international cooperation extends also to another subject of concern about growing worldwide interdependence—namely, threats to the environment. (See Chapter 6.) So far, the focus has been on damage caused by processes of industrialization, centered primarily in rich countries. Yet, at some point, it is clear that development and industrialization in poor countries will also have a substantial and growing effect.

It will profit the rich countries little, for example, if they eliminate use of DDT, while its use expands in countries that are tied together with us in the same ecosystem. And, of course—even beyond the problems of retarding environmental damage—there will be growing competition between rich and poor countries for the raw materials that make industrial advance and prosperity possible. At some point, therefore, some division of resources—and some agreement on environmental damage that the world can tolerate—will need to be worked out, if any country, rich or poor, is to be able to plan on achieving or maintaining a high level of prosperity. This problem is complicated by the worldwide growth of population, centered primarily in poor countries but threatening both rich and poor.

Worse still is the obvious fact that a world of even today's population, and using current technology, could not support all nations in the style of living found in the United States, Europe, and Japan. The massive worldwide economic growth that would create this pressure on the ecosystem and supply of raw materials is a long way off—but its prospect does raise profound questions about the interrelation of development in all countries. And some day these questions must be answered by the rich and the poor countries in common, even if that time is not now.

## PROBLEMS FOR U.S. SECURITY

For the rich countries, therefore, some cooperation by the poor will eventually be required if we are to solve our own domestic problems, meet both short-run needs like international narcotics control and longer-run needs to protect the environment, and be free to trade and invest abroad—indeed, to have a system of international trade and finance that works effectively. Moreover, threats may emanate from the poor countries to our own security, as it is traditionally conceived.

It is now clear that a cold war rationale for interest in poor countries (that is, to keep them from "going Communist") is no longer valid—if it ever was. But that does not mean that there will be *no* threats to our security emerging from the Third World. Of course, neither Latin America nor Africa should present security problems for us during this decade, unless circumstances change radically, because of events in Southern Africa or (most unlikely) because of outside involvement by Russia or China in Latin America. (See Chapter 4.)

But in other parts of the Third World there is less certainty. For example, the stability of the Indian subcontinent is of some importance to the United States. How important is in some doubt: There will be no *direct* threat posed to the United States from any of the states in that region, or from the Indian Ocean. Yet *indirectly* we can be less confident. In particular, we should take a greater interest in the sheer survival of India, as the most important country in the region, the world's second largest state, and the largest working democracy. India's importance has been increased by the breakup of Pakistan and the emergence of Bangladesh—a situation that is becoming a factor in the triangular relations among the United States, the Soviet Union, and China. How these relationships work themselves out in the Indian subcontinent could have implications for what happens to them elsewhere, although where and how is not at all clear.

Whatever the uncertainties of the subcontinent's future, the United States does have an opportunity—if only one of helping to prevent future, unspecified trouble. And that means taking a greater part in the development of the region, and particularly of India. Indeed, development is the key to survival here. Rich-country support for economic development may be the best way of helping the subcontinent resist being sucked too deeply into the maelstrom of great power rivalries. Here, for a relatively minor investment of effort and resources, we could help to prevent the emergence of conditions and trends that would cause us greater difficulties in the future.

Farther east, in Southeast and East Asia, the importance of our efforts is even more apparent and related to our own security. As indicated above, the growth of its economic power will lead Japan to deep involvement in the political and economic life of a dozen countries in the region. Yet, because of memories of Japanese occupation—as well as fears of being dominated economically—there is a strong need for the presence of some other country to help soften the impact of Japan. For the present, this means the United States, as part of our continuing interest in seeing as little additional trouble as possible develop in East and Southeast Asia during the next few years. And, of course, we have a strong commercial interest in preventing the emergence of a "Japanese lake."

Here, too, the tools for acting are economic ones and relate directly to the development of poor countries in the region. Whether with trade, aid, or investment—or with some combination of all three—the United States has both an opportunity and a need to be involved in the poor countries of the region as a means of helping to provide whatever political and economic stability is possible and to work out a joint relationship with Japan in the area. Again, economic instruments can be a relatively inexpensive way of pursuing interests that are at least partly oriented to our own long-range security.

## THE MIDDLE EAST

Finally, the United States will continue to have interests in the Middle East, whether to preserve Israel for its own sake, to help ensure the flow of oil to Western Europe and Japan, or to prevent the dominance of the area by the Soviet Union. And here, too, at least one instrument of policy lies in development. Of course, the Arab-Israeli conflict cannot be solved by development assistance. If such assistance were directly linked with peace, it would be rejected out of hand by all Arab states as a Western trick. And even if it were pursued indirectly (as it is through the World Bank, for example), development would have little impact on this intractable conflict.

In the very long run, however, development could be an important adjunct to other efforts, as part of the eventual mitigation of a conflict based, in part, upon the economic disparities between Israel and its Arab neighbors as well as on the difficulties most Arab countries face in trying to develop economically.

With regard to oil and general U.S. relations with Arab states and Iran, development is also important. In the oil-rich states, it is not so much a matter of resources as it is of technical assistance. Even more, it is a matter of showing that the United States takes the economic needs of local countries seriously— and that it is prepared to work amicably with them as the terms of economic power in oil shift toward the producers.

Obviously, in the interests of peace, the United States would benefit from trying to shift its competition for influence with the Soviet Union from the military to the economic realm. Doing this may not be possible now. But, over time, the more that can be done to play down military involvements of the outside powers —and play up their commercial and development roles—the less likely it is that that part of the world will continue causing significant security problems for concerned outside states.

## VIOLENCE IN THE THIRD WORLD

United States security interests in the developing countries are hardly as compelling as the old cold war arguments made them out to be. Yet, especially in view of the relatively small amount of resources that would be required in the form of economic tools of foreign policy to protect and advance them, these security interests are not to be dismissed lightly. Even more important is a related problem: the growth and spread of violence in the developing world. (See Chapter 5.)

Again, it is difficult to predict just what connection violence in poor countries might have with our own direct security. The civil war in Nigeria-Biafra, for example, meant little to the security of the United States, even though it was a human tragedy ranking with the worst in this century. Of course, there are some problems that must be borne in mind: They begin with personal security for our diplomatic corps and for travelers and proceed to commercial security for trade and investment. There is also a continuing moral concern in the United States to see inevitable change take place with as little violence as possible. Whether this concern will strongly affect American foreign policy is another question. We have already seen the tragic consequences of our trying to prevent violent change in Southeast Asia. Yet, it is likely that we will not be indifferent, as a people, to suffering in places like East Pakistan, even if we do little about it.

How much we could do about it is a matter for debate. Indeed, in many cases, processes of development can promote violence instead of retarding it, at least at first, especially where certain groups benefit to the exclusion of others. Yet, it may be that development assistance will help countries get through the difficult periods of instability that usually occur between abject poverty and reasonable success of development. This means helping to get at some direct causes of violence, including pressures of overpopulation, urban growth and decay, a lack of social justice, and widespread unemployment. And the very fact that these problems are so massive, and that efforts to combat them are so long-range in their effects, does not mean that the problems themselves should be left to find their own violent "solutions."

More broadly, the issue is whether the present system of international relations will work. Like the system of international trade and finance, it is not clear that there can be a fractured political system—with rich countries more or less ordering their relations with one another without conflict, and with poor countries torn apart internally, warring with one another, or posing what limited economic and strategic threats they can to the developed world. Again, can the rich countries really isolate themselves from the products of violence taking place elsewhere? Or will they inevitably be affected, perhaps in ways that are not yet clear? Or, to put it another way, is there a broad enough sense of an international political system to lead rich countries to take part in development, even though development is no sure way to decrease the incidence of violence in the Third World? There may be a simple case for trying, especially with economic instruments, even if there is no guarantee of results.

The United States should also view the problem as another example of maintaining a general sense of responsibility for what happens in the outside world. At the simplest level, taking part in development assistance has become part of the system of cooperation among the rich countries, and they have managed to agree on formulas for sharing the burden of foreign aid. Our defaulting on these agreements—which have implications for trade and investment as well—must have some impact on other forms of international cooperation among the rich. And, at a higher level, the interdependence of all nations in a single political system cannot be neglected.

We in the United States need to fit our relations with poor countries into a larger moral view of the world and our place in it. Indifference to the problems of poor countries may be sanctioned by hard-headed analyses of what they could do to us and what we want from them. Yet, we still have to consider what kind of world it is in which we want to live, and what we, as citizens of the richest country on earth, feel is our responsibility to people generally. Of course, foreign policy cannot be based on a moral view alone—especially since, as will be noted below, it is not always clear that acts we consider "moral" are seen as such by others. Yet this dimension of foreign policy should not be neglected, even if it does not fit conventional views of power politics.

## THE NIXON DOCTRINE

These questions are of some importance to the United States because of what we are actually doing. Today, our relations with the developing world are dominated by the so-called Nixon Doctrine, a loose collection of attitudes and methods about our foreign policy that are designed to tide us over during the necessary period of debate and new decision. The chief cornerstone of this doctrine provides for a reduced U.S. involvement in many countries of the world—what is called a "low profile." This should mean less emphasis on American military deployments overseas (although, paradoxically, the U.S. military budget is going up). With regard to the poor countries, low profile means a reduction in the size of U.S. bilateral aid missions maintained abroad. And it means shifting the emphasis in foreign aid from bilateral administration to a reliance upon international organizations. In addition, the Nixon Doctrine places considerable reliance on U.S. cooperation with other developed countries, and on recognizing their greatly increased capabilities, rather than on our taking independent initiatives. And there is a principle of "self-help" whereby poor countries are expected to bear most of the responsibility for their own development.

These are worthy objectives, in theory. In practice, however, the Nixon Doctrine also appears to mean placing little emphasis on maintaining—let alone increasing—today's volume of resources transferred to poor countries. Furthermore, in practice the doctrine currently gives *military* assistance precedence over *economic* assistance, in programs reminiscent of those that served us so inadequately during the 1950's. This precedence has been set despite the growing importance of economic instruments throughout our foreign policy and their potential for decreasing our tendency to react hastily to security problems with military "solutions." Yet awareness of this growing importance of economic factors and tools so far has not penetrated deeply within the U.S. Government, where emphasis is still placed on more traditional patterns of military security as the cornerstone of foreign policy.

It is doubtful, therefore, that the Nixon Doctrine, as currently practiced, can provide a satisfactory basis for our relations with poor countries. The simple reason is that the primary threats that those countries face—and that face us indirectly, as outlined above—do not lie in the traditional concept of "security" that underlies the Nixon Doctrine. Rather, both the problems and the promise lie in the area of development—either its failures or the successes that could emerge from it. At the very least, therefore, any successor to the Nixon Doctrine (as it applies to the poor countries) needs to be based on the broad view of U.S. interests in them that is discussed here and on the use of economic instruments. Thus questions of means and ends in our relations with poor countries are inseparable.

## OPPOSITION TO DEVELOPMENT ASSISTANCE

The issue of means is also central to the way in which American involvement in many poor countries is viewed. We are finding that what we have done in the past is open to new criticisms—sometimes by leaders in Congress (see chapters 12 and 13) or other domestic critics of U.S. policy, sometimes by poor-country governments, and sometimes by people in the poor countries who are excluded from power. Among other things, there is growing concern that the aid relationship (whether military or economic) neither gets at problems of international equity nor contributes to goals of social justice within the poor countries themselves. This concern is also applied to trade and investment between rich countries and poor. There are, of course, examples of countries that are achieving social justice—such as India. Yet the point remains: The methods of rich-country involvement in the developing world are becoming increasingly suspect. This, too, is a problem with a moral dimension. Moreover, excessive preoccupation with economic growth is coming under attack. Growth itself has done little to get at basic problems of income distribution and social justice; economic growth alone does not guarantee that there will be an attack on fundamental problems of social and economic development; the United States is an example of this sad fact.

Within many poor countries, there is increasing fear of apparent neo-imperialist aspects of some outside assistance, particularly where it has not contributed to social goals that are gaining in importance and popularity. At the same time, in the United States disillusionment with the results of development assistance—however these results are defined—is leading to a dwindling in support for the very idea. This trend is evident on the political Right in America, where there has always been opposition to "give-away" programs for the developing world. Today, it is also evident among liberals, who are concerned either that resources should be spent solving problems at home rather than permitted to go abroad, or that the aid relationship contains inherent dilemmas, such as the growing gap between rich and poor as a part of society is left out of the modernization process. Finally, there is growing opposition from the Left, from people who point to the inadequacies and contradictions in many of our past policies and attitudes and argue, on the basis of these examples, that we should cease foreign aid altogether—economic or military.

The Nixon Doctrine, therefore, is at best a stop-gap measure that will have to be changed continuously as conditions change during the 1970's. This will be true whether we decide to take a major part in helping poor countries work on their problems of development or retreat further into our own preoccupations and problems. Doing nothing is also a policy that carries major implications with it.

## THE CHALLENGE

At present, we have both a challenge and an opportunity. The challenge is to restructure U.S. foreign policy toward many areas of the world, including the poor countries, in order to take into account our changing interests and to make use of the best means available to accomplish our objectives. If so, both we and they will benefit. But this is simple to say and difficult to work out. We also have an opportunity to use today's widespread uncertainty about our place in the world as a basis for reopening old questions and asking new ones about the kind of world in which we want to live, and what we have to do to bring it about. With regard to the poor countries, this means taking a new look at trade, aid, investment, and military policies, as well as at issues of growing worldwide interdependence, international equity, and the over-all relationship of rich countries to poor.

The generally dwindling support for foreign aid coupled with the Senate's warning, temporary defeat of bilateral aid legislation on October 29, 1971, could prove a blessing in diguise by forcing the questions out in the open. But there are some big "if's" here —*if* we are willing to bring hard thought to bear upon both the poor countries and our relations to them; *if* we can develop the political will to act upon what we learn and decide. Of course, all foreign policy is chiefly an aggregation of discrete problems that have to be met from day to day, and discrete acts designed to meet these problems. Nonetheless, some broader framework is useful. There is also a need for debate and understanding about specific issues, especially since the outside world will not wait for us to put our own house in order. The sooner the debate begins, the more likely we are to have a foreign policy toward the poor countries that can meet some of their needs— and ours.

# 2

# Foreign Aid:
# For What and for Whom?

## SAMUEL P. HUNTINGTON

*The debate on development assistance that is taking place in the United States suffers most often from a lack of clarity and precision—not surprisingly, in view of the different foreign aid programs that have proliferated to serve many ends, justified by many and changing rationales. In this essay, Professor Huntington seeks to untangle some of the complex threads of argument and presents an analysis of U.S. relations with developing countries that relates directly to our foreign-policy interests. The first portion surveys the past and questions the rationale that has been advanced for aid in relation to economic development. The latter part analyzes the various goals that aid may serve and offers a new approach for understanding and organizing aid programs to make them serve these goals.—*THE EDITORS

"Foreign Aid: Billions in Search of a Good Reason" was the title of a 1963 *Fortune* article by Charles J. V. Murphy. Seven years later, the billions may be fewer in number, but the search for the good reason is all the more intense. The continued quest

This chapter is adopted from *Foreign Policy*, Winter, 1970–71, and Spring, 1971. Reprinted by permission.

for a rationale for foreign aid is one of its distinguishing characteristics as an area of public policy. It is a quest that has been pursued through countless commissions, study groups, conferences, reports, and memoranda. President Nixon told the most recent Presidential task force that its primary mission was to come up with a new concept or purpose for foreign aid.

One would expect the *opponents* of foreign aid to ask: "What's its rationale?" Instead, it is those most fervently committed to foreign aid who most often raise the question. Here is a marked reversal of the usual pattern. For, in other areas of public policy, the purposes of a program are fairly clear: There is, for instance, obvious good reason to improve the economic well-being of the urban Negro; the problem is to come up with the right program or programs—equal job opportunity, job training, black capitalism, welfare—to achieve that goal. Similarly, there are obvious reasons why the United States conducts intelligence activities, engages in overseas public information and propaganda, and maintains a nuclear retaliatory force and a Marine Corps. One may or may not agree with the reasons for engaging in these activities, but at least there is little doubt as to what those reasons are.

With respect to foreign aid, however, many people seem to feel that it is a good thing, but they cannot call up convincing reasons why it is a good thing. It is a tribute to the emotional dedication and loyalty of the supporters of foreign aid that it has staggered along as well as it has during the past few years. Both the strength and the weakness of foreign aid stem from the fact that its supporters remain firmly committed to it, despite their difficulties in finding a rationale. To the dedicated, foreign aid is a good in itself—and the more of it the better. The criterion of progress and of the wisdom of Congress as a legislative body is the size of the annual foreign aid appropriation.

Supporters of foreign aid agree that its rationale is inadequate. They do not, however, draw the obvious conclusion: namely, that if its rationale is inadequate, foreign aid should be reduced. Instead of scaling down the program, they seek to beef up the rationale. At the same time, they castigate Congress for taking the inadequate rationale at its face value. The development of the rationale becomes the means of preserving and expanding a program good in itself, whatever the weakness of the arguments for it. The psychology of the foreign-aid devotee often bears a striking resemblance to that of the battleship admiral or bomber general who views American ships and airplanes as good in themselves quite apart from any national purposes they might serve.

Those who do not belong to the select, articulate corps of aid's true believers may look at the program slightly differently. To what extent is foreign aid something good in itself? If we had not inherited a foreign-aid program from the past, would there be any clear national need to create one? If there were such a need, would we create a program resembling the current one?

The only way to deal with these questions is to reverse the implicit means-end relationship of aid's true believers. Foreign aid involves the concessional transfer of resources—capital, commodities, expertise—from the United States to other countries. Foreign aid is, in some sense, the foreign counterpart of federal grants-in-aid to the states. These latter programs may be devoted to a variety of purposes—from road-building to public housing to welfare to education. In the domestic context, grants-in-aid are recognized as simply one means of achieving a number of goals. Aid is a means that can serve a variety of ends, most of which can also be served by other means. The scope and nature of U.S. foreign aid presumably should reflect (1) the relative importance of the ends to be served by foreign aid in comparison with other goals and (2) the relative effectiveness of foreign aid as a means to achieve those ends in comparison with other means.

In analyzing the purposes to which foreign aid may be relevant in the 1970's, it will be desirable (1) to reconsider and to restate the U.S. interest in the principal purpose to which foreign aid has been devoted in the 1960's—*i.e.,* the economic development of poor countries;* (2) to disentangle from one another this and other purposes served by foreign aid and to realign programs and organizations in terms of major purposes; and (3) to identify any new purposes of high priority for the United States that might be promoted by some form of foreign aid.

* Those who prefer bureaucratese should think "LDC," or "less developed country," when they read "poor country" in this essay.—S.P.H.

## TRENDS IN THE 1960'S

Sensitivity to the problems of economic development mani-
fested itself in the higher echelons of the U.S. Government in the
late 1950's. In 1961, the Foreign Assistance Act replaced the old
Mutual Security Act as the legislative basis for aid programs. The
new Act declared that emphasis should be given to long-range
assistance to promote economic and social development. Two
years later, Congress warned that such assistance should not be
diverted to "short term emergency purposes . . . or any other
purpose not essential to the long range economic development of
recipient countries." Economic development thus became the
prime rationale for American economic-assistance programs. There
was, as Edward S. Mason observed in a speech delivered at Middlebury College in 1966, "a growing conviction that the primary
objective of aid was the promotion of economic development." In
the years after 1961, this conviction became an increasingly accepted assumption for most people actively concerned with the
aid program. Indeed, "aid" and "development" came to be so
closely linked as to be almost interchangeable.*

The growing emphasis on economic development of poor countries as the purpose of U.S. foreign aid more or less coincided with
two other trends in the quantity and quality of U.S. foreign assistance. The amount of U.S. economic assistance moved sharply
upward in the very early 1960's, when the economic development
rationale was new, peaked in the mid-1960's (somewhere between
1963 and 1966, depending on what statistics are used), and then
declined slowly but regularly to the end of the decade. Perhaps
more significantly, congressional appropriations for the central
economic-development assistance program in the Agency for International Development (AID) declined much more sharply. At

* Note the changing styles in the names of Presidential study groups
concerned with foreign aid. The Clay Committee (1963) was officially
"The Committee to Strengthen the Security of the Free World." In 1968,
however, the Perkins Committee was the "President's General Advisory
Committee on Foreign Assistance Programs," and, by 1969, the transition
was complete with the Peterson "Presidential Task Force on International
Development."

the same time that there was such over-all decline in the quantity of economic development assistance, there was also a marked deterioration in what is generally called the quality of such assistance. In successive annual authorization and appropriation acts, Congress wrote in more and more restrictions as to how, where, and for what aid could be used. The restrictions ranged from those designed to prohibit aid to certain countries (*e.g.*, those who trade with Cuba, who fail to prevent mob destruction of U.S. property, who expropriate U.S. property, or who are delinquent in debt repayments) to those that were designed to safeguard the U.S. balance of payments and provide minimum interest rates for U.S. loans, to those that benefit specific U.S. industries. The 1969 Foreign Assistance Act took eighty-four pages to spell out restrictions that had accumulated over the years in response to the special-interest demands of legislators and lobbies. There were, at that point, some sixty-five individual restrictions on the checklist for the making of loans. "It is probably not an overstatement to suggest," one AID report put it, "that perhaps as much manpower, talent, and energy are spent in ensuring compliance with specifically imposed restrictions as is spent in the execution of programs and projects."

The declining level of aid since the mid-1960's and the multiplying restrictions on aid since the early 1960's suggest that economic development as a purpose lacked a certain appeal among key policy-making groups, most notably in Congress. This apparent conclusion is not surprising. U.S. aid programs in the 1940's and early 1950's were devoted largely to the reconstruction and recovery of an area of the world (Western Europe) whose independence, defensibility, and prosperity were obviously of crucial importance to the United States. The Mutual Security programs of the later 1950's were devoted largely to strengthening "forward defense" countries, like Korea, Taiwan, Iran, Turkey, and Greece, whose security appeared to be essential to that of the United States, and who appeared to be threatened by Soviet or Chinese expansion. Compared to the national interest in European recovery and in containing communism, the U.S. interest in the general economic development of poor foreign countries could easily seem somewhat remote. If a country is threatened by 50,000 Communist troops, the rationale for U.S. economic and military aid to that country is fairly clear. If a country is threatened by a 3 per cent rate of economic growth, the implications for American national interests are not quite so obvious, to put it mildly. In addition, so long as the rationale for aid is primarily in terms of *economic* benefits to a *foreign* country, it is hard to defend the aid program against restrictions and conditions designed to provide economic benefits for the United States (*e.g.,* tying aid, shipping restrictions, the Hickenlooper Amendment). Why, indeed, should we put economic advantages for other countries ahead of the protection of seemingly legitimate U.S. economic interests?

## FOREIGN AID WITHOUT FOREIGN POLICY: THE PURIST RATIONALE

The general weakening of U.S. support for economic assistance reflected, in part, the belief that the economic development of poor foreign countries was not and could not be a very high-priority goal for the United States. It also, in part, reflected the negative impact of one type of rationale advanced in support of developmental aid. An argument often eloquently made was that economic development should itself be a high-priority goal of U.S. foreign policy, but that economic development assistance should not reflect U.S. foreign policy. Thus, economic development became an end in itself, just as, at a lower level of abstraction, foreign aid was considered an end in itself. The organizational implication of this "purist" rationale was that the administration of developmental assistance should have an autonomous status (in an independent bank or institute) divorced from the State Department. The argument undoubtedly reassured aid supporters of the morality and importance of their cause at the same time that it weakened that cause. Three aspects of this approach are worth noting.

First, the purist rationale emphasized the general relation between the developed and the underdeveloped world, stressing the extent to which development is an extraordinarily long-term process. It abstracted the whole question of development from the particular interests that the United States may have in particular countries for particular periods of time. The case for aid was typically phrased in terms of foreign needs rather than U.S. purposes. As portrayed by the supporters of aid, the needs of the poor countries were so great that anything the United States might do would make little difference. The 1969 Pearson Commission report, *Partners in Development*, begins by saying, "The widening gap between the developed and developing countries has become a central issue of our time." According to the analysis made by Richard Jolly in a paper prepared for the Columbia University Conference on International Economic Development, February, 1970, even if the Pearson Commission recommendations were implemented, however, the gap would "continue to increase to three or four times its present size by the end of the century."

If so, then the case for not bothering to do anything becomes overpowering. Ambassador Edward Korry, in the *New York Times*, March 8, 1970, put it neatly: "By not differentiating our development objectives in accordance with realities, we appear to be engaged in developing virtually the entire less-developed world. An undertaking of that kind is simply not credible."

Not only has the purist rationale typically been formulated in universal terms so far as geography is concerned, it also has been formulated in indefinite terms so far as time is concerned. Indeed, the promoters of aid have gone out of their way to emphasize that development is a long-term process—which, to be sure, it is. But a government aid program needs to be directed to specific objectives that can be achieved in particular periods of time. The indefinite, universal quality that adheres to the goal of economic development contrasts with the limited, specific character of the most successful U.S. aid effort. The Marshall Plan was (1) directed to specific and well-defined goals, (2) limited to a geographical area of vital concern to the United States, and (3) designed for a limited period of time. U.S. efforts to promote economic development in Third World countries have lacked all three of these characteristics. As a result, those efforts appear to have little relation to U.S. foreign-policy purposes.

A second key proposition in the purist rationale is that economic-development assistance should, as one memorandum put it, "be treated as separate and independent from the shorter-term political and economic goals which both donors and recipients pursue as a matter of immediate national advantage." Indeed, if any cliché is regularly invoked in almost every report and analysis of aid, it is this: Economic development programs must be separated from "short-term political objectives." Nothing could better illustrate the self-defeating character of the purist rationale. As anyone having even a marginal familiarity with government knows, "short-term political objectives" are precisely the thing to which political leaders devote most of their time. By proclaiming that economic development is divorced from "short-term political goals," the aid enthusiasts are saying that it should be divorced from the main concerns of political leaders. It is a little peculiar to try to mobilize the support of politicians for something by arguing that it has no relevance to politics. In economic-development assistance, as elsewhere, those who wish to be pure in spirit are usually doomed to be poor in pocket.

In fact, of course, economic-development assistance can be very relevant to politics, just as aid that is given for political purposes has been very relevant to economic development. By stressing again and again that economic development must be pursued as an end in itself, apart from all other goals, the proponents of economic development limit the potential supporters of aid. The proponents of aid in the United States might well have learned something from those other countries that have had relatively high or increasing aid levels in recent years. French official economic assistance has consistently been 50 to almost 100 per cent higher than U.S. assistance as a ratio of gross national product (GNP). One reason for this may well be that French aid has had the very consciously defined political purpose of maintaining French influence in its former colonies, and that it has been almost exclusively concentrated in those former colonies. Such purposes make sense to chief executives and legislatures. In a somewhat similar fashion, the rapidly increasing Japanese aid has been directly tied to the efforts of Tokyo to extend Japanese commerce and investments in Asia. It seems highly unlikely that the foreign-aid administrators of France, Japan, or any other country would ever repeat the statement of the U.S. AID administrator who declared it absolutely false that "the foreign aid program can and should win friends for the United States and increase our bargaining power in the United Nations and other international forums." If supporters of economic development want the United States to spend the same proportion of its GNP on aid that France does, they might well forgo their ideological purity and graciously endorse aid being used for purposes similar to those that French aid serves.

The third and most extreme version of the purist rationale argues not only that economic development should be pursued independently of political goals, but that economic development is the only legitimate goal of economic assistance. The use of economic assistance for other purposes is either immoral or ineffective. "If the objective of economic assistance is to have an immediate influence on the political behavior of aid-receiving countries," in Professor Mason's words at Middlebury, "we had better get out of the aid business now." In practice, however, the United States has frequently given economic assistance to achieve noneconomic objectives, and with results that have been at least as relatively successful as its efforts to promote economic development. This assistance has generally tended to take three forms:

1. The granting of economic assistance to a friendly government to help it consolidate its position after initially coming to power (*e.g.*, Brazil, 1964), to help it survive a temporary period of financial crisis (Iran, 1961), or to help it win an election against somebody we would rather not see in power (Chile, 1964). In these cases, there is mutuality of interest between the government of the country and the U.S. Government.

2. The granting of economic assistance to a government that may or may not be very friendly to the United States in return for that government's giving us something we want, such as base rights, a U.N. vote, troops in Vietnam, the rejection of aid from another country. In this case, there is a reciprocity of interest between the government of the United States and the other government; the relationship depends simply on each feeling that it has gotten what it wanted from the bargain.

3. The denying of economic assistance to governments that do things we do not like or refuse to do things we want done. Often, the United States has, for instance, suspended assistance to governments that have come to power through *coups d'état* until such governments have scheduled elections. At other times, the United States has attempted to use the threat of suspending assistance to induce governments to settle controversies or refrain from other political acts.

The desirability of economic assistance for political purposes in situations (1) and (2) depends on how one rates the purpose to be achieved and the price that is paid to achieve it. Such aid is almost always effective. Conversely, efforts to induce other governments to change their behavior by threatening to deny them aid—situation (3)—are often not effective. Psychologically and politically, it is easier for another government to accept aid in return for performing some service to the United States than it is for that government to allow itself to be "coerced" into doing something by the threat that the United States will take away aid.

The exchange of economic assistance for political benefits between the United States and poor governments during the past decade has rested on the fact that the U.S. Government has had hard currency, which other governments lacked and wanted, while poor governments have had other things (*e.g.*, strategic locations) that the U.S. Government lacked and wanted. In the future, as the United States increasingly assumes a "low posture" in many parts of the world, presumably there will be fewer other things that the U.S. Government would consider worth a lot of economic assistance. To the extent that other governments also come to place less value on economic assistance, they will, presumably, be less willing to perform services for the United States in exchange for such assistance. Thus, the use of economic assistance purely for "short-term political objectives" is likely to decrease. Given the difference in resources and goals among governments, however, such assistance will appropriately and naturally continue to exist in one form or another, and it does not serve any useful purpose to argue that there is something inherently illegitimate about it.

## Pick a Number, Any Dramatic Number

The purist rationale also divorces economic-development assistance from foreign policy by defining the goal as a level of foreign aid equal to some percentage, usually 1 per cent (for all resource flows) or .7 per cent (for official aid) of GNP. It is difficult to conceive of a more telling admission of bankruptcy of purpose than the enthusiasm with which the proponents of economic development have espoused this target. Such a figure is, of course, completely unrelated to the differing and changing interests and purposes of the aid donors; it is almost equally unrelated to the differing and changing requirements of the aid-receivers. The amount of aid that poor countries could effectively use for development has to be worked out on a country-by-country basis. Their total needs might or might not be more than 1 per cent of the GNP of the developed countries. Estimates of the probable needs of the poor countries in 1973, for instance, range from a low of $13 billion to a high of $22 billion. The latter figure is somewhat more than 1 per cent of the probable GNP of the developed countries in 1973; the former is about two-thirds of 1 per cent, or just about the level of U.S. aid in 1968. In addition, of course, as noted by the Task Force on International Development in its 1970 report, *U.S. Foreign Assistance in the 1970's: A New Approach*, a target such as this "puts the emphasis on the wrong side of the partnership" for yet another reason: A decrease in the GNP of the rich countries could well coincide with an increase in the development-assistance needs of the poor countries.

There is something basically wrong with a program when its supporters define its goals in terms of how much should be spent on it rather than what should be achieved by it. The establishment of percentage goals reflects the view that foreign aid is a good in itself: Pick a nice round figure, which can be easily dramatized, is substantially higher than existing levels, but is not entirely beyond the range of the economically and politically feasible, and make it your target! In the absence of a clear relationship between foreign-aid spending and some vital national purpose, however, the percentage goal becomes highly unreal. Expenditures are justified only insofar as they serve some important objective, and the national interest in them will presumably change over time. Thus, it is not surprising that at one time some countries (Japan, Germany) may find it in their interest to increase their aid efforts significantly, while another country (the United States) may find it in its interest to cut back on aid because it is moving into a "low posture" in foreign affairs and giving increased attention to domestic needs. The foreign-aid programs of different countries are designed to serve different ends. It makes little sense to add together apples and oranges to produce international comparisons of aid levels when the resulting totals obscure crucial differences in content, quality, scope, and purpose.

A percentage can be a target. It is not a purpose. The aid proponents' enthusiasm for a fixed level of aid underlines a desire to escape from politics and a reluctance to develop a rationale relating aid and development to other U.S. foreign-policy goals. Precisely such a statement of relationships is what is required today.

## ECONOMIC DEVELOPMENT AND FOREIGN POLICY: U.S. INTERESTS

A more conscious effort than has been made in the past is needed to place economic development in the over-all context of U.S. foreign policy. Although many arguments and analyses have been devoted to this purpose, and much of what has been said has been quite persuasive, some of it has been rather extravagant in the claims made for a U.S. interest in economic development. What follows in this section is an effort to take a cold, hard look at these claims and come up with an honest answer to the question: To what extent is the promotion of the economic development of poor foreign countries a desirable and important goal for U.S. foreign policy?

America's concern with the economic development of poor foreign countries can presumably be analyzed in terms of moral obligation and national interest.

The moral obligation is clearly that of the rich to be concerned with alleviating the poverty of the poor. In the words of the Pearson Commission, "The simplest answer to the question (Why aid?) is the moral one: that it is only right for those who have to share with those who have not." This argument is persuasive and unchallengeable. The problem is that, in its simple form, it does not reach very far. Those who can help have the obvious responsibility to help eliminate the obvious evils of hunger, disease, illiteracy, inadequate housing. The moral obligation to attack such evils furnishes an effective justification for many elements of U.S. foreign aid, including the Peace Corps, food programs, relief programs, health programs, and, perhaps, population control. The justification for long-term and, usually, larger projects and programs oriented more specifically toward economic development is, however, more tenuous. The moral obligation to feed the hungry in India is fairly obvious. The moral obligation to ensure that India's economy grows at 6 per cent per annum is considerably less obvious.

The moral obligation is further weakened by the nature of the public aid-giving process, which, typically, involves the transfer of resources or credit from one government to another. The moral obligation, however, is to help the poor people of poor countries, not the governments of poor countries. Yet, aid given to the government of a poor country may well yield little direct or indirect benefit to the poor people in that country. This is the reason that private relief programs and public programs, such as the Peace Corps, which can show direct results in aid-to-people, advance greater moral claim for support than those that involve aid processed from the "power structure" and upper- or middle-class bureaucracy of one country to comparable institutions in another country.

The moral argument is thus persuasive when it comes to providing minimum economic well-being for individuals, but much less so when it comes to promoting optimal economic growth of societies. Indeed, in some sense, the goal of promoting economic development may conflict with assumptions underlying the case for moral concern. It is, for instance, generally agreed that aid for economic development should be given primarily on the basis of past or prospective economic performance. Donors should help those who help themselves. The moral case for aid, on the other hand, normally is made in terms of need, not performance, which means helping those who are not able to help themselves.*

What, then, is the U.S. national interest in promoting economic development in the Third World? Three arguments—economic, security, political—are usually advanced. First, economically developed countries are better markets for U.S. goods and better locations for U.S. investments than less-developed countries. This proposition is indisputable. The extent to which it necessarily follows that the United States has a clear economic interest in the economic development of Third World countries is not quite so obvious. Economic development of those countries will not only open up sales and investment outlets, it will also produce many industries that may compete with U.S. products in foreign markets and, conceivably, in the U.S. market as well. Economic development may also have other consequences that could counterbalance the benefits of new sales and investment outlets. Nonetheless, it seems likely that the long-term effects of the economic development of the Third World would probably be more beneficial than otherwise to the economic interests of the United States.

The second, or security, argument for a U.S. interest in the economic development of poor foreign countries revolves around the inherent instability of a situation in which a tremendous gap exists between a small proportion of the people of the world who are rich and a large majority who are poor. Reducing this gap is essential to the security of the affluent minority. If the reduction does not occur, resentment, frustration, and hostility will escalate, and violence will inevitably result.

This argument is not very persuasive. In fact, poor countries are less likely to have either the desire or the capacity to threaten the security of others than are countries engaged in rapid economic and social development. Only countries that have reached a minimum level of economic strength are in a position to under-

---

* There is some question whether either of these criteria has been consistently applied in the U.S. economic-aid program. One index of need, presumably, is the level of per capita GNP in a society. One index of performance, presumably, is the rate of growth of GNP in a society. In terms of these measures of both need and performance, the East Asian societies where the United States is eliminating aid are far more deserving of assistance than the Latin American societies (with higher per capita GNP and lower growth rates) where the United States is continuing aid.

take aggression. Historically, war and economic development have been closely related. Economic development of a poor country contributes to U.S. security only where the security of that country is essential to the security of the United States. By and large, poor countries, so long as they are poor, lack the capability to threaten U.S. security, whatever their desires may be. Once they are richer, they will have greater capability to be a threat to the United States; and there is little or no basis in logic or history to think that any desire to threaten the United States will be significantly lowered simply because they are richer.

Finally, the political argument for U.S. help for Third World economic development is that the current poor countries are going to develop economically by hook or by crook, anyway, and that it is in the long-term interest of the United States to help them in order to win their friendship and understanding, or at least to minimize the bitterness that a failure to aid them would engender. On the surface, this argument has a persuasive simplicity to it, and one can think of cases (the United Arab Republic, Cuba) where U.S. refusal to give aid probably contributed to subsequent hostility toward the United States. But, as with most commonsensical propositions, there is also a commonsensical counterproposition. How many times have we heard that one cannot buy friends by giving them aid; that it is a mistake to think that other people are going to like us because we help them; that such relationships are more likely to breed feelings of resentment, guilt, and frustration on both sides?

More generally, the gratitude of nations and governments is normally a transient thing, at best, and is apt to approximate the classic expression of the ward heeler to the political boss: "What have you done for me lately?" France, the country that received more U.S. aid after World War II than any other, was, after all, hardly a model ally for many years thereafter. Insofar as the governments of both rich and poor countries expect the United States to demonstrate an interest in the economic development of poor countries, however, the United States may well have a political interest in demonstrating such an interest in order to avoid the critical opinions and antagonistic behavior that might result if such expectations were disappointed. This derived, or secondary, political interest could lead the United States to promote such development even if the direct political benefits that might result therefrom were minimally positive or minimally negative.

This political argument is often based on the explicit proposition that economic development is the overriding goal of the people and governments in the poor countries. That it is a goal is quite clear. That it transcends all other goals is not at all clear. Governments, in particular, have to be concerned with many other things that often conflict with economic development and often must take precedence over it. The prime requisite of any government is to remain a government, and political leaders give first priority to staying in power. They are likely to rate the goals of internal order and external security above the goal of economic development. They may prefer to have a greater degree of national independence than a higher growth rate. Some may be more interested in ideological and symbolic goals than in the more mundane demands of economic development. In fact, of course, some political leaders of poor countries clearly have not given very high priority to economic development. The extent to which the World Bank, the U.S. Agency for International Development (AID), and the consortia have found it necessary to impose conditions for aid in the form of demands for fiscal and economic reforms suggests that the recipient governments, if left to their own devices, would give priority to other needs. Donors of foreign and international aid often appear more interested in the economic development of the aid recipient than is the recipient government itself. Since the donor agencies have that very fact as their *raison d'être*, and since governments are inherently multipurposed, this situation should cause neither surprise nor alarm. It does mean, however, that the economic development goal, which may be the be-all and end-all for donor agency officials, is only one of several targets for the harassed and cross-pressured political leaders of the recipient government.

When viewed from a somewhat broader perspective than that of the aid agencies, economic development is also unlikely to be the overriding American interest in most poor countries. Take India, for example: The United States has a definite interest in promoting Indian economic development; but it also has at least three other important interests in India—(a) the military security of India against external attack, particularly from Communist China; (b) the national integration of India, preventing its break-up into half a dozen or more squabbling ethnic-linguistic states; and (c) the political stability of India as the largest democracy in the world and one of the few effectively functioning democracies in the Third World. Each of these three goals, it can be argued, is considerably more important to the United States than the economic development of India.

The general point, simply, is that the U.S. interest in the economic development of India or any other part of the Third World has to be viewed in the context of other U.S. interests in those areas. Economic development cannot be presumed to be the only U.S. interest, or even the primary U.S. interest, in developing countries.

## Where and How Much

Assuming that the United States does have an interest in the economic development of at least certain Third World countries, there is still the question of how great an interest it has. How important is it to the United States that India achieve a 6 per cent rate of economic growth rather than a 5 per cent rate of growth? If that 1 per cent higher rate of growth were clearly dependent upon $300 million or $500 million or $1 billion aid from the United States during the next five years, what case could be made for giving that use priority over, say, (1) investing the money in U.S. urban ghettos, (2) granting additional tax cuts to the U.S. poor, (3) allocating the amount to medical and scientific research, or (4) reducing inflationary pressures by not spending the money at all? There probably is no way of answering this question that is both rational and persuasive; but it is clearly the sort of question that is in the minds of many critics of aid and has to be grappled with one way or another.

Assuming that the United States has some general interest in the economic development of poor countries, there is still the question of its *particular* interest in the development of individual countries. Recent arguments on behalf of development assistance have generally not been framed in terms of individual countries. Pre-

sumably, however, the United States does have a greater interest
in promoting the economic development of some countries than
of others. What criteria might be used to distinguish between
countries in terms of the extent of U.S. interest in their economic
development? The obvious answer furnished by the logic of economic development is the manifest interest of the recipient government in promoting its own economic development, measured
by past or prospective economic performance. Yet, even the enthusiasts for economic development recognize that, while they
may be able to make a case for the use of purely economic
criteria in allocating resources within a country, they clearly cannot hope to persuade political leaders that purely economic
criteria should be used in allocating resources among countries.
These criteria may play some role, but other factors necessarily,
and indeed appropriately, also come into the picture. Perhaps
five criteria are relevant:

1. Economic performance—the demonstrated or probable ability
of the country to make effective use of aid for economic development and its willingness to commit its own resources and adapt
its own politics to this goal;

2. Security relevance—the extent to which a country's external
security is of major interest to the United States and the extent
to which that security is or could be threatened by another
power;

3. Political democracy—the extent to which the country has
a broad-based, democratic political system with meaningful elections and protection of individual civil liberties;

4. Historical association—the extent to which some special,
historical relationship has existed between the country and the
United States, giving that country an extra claim on U.S. consideration and help;

5. Global importance—the relative weight that the country
has or potentially may have in world politics.

Presumably, the U.S. interest in the economic development of
countries that meet several of these criteria is considerably higher
than its interest in those that meet none, or only a few, of them.

The critical point is that the U.S. interest in the economic development of a country is one aspect of the over-all U.S. interest in that country and has to be meshed with the totality of U.S. foreign policy toward that country.

## Economic Aid as a Means of Economic Development

If the United States does have some interest in promoting the economic development of Third World countries, to what extent is economic assistance an effective way of achieving that goal? Are there other means, such as tariff preferences or investment guarantees, that may be as effective as, or more effective than, capital and technical assistance in promoting economic growth? Economists may provide academic answers regarding the relative effectiveness of differing means of economic development, but the U.S. Government is singularly ill-equipped to consider this issue on a policy basis. AID is the only agency concerned primarily with the economic development of poor countries; the only way it can promote this goal, however, is, in effect, through capital and technical assistance. It is in no position to consider the trade-offs between aid and other ways of achieving economic development. These other means fall within the jurisdiction of the Treasury Department, the U.S. Tariff Commission, or the Commerce Department, for all of which the economic development of poor countries is a relatively low-priority concern.

In practice, therefore, economic assistance becomes the principal means of promoting economic development. How effective has it been in this effort? Here again, the talents of the economist are essential for assessment. It cannot be blindly assumed that there is a direct, positive relationship between economic assistance and economic development. The relationship may exist, but it has to be demonstrated. During the 1960's, aid financed 10 per cent of the capital investment in the poor countries and 20 per cent of their imports. According to a paper prepared for the Brookings Institution, "Foreign Capital and Economic Growth," December, 1969, Alan Strout has evidence that, in developing countries, "the GNP contribution of foreign capital has equaled or exceeded that of exports in spite of the fact that export earnings were larger than foreign capital receipts by a factor of 5:1," and that it was also greater than the contribution of all of agriculture. In a few countries (Korea, Taiwan, Iran, Turkey), massive doses of aid apparently led to high rates of growth, which either have freed or promise to free these countries from reliance on concessional aid. In Pakistan, between 1960 and 1965, as Professor Mason has pointed out, 40 per cent of the total developmental expenditures and 70 per cent of developmental imports were made possible by foreign aid. Technical assistance has contributed enormously to the ability of poor countries to plan and manage their development and to educate the additional man power needed for development. In agriculture, foreign assistance has made possible the "Green Revolution," which promises to render many countries self-sufficient in food, thus freeing foreign exchange for other developmental purposes.

At the same time that a case of this sort can be made for the role of aid in promoting economic development, it is also necessary to note that there may be a few holes in the relationship. Even the Pearson Commission is forced to admit that, despite the contribution of aid, "the correlation between the amounts of aid received in the past decades and the growth performance is very weak." And, in his book, *The Economics of Foreign Aid,* Raymond Mikesell argues that

> Historically, some countries have developed without significant capital imports and, in some cases, the achievement of sustained growth preceded a substantial capital inflow. On the other hand, large capital inflows have frequently made little contribution to development. As a general proposition, external capital or aid is neither a necessary nor a sufficient condition for development.

In a similar vein, Professor Mason has pointed out that external assistance to India under the Third Five Year Plan was double that under the Second Five Year Plan; yet, there was no significant increase in the Indian growth rate. This testimony would seem to suggest that, in some situations, high rates of economic development may be achieved with low levels of foreign aid, and that, in other situations, high levels of foreign aid may not alter low rates of economic development.

The impact of different types of economic aid on economic development also does not appear entirely predictable. Economists tend, for instance, to view defense support or supporting assistance as a somewhat dubious form of foreign aid that clearly does not have the same impact as project aid or technical assistance. On commodity assistance, they seem to be of a divided mind. As Joan M. Nelson has observed in her book, *Aid, Influence, and Foreign Policy:*

> It is striking that among the countries receiving sizeable U.S. assistance, those that have recently achieved or are expected to achieve self-sustaining growth are the countries in which U.S. aid was initially and for some years after directed to security problems. The outstanding characteristic of these programs was sustained large-scale commodity assistance. This assistance almost surely served as a powerful catalyst for later rapid growth.

That this aid would have such effect apparently was not anticipated by most economists. Nor does there seem to be any general agreement now among the economists regarding the relative value of program and project assistance. Noneconomists, consequently, may perhaps be excused if they remain somewhat perplexed about the real efficacy of different types of aid in promoting economic development.

## THE OPPONENTS OF AID

One question deserving more attention than it has been given in the United States is the increasingly hostile attitude of groups within recipient countries toward foreign aid. While American thinkers have been searching for a new rationale for aid, Third World thinkers have been developing a new rationale against aid. This anti-aid rationale is rooted in three increasingly important intellectual currents: nationalism, socialism, and traditionalism or anti-Westernism. The intellectual opposition to aid generally accepts the view that aid makes a difference—that it has an effect, which, however, is more negative than positive. As one representative Brazilian intellectual has argued, foreign aid is good for the United States because it helps to maintain a channel for the exercise of U.S. influence in Brazil—to keep in power a Brazilian Government friendly to the U.S. private investment. (This latter point, that a main purpose of U.S. aid was to create a favorable environment for U.S. private investment, was widely endorsed by AID officials in Brazil.)

So far as Brazil was concerned, however, U.S. aid impeded development and sustained the *status quo*. Development in Brazil could come about either through the emergence of a vigorous national bourgeoisie or by the overthrow of the existing system by a revolutionary elite. American aid encouraged U.S. private investment, which, with its superior resources and managerial talent, now dominated the dynamic sectors of Brazilian industry. (This judgment, too, was confirmed by U.S. aid officials in Brazil.) Hence, there were increasing obstacles to the emergence of an autonomous Brazilian entrepreneurial class. The absence of such a class would place a ceiling on the extent to which Brazil could develop under a capitalistic or mixed economy. At the same time, U.S. military and economic assistance strengthened the repressive powers of the government and, consequently, made it more difficult for a revolutionary movement to overthrow the existing system. United States aid thus condemned Brazil to economic and social backwardness.

In one form or another, this type of argument has been expressed by intellectuals, not all of them Communist or Marxist, in almost every developing country. These expressions range from the argument of the Chilean psychiatrist Vincent Sanchez, quoted by Oswaldo Sunkel in "National Development Policy and External Dependence in Latin America," *Journal of Development Studies,* October, 1969, that U.S. aid created a "cultural psychosis" in Chile to that elaborated by Ivan Illich in the *New York Review of Books,* November, 1969, that the export of Western concepts, aspirations, and techniques of mass production and consumerism induces "chronic underdevelopment" in poor countries from which the latter can escape only by evolving some fundamentally different alternatives unknown to developed Western societies.

Not only is there an anti-aid rationale developing among Third World intellectuals, but there are also some second thoughts on aid appearing among Third World governments. In Brazil, for instance, the United States suspended aid in December, 1968, in response to the Institutional Acts disbanding Congress and severely restricting individual liberties. The effects of this action on the Brazilian Government, however, were nil. United States aid was largely directed toward education and agriculture, and these apparently did not rate very high among the concerns of the military officers running Brazil. The willingness of the governments of Peru, Bolivia, and other countries to risk aid cutoffs under the Hickenlooper Amendment suggests that aid in itself occupies a subordinate position in their hierarchy of values. Such attitudes may seem perverse to Americans preoccupied with development as the overriding goal. Yet, it is perfectly natural and rational for the government of a poor country to be as much concerned with how its economy develops as with how fast it develops. All aid involves some costs for the recipient, and the additional 10 per cent investment (supplied by aid) may simply not be worth those costs to many governments.

## AID AND DEVELOPMENT

United States assistance to the economic development of poor countries has suffered from the tendencies of its supporters to divorce economic development from over-all U.S. foreign-policy objectives and, more generally, to make the case for U.S. economic-development assistance in terms of the needs of the poor countries rather than in terms of the interests of the United States. Economic-development assistance has been underfunded in part because it has been undersold. In this essay, we have attempted to escape from the rhetoric and sentimentality so often adduced on behalf of foreign aid and, instead, to take a cold, hard look at the interest of the United States in the economic development of poor countries. Three general conclusions seem to flow from this discussion:

1. As the wealthiest country in the world, the United States has a moral obligation to help alleviate the sufferings of poor people in poor countries.

2. The United States has some real but not overriding interest, primarily economic and long-term, in the economic development of poor countries generally; it also has some derived political interest in not disappointing the expectations of other governments that it ought to be interested in the economic development of poor countries.

3. The United States has special interest in the economic development of individual countries that are of particular concern to the United States, usually for noneconomic reasons, and the promotion of whose development is an integral part of the overall U.S. foreign policy toward those countries. Rarely, however, is the economic development of a country the *primary* interest that the United States has in it.

From the foregoing, one can conclude that the United States ought to maintain at least three different types of economic assistance programs: humanitarian and related programs aimed primarily at alleviating immediate evils to poor peoples; general economic assistance grants channeled through the World Bank and other multilateral agencies to assist in the over-all economic development of the Third World; and bilateral programs that are an integral part of U.S. foreign policy toward countries where the United States has special political, economic, or security interests.

Economic development and related purposes do not, however, exhaust the goals that the United States pursues by means of foreign aid. Aid is also used to promote military security, U.S. exports, disposal of agricultural surpluses, U.S. overseas investment, private enterprise abroad, social welfare, political participation and democratic government, diplomatic support for the United States, and political support for friendly regimes.

An activity that has a multiplicity of goals should command support, one would think, from a multiplicity of sources. Multiple support is, however, rarely given to bureaucratic programs and governmental agencies. Best off are those in which there is a clear identification of one major purpose with one particular program and that particular program with one distinctive agency. When an agency serves a large number of purposes, no one constituency feels that it has any great stake in its program, and the general public lacks a clear perception of the public needs met by the agency. Most important of all, the agency's personnel tend to become demoralized as they find themselves having to serve a variety of often conflicting purposes. They also feel vulnerable to criticism by Congress and the public, because they can always be attacked for not making sufficient effort to achieve one goal when they have been preoccupied in trying to achieve several others. An agency asked to serve many different purposes tends to lose its sense of commitment to any one of them.

This multiplicity of aid goals has been reflected in the multi-functionality of the Agency for International Development, the only comprehensive aid agency in the world. AID is simultaneously a bank, foundation, management consultant service, operations agency, economic developer and planner, political manipulator, and technical adviser. Organizationally, this situation in a way resembles that of the pre-McNamara Pentagon.

Until the Defense Department reforms, begun in 1958 and completed in 1961, our military system was organized around multipurpose, multifunctional agencies; the key elements were the Army, Navy, and Air Force. Thus, for example, the Air Force included strategic retaliatory forces, tactical support forces, continental defense forces, air transport forces, and antisubmarine planes—and the Navy and Army each duplicated some of these functions. In the Pentagon of the 1950's, as in AID in the 1960's, the multipurpose means of policy were stressed at the expense of the ends of policy. In bidding for funds and support, the Navy repeated *ad nauseam* that 70 per cent of the earth's surface was water; the Army reminded everyone that man was a land animal; the Air Force pointed to the speed and flexibility of moving through the air. But the nation had no intrinsic interest in any of these three methods; they were valuable only insofar as they served more general purposes, such as strategic deterrence and continental defense, limited war capability, and the protection of Europe from attack. The McNamara reforms restructured military planning in terms of ends rather than means. Each service now had to justify its weapons and forces not according to the "needs of the service" but according to how they contributed to over-all national objectives.

The multifunction, multipurpose aid program of today is a prime target for similar changes. Aid, like air power, needs the McNamara treatment. The disaggregation of aid programs will help identify what goals aid may serve and to what extent those goals may be justified. Disaggregation involves, as a first step, doing away with the annual omnibus foreign-aid bill and with the omnibus economic-assistance agency. Both these hallowed institutions have lived beyond their time. They no longer play the critical role they once did in either aid or development, and they need to be replaced by more flexible, specialized, and purposeful mechanisms.

*From AID to Aid*

In the early 1960's, both the Foreign Assistance Act and the Agency for International Development were the central institutions of U.S. foreign aid. This is no longer true. For fiscal year (FY) 1962, the Foreign Assistance Act's first year, total U.S. economic assistance to poor countries was $4.5 billion; for FY 1970, it was $4.1 billion—a decline of only 8.5 per cent. For FY 1962, AID grants and loans were $2.5 billion; for FY 1970, they were $1.7 billion—a drop of 33 per cent. In FY 1962, 55 per cent of the total U.S. economic assistance to poor countries was administered through AID. In FY 1970, a bare 40 per cent went through AID. In FY 1969, only 43 per cent of all U.S. development assistance was authorized in the Foreign Assistance Act. While over-all U.S. contributions to economic development declined somewhat during the 1960's, this decline was concentrated entirely in AID appropriations and expenditures. Non-AID economic loans and grants to poor countries, indeed, went up 22 per cent—from $2,015 million in FY 1962 to $2,470 million in FY 1970. The most significant increase took place in U.S. contributions to international organizations. Such contributions accounted for an average of $207 million a year between FY 1960 and FY 1963. They rose to $571 million in FY 1968 and $627 million in FY 1969. Of this FY 1969 total, $480 million went to international lending agencies, nearly as much as the $570 million that AID itself lent that year. In a somewhat similar manner, both AID and the Foreign Assistance Act also played a declining role in security assistance. In FY 1969, only 29 per cent of the total U.S. security assistance was provided in the Act and only 13 per cent was administered through AID.

A major contrast thus exists between the AID portion of U.S. development assistance and the other portions of that assistance, particularly those handled through international agencies. This contrast is highlighted by the fact that, between FY 1957 and FY 1968, the International Development Association (a World Bank affiliate) and the Inter-American Development Bank had perfect records in congressional appropriations, getting 100 per cent of the funds requested; while AID had the worst record of seventeen foreign-affairs agencies, obtaining only 81 per cent of its requested funds, according to David Howard Davis in "The Price of Power: The Appropriations Process for Seventeen Foreign Affairs Agencies," *Public Policy*, 18 (Spring, 1970).* What declined during the 1960's was assistance administered through the Agency for International Development; other forms of economic assistance increased. What developed up until 1971, in short, was not so much an aid crisis as an AID crisis.

This decline in the importance of the omnibus Foreign Assistance Act and the multipurpose economic assistance agency was the natural result of the diversification of U.S. aims in world politics and of the multiplication of means by which these aims could be achieved. It has been noted that the business corporation in which the vice president for international affairs is important does not itself normally play a major international role. Once a major share of a corporation's business is international business, the vice president for international affairs becomes superfluous, as its regular vice presidents and division managers discharge their functions abroad as well as at home. Something similar may be true of the foreign-aid organization of the U.S. Government. Aid is an instrument that can be used for many purposes and has proliferated in so many different forms that it now cannot be encompassed within the confines of a single agency or a single piece of legislation. Aid is a means that almost any govern-

* Recent congressional actions, however, suggest that, as multilateral programs become more important, they may also become more vulnerable to appropriations cuts.

ment agency may use to achieve goals that cut across national boundaries. (The CIA, for instance, has for years presumably given "foreign aid" worth millions of dollars to foreign governments in the form of intelligence information.) The abolition of the omnibus act, as well as of the omnibus agency, will simply bring to a culmination a process that has been under way for some time.

## The Pros and Cons of Disaggregation

The principal arguments against disaggregation (apart from those rooted in the vested interests of congressional committees and bureaucratic bodies) are twofold. First, it is said, in defense of a multipurpose aid agency, that any specific activity can accomplish several ends. It is, of course, true that building a road serves both military security and economic deveopment. The fact of political-bureaucratic life, however, is that no road will ever be built unless a development administrator or a military adviser sees it as necessary to achieve his purpose. Someone has to have a primary interest in the activity and to perceive it as related to some major goal. It may also make important collateral contributions to other ends. Many of these consequences, however, will be unanticipated by the original promoters of the project and even by its subsequent collateral beneficiaries. The effects of any activity are normally more diffuse and varied than its purposes. The point here, simply, is that all those activities that are related primarily to one purpose should be grouped together, no matter what their more varied consequences may be.

The second argument against disaggregation is that it may often be politically desirable for the donor government or the recipient government, or both, to conceal, or be ambivalent about, what purposes aid may serve. Some purposes at some times appear to be more legitimate than others. It is generally thought to be illegitimate for one government to give another government money simply to keep it in power. Hence, while it might make sense to have separate agencies handling aid for security and aid for development, an agency designed publicly to give aid for "short-term political purposes" simply would not have any customers. Aid that directly serves political purposes either has to be given covertly or commingled with aid given for other more legitimate ends, like security or development. Disaggregation means relating programs to purposes; and, if purposes cannot be publicly acknowledged, then the programs cannot be disaggregated. This restriction imposes a limit on disaggregation, but it does not invalidate it as a general principle.

Some critics of disaggregation also argue that it would reverse the major advance made in 1961, when capital assistance, technical assistance, and supporting assistance were all brought together under one roof in AID. In part, the 1961 consolidation of functions (capital assistance and technical assistance) related to a single purpose (development); in part, it was a bringing together under the same umbrella of programs related to different primary purposes (development assistance and supporting assistance). The aggregation of capital and technical assistance was clearly desirable at that time. Whether it is still desirable today is debatable. Purposive disaggregation, however, would not necessarily affect the relation between capital and technical assistance. Its principal aim is to separate functions related to different purposes, not those related to the same purposes.

These objections to disaggregation thus do not carry much weight. On the other side, the positive advantages of disaggregation are that it

1. Focuses attention on the goals of policy rather than upon one means (foreign aid) by which those goals may be achieved;
2. Makes possible a more considered and informed choice among goals;
3. Makes possible a more rational choice among the means appropriate to achieve each goal;
4. Brings together, in both the legislature and the executive, decision-making responsibility for the achievement of each goal;
5. Clarifies and highlights priorities for officials and thus should improve their morale, efficiency, and performance.

## Four Main Goals of Aid

The multiplicity of goals that foreign aid may serve cannot be analyzed in detail. Some of the more important goals can, however, be distinguished from each other, and institutional mechanisms can be suggested for promoting them. Four goals that seem particularly important are discussed below:

### 1. *To enhance the military security of selected countries*

The United States has had, and presumably will continue to have, an interest in giving assistance to selected countries to enhance their security against attack by hostile powers. The number of countries in which this is a major U.S. interest may well increase somewhat in the near future as the United States reduces its own troop deployments and bases overseas. In the longer run, however, U.S. military assistance is likely to decline.

Currently, the Foreign Assistance Act authorizes appropriations for military assistance, supporting assistance, budget support for political purposes, and public-safety programs (all of which are justifiable in terms of security), in addition to economic assistance justified in terms of development. Military assistance is administered by the Defense Department, with policy guidance from the State Department. Military assistance for Vietnam, however, is appropriated, not along with military assistance to other countries in the foreign-aid bill, but, instead, in the Defense Department appropriation bill. Loans to foreign governments to buy military equipment are authorized in a separate Foreign Military Sales Act, also administered by the Defense Department. Supporting assistance (which in recent years has been almost exclusively for Southeast Asia), budget support, and public-safety aid are administered by AID. Thus, AID, which is supposed to be concerned with development, has substantial programs aimed at security—and security assistance each year involves four different pieces of legislation.

This tangle of authority and administration has led almost every recent study group to urge a separation of security assistance from developmental assistance. In the 1950's, the latter was supposedly tied to the former in order to benefit from the greater popular and congressional support for security. This consideration, if it was ever valid, certainly is no longer so today. Security assistance programs, and particularly military assistance and military credits, serve the same purpose as U.S. military forces and programs; there are obvious trade-offs between military assistance to a country like South Korea and the size of U.S. forces deployed in, or committed to, Korea. Hence, authority for security activity should be contained in one piece, or closely related pieces, of legislation, and responsibility for security programs should rest in agencies not concerned with economic development. The general principle is that all military-assistance programs should be in the Department of Defense and all nonmilitary security-assistance programs in the Department of State. On the legislative side, either all military assistance should be in the Defense Department budget and security assistance in the State Department appropriation, or, as was suggested by the Task Force on International Development, headed by Rudolph A. Peterson, in *U.S. Foreign Assistance in the 1970's: A New Approach*, its report to the President, all forms of security assistance (military and nonmilitary) should be grouped together in an International Security Cooperation Act.

## 2. To encourage the economic development of the Third World in general

I argued earlier that the United States has a limited but real interest in the general economic development of the Third World. This goal has widely shared international support, and the most appropriate means of achieving it is through international agencies. The number, activities, and lending operations of the multilateral aid-giving agencies, the World Bank Group and the regional banks, have been increasing significantly in recent years. Gross disbursements for economic development by multilateral agencies totaled $483 million in 1960 and $1.5 billion in 1968. The international agencies, particularly the World Bank, have also been expanding their capacity to provide more diversified forms of developmental assistance. In this context, the United States should follow the recommendations of the Peterson Task Force and (1) rely on international organizations to develop aid programs and performance standards with developing countries, (2) increase its contributions to the multilateral agencies —provided other countries make proportional increases—and (3) cooperate with other governments in strengthening the capabilities of the multilateral agencies.

One controversial issue remains. What level of U.S. aid is warranted by the U.S. interest in promoting the economic development of poor foreign countries generally? Any answer necessarily requires a weighing of this interest against other goals that the United States should pursue at home and abroad. Even a narrow definition of the U.S. interest in the economic development of poor foreign countries, however, would seem to argue for more rather than less U.S. effort. The Peterson Task Force proposed a doubling of the annual U.S. contribution to multilateral development institutions—from the present $500 million to a new total of $1 billion. In terms of the rather hardheaded definition of the general U.S. interest in the economic development of poor foreign countries advanced earlier in this essay, the Peterson recommendation would appear to be a reasonable target.

3. *To promote the economic development of selected countries as one element of over-all U.S. foreign policy toward those countries*

For the foreseeable future, the United States will continue to have special interests in the development of particular countries that cannot be satisfactorily met through multilateral aid programs. Bilateral action to promote the development of these countries will remain a necessity, although in many cases it should also be closely coordinated with multilateral assistance. U.S. promotion of the economic development of these countries or regions would be one aspect of its over-all foreign policy. The rationale for a bilateral aid program, in short, is not that the economic development of the Third World is important to the United States, but, rather, that Country X is important to the United States. The rationale stems from a general concern with a limited territory rather than from a limited concern with the Third World generally.

United States bilateral aid programs in particular countries and regions should thus reflect U.S. foreign-policy goals in those countries. They should be designed to achieve specified ends in specified countries within specified periods of time. This would mark a return to the original pattern of U.S. foreign assistance in the Marshall Plan and the Greek-Turkish aid programs. The objectives and the countries involved in such programs would change over time within the changing context of U.S. foreign-policy goals and needs.

How should such aid be organized and administered? The general disaggregation of foreign aid will involve the transfer of nonmilitary security assistance and, possibly, of much technical assistance from AID to other agencies. Little reason exists to maintain AID simply to administer bilateral capital-assistance programs. The Peterson Task Force proposed that these programs be handled through a U.S. International Development Bank, which would be an independent governmental body with a board of directors composed of government officials and private citizens. This would provide a more rational and effective organization than any that exists at the present time. If, however, major reliance is to be placed upon the increased role of international, multilateral lending agencies to meet the general needs of Third World countries, the reasons for creating a parallel banking organization to handle bilateral U.S. capital assistance decrease in persuasiveness. This U.S. development bank either would function primarily like a bank (in which case it should not, and would not, be sensitive to changing U.S. foreign policy needs) or would not function like a bank (in which case it should not be mislabeled a bank).

If bilateral aid is to be an integral part of U.S. foreign policy, it ought to be administered by and through the agency responsible for U.S. foreign policy—the Department of State. At present, AID and State work closely together. Under the reorganization I would propose, that portion of U.S. economic assistance that should be carried out relatively independently of other U.S. foreign-policy goals would be handled through multilateral agencies or through other instrumentalities independent of the State Department. That portion of U.S. economic assistance that was designed to be an integral part of the U.S. foreign policy would be handled directly through the Department of State. The number of people necessary to perform these functions would not be great. The large-scale overseas AID mission would disappear, and the small number of people with the economic and administrative skills necessary for a modest bilateral lending program would be assimilated into the regular embassy staff.

Because these bilateral assistance programs would be focused on particular objectives for particular countries, legislative authorization for them would appropriately take the form of individual acts for individual countries or regions that would remain valid for designated periods of time. The State Department might, for instance, draw up a four-year country program for Indian economic development that would reflect over-all U.S. foreign-policy objectives and include, as appropriate, legislative proposals not only for aid but also for trading arrangements, debt moratoria, incentives to private investment, primary-products quotas, and any other ways in which the United States might contribute to Indian development. Congress would then consider and act on an India Development Act designed to help India achieve specified economic goals within a four-year period and authorizing annual aid appropriations and other measures in support of this purpose. At the end of the period, the State Department could propose an extension or renewal of the Act or a new three- or four-year program designed to help India achieve additional goals in its next phase of economic development. In any event, the foreign-affairs committees of Congress, at that point, would have the opportunity to review thoroughly the success or failure of the program over the preceding three- or four-year period and to take whatever action they thought appropriate in the light of that record.

### 4. *To encourage the emergence of pluralistic societies*

In the past, the U.S. Government has been caught between two beliefs, each of which is undoubtedly supported by large elements of American opinion, and each of which is undoubtedly in part true: first, that the people of a country have a right to shape their own political, economic, and social institutions free from outside interference; and second, that the most desirable society is a pluralistic one characterized by private enterprise, social equity, and political democracy. The conflicting demands of these two propositions have come to a head again and again as U.S. officials debate whether to recognize a military junta, to suspend aid to a government that suppresses liberties or expropriates property, or to use "leverage" to promote economic and social reforms in another land.

On the one hand, Americans, like most people, feel not only

that their institutions are right and good for them, but that they also have a more universal moral validity and practical applicability. The need to express this belief stems in large part from the need to have confidence in one's own society and its forms of social, political, and economic organization. More objectively, cases can be made that private enterprise, social equity, and democratic politics may also contribute to other goals, such as economic development and peaceful political development. In addition, to the extent that private enterprise, social equity, and democratic politics do exist in other states, the leaders of those states are more likely to identify their interests with the United States and to be sympathetic to American aims. Hence, it is argued that the United States has an interest in using foreign aid as a means for the promotion of these goals in other countries.

On the other hand, the problems of attempting to induce, bribe, coerce, or persuade another government to make changes that it would otherwise be reluctant to make in its economic, political, and social institutions usually ends only in frustration for all concerned. It thus seems generally desirable not to use economic-development assistance or military assistance, warranted on other grounds, as levers to attempt to produce significant changes in the basic structures of other societies. Since the changes that the United States is interested in making often involve restricting or cutting back on the scope of government, there is, indeed, an inherent contradiction in attempting to do so through that very government.

The conclusion, consequently, is that promotion of greater pluralism and equity in other societies is not only an important and legitimate purpose for the United States, but one that is quite separate from its interests in the promotion of the economic development or military security of particular societies that are of special concern to it. The U.S. interest in pluralism embodies a more general concern, reflecting the type of organization we prefer and would like to encourage other societies to adopt. The most effective way for the United States to promote this goal is indirectly, rather than on a government-to-government basis. The United States should, as the Peterson Task Force recommended, promote local private investment overseas by investing more capital in local development banks, supporting regional private investment companies, and helping to develop capital and credit markets in poor countries. In addition, the United States should promote measures for social equity, like land reform, by encouraging the development in other societies of democratic social and civic organizations, such as trade unions, cooperatives, peasant associations, and professional groups. The Inter-American Social Development Institute authorized by Congress in 1969 and established in the fall of 1970 is one means of promoting this goal in Latin America. No reason exists to restrict this type of operation to that region. Such an organization can provide a way for getting resources directly to private groups, bypassing governmental bureaucracy, and it could help bring about fundamental social change in modernizing societies.

## TOWARD A LIVABLE WORLD

Foreign aid is a means that has served many purposes in the years since World War II. In the late 1940's, the primary purpose was European recovery. In the 1950's, it was mutual security. In the 1960's, it was economic development. Are there other purposes that might be served by foreign aid in the 1970's?

One such set of new purposes stems from the real interest that the United States will increasingly have in the maintenance of a benign world environment. This interest derives from the simple fact that we live in a shrinking and increasingly crowded world. Perhaps the most fundamental change that has occurred on a global scale during the past twenty years has been the compression of the world, brought about by population growth and the revolutions in transportation and communication. This increased interaction means that the United States has a new and fundamental interest in the promotion of a human and physical environment suitable for the survival and improvement of the conditions of life on this planet. This interest did not exist in the past; it will become increasingly vital in the future.

It follows that the United States should take the lead in developing programs to attack some of the common problems that confront mankind as a whole. The focus here should be on "problem programs" instead of "country programs." Such programs should operate on a global basis, tackling problems where they are most serious, and where there is greatest likelihood that something can be done about them. In terms of the familiar types of aid, these programs would consist primarily of technical assistance and, to a much lesser extent, of capital and commodity assistance. Starting from present U.S. technical assistance efforts, they would involve the creation over the years of new programs designed to deal with new problems of global maintenance as they arise. The type of initiative needed is comparable to that which the United States took in May, 1970, when it proposed a new international treaty establishing international control over seabed resources beyond the 200-meter depth. George Kennan's proposal (in *Foreign Affairs*, April, 1970) that the industrial nations take the lead in creating an "International Environmental Agency" is a suggestion for somewhat parallel action with respect to another major global problem. A major element in these programs would be research on how to solve environmental problems. The results of this research would, of course, be disseminated rapidly throughout the world. The object would be to duplicate in other fields the "Green Revolution" in agriculture and the lesser revolutions in birth-control techniques. The payoff of such programs can be big, and the benefits can come more or less simultaneously to those who need them, in whatever country they may be.

The growing U.S. interest in the promotion and maintenance of a "livable world" would, in many respects, be a natural next step in the evolution of the U.S. purposes served by foreign aid. These purposes and the accompanying aid programs have reflected a gradually expanding geographical concern on the part of the United States that has, in turn, reflected the extent to which changes in transportation and communication have brought the rest of the world to the American doorstep. In the 1940's, the principal purposes served by aid were limited to Western Europe. In the 1950's, the mutual security program saw an expansion of U.S. geographical concern to the rim countries of Asia, stretching from Iran to Korea, which appeared to be threatened by Soviet or Chinese expansion. In the 1960's, with the shift to economic development, the geographical focus of American concern similarly broadened to encompass almost all areas of the Third World, including Africa and Latin America. (By the end of that decade, the fifteen major recipients of AID assistance included five Latin American, five East Asian, three South Asian and Middle Eastern, and two African countries.) In the 1970's, the U.S. interest in global maintenance could carry this process of broadening the geographical scope of U.S. concern to the globe as a whole.

The organizational means for expressing the interest of all nations in human survival may take a variety of forms. New international structures, with adequate financial support and legal authority, will be necessary. At present, the international capability for action is limited, and the United States must take the lead. United States participation in these programs would reflect our general and continuing interest in promoting a benign world environment. The heart of foreign policy, however, is the definition and implementation of changing U.S. attitudes and commitments toward, as well as involvements in, different countries and regions. World maintenance programs consequently could not be thought of as instruments of U.S. foreign policy, as foreign policy is commonly conceived. The actual operation of many of the programs would involve techniques, skills, and resources that, at present, are concentrated in U.S. domestic agencies. Very possibly, these agencies could expand their operations to the international scene, channeling the U.S. contribution to international agencies. Alternatively, some of these new programs might be organized and administered through a new executive agency, responsible to the President and completely independent of the Department of State.

## THE ENDS—AND END—OF FOREIGN AID

Except for those who oppose all forms of "foreign aid" no matter what purpose it serves, little reason exists to talk about foreign aid as an end in itself. The discussion of policy should be in terms of, first, the desirability and importance of the goals that may be served by foreign aid and, then, the relative effectiveness of aid as measured against other means for achieving those goals. Given the multifarious purposes to which aid may contribute, a "foreign-aid act" and a "foreign-aid agency" are clearly anachronisms. Current aid programs need to be disaggregated in terms of their purposes and new programs inaugurated to reflect emerging U.S. interests in global maintenance.

By focusing on these purposes, the supporters of foreign aid would shift the focus of attention from a means that has politically negative connotations to ends more likely to have positive appeal. In addition, they would transform the effort to develop a "constituency" for foreign aid (which is the equivalent of developing a constituency for "subsidies") into more meaningful and successful efforts to develop special constituencies for the particular purposes that foreign aid may serve. The net result of this disaggregation could be more or less foreign aid than there has been in the recent past, but, happily, no one would know for sure which it was.

Focusing on the ends of aid should thus clarify both purpose and understanding. Above and beyond this, however, there is the possibility that foreign aid, even as a means, may be in the process of becoming less meaningful. Foreign aid, as it is commonly conceived and practiced, was a product of the emergence of the Western state system in the sixteenth and seventeenth centuries. It has normally meant military, economic, or political assistance from one government to another.

In many areas of policy, however, the distinction between foreign and domestic programs has already become blurred. Private organizations, international bodies, and "domestic" agencies of different governments blithely pursue their objectives across international boundaries. As these transnational operations expand, the identification of "aid flows" themselves becomes increasingly difficult, and trying to pinpoint the net benefits and costs of any particular transaction to national territories becomes practically impossible. When an American-based, multinational corporation uses profits from a plant it has previously constructed in, say, Brazil to build a new one in, say, Peru, who is contributing to the development of whom? When one government lends to another at less than commercial interest rates, so that the borrower can buy capital goods from the lending government's country, how much of the loan is aid, how much of it is an export subsidy, and how much of it is just a straight business deal? Such questions are becoming more and more frequent, and more and more difficult to answer. As such relationships become increasingly complex and diversified, the entire concept of foreign aid could itself become anomalous and irrelevant.

# 3

# Foreign Aid:
# A Report on the Reports

## WILLARD L. THORP

*As part of the soul-searching in the United States and elsewhere about rich-country relations with the poor, a number of studies on foreign aid have been commissioned both here and abroad. In this chapter, the author goes through the major reports that have come out, and analyzes their basic provisions. Beyond doubt, the long process of "thinking again" about foreign aid will help to shape the way in which problems of development are treated during the decade.*—THE EDITORS

The phrase "foreign aid" has been used to cover many activities —missionary enterprises, disaster relief, general postwar rehabilitation, aid to refugees, defense support, market expansion, foreign investment, political intervention, cultural extension, and multilateralism. However, with the breakup of empires and the acceptance of the relatively new concept of government responsibility for social and economic conditions, aid has become focused on the development of the less-developed world.

At first, there was full confidence that this could easily be done. Since there already were advanced countries, all that was needed

This chapter is adapted by permission from *Foreign Affairs*, April, 1970. Copyright held by the Council on Foreign Relations, Inc., New York.

was to follow in their footsteps. And the extraordinary success of that fortunate improvisation, the Marshall Plan, was also a source of optimism. But where the Marshall Plan involved the rehabilitation of societies already modernized, a repair job rather than a transformation, the less-developed countries started off with few of the essential requirements for a modern society. Nor were they homogeneous but large and small, new and old, far and near, rich and poor in physical resources. They differed in traditions, religions, languages, unity and character of leadership. Some already were in the process of changing while others had hardly started.

Both the League of Nations and the United Nations had procedures for a temporary, tutelary status to deal with situations where preparation was needed between the colonial condition and full independence. However, after World War II, with India as the exemplar, the insistence on instant independence in colony after colony was so strong that almost all skipped any transitional stage. And they wanted to parallel the sudden political change with a similar social and economic mutation.

Nor were the developed countries much better prepared for giving assistance. There existed no body of recorded experience and knowledge to provide answers to the obvious questions of how, where, how much, and on what terms, or to the more subtle problems created by national sensitivities and pride of sovereignty and by uncertainties about the development process itself. Aside from anthropologists, social scientists had paid little attention to the problems of less-developed areas. And the colonial powers were equally at a loss. They had considered their main function to be preserving order rather than inducing widespread change.

During the 1940's and 1950's, foreign aid was regarded as a temporary phenomenon. The metropolitan powers often agreed to give assistance to the newly independent for a few years. The initial Common Market agreement with former colonies was for five years. And in the United States, not only has the central foreign-aid legislation been of one-year duration, until 1969–71, but also, in extending the Mutual Security Act in 1953, Congress stipulated that economic aid was to end within twenty-four months and military aid within thirty-six. That particular death sentence, however, was commuted and the early years of the 1960's saw economic assistance at much higher levels for nearly all supplier countries. Under U.S. leadership, they formed the Development Assistance Committee in 1961, agreeing "to secure an expansion of the aggregate volume of resources made available to less-developed countries and to improve their effectiveness."

## THE EXPERTS GATHER

The last twenty years have greatly increased the awareness of the difficulties of speeding up the growth process in the less-developed countries. The disappointment of exaggerated expectations has led to a sense of frustration in many quarters. Aid itself has been increasingly challenged as ineffective and unjustified. As a consequence, a number of full-scale appraisals of foreign aid appeared over a period of about two years.

The most comprehensive examination is that by the Commission on International Development, sponsored by the World Bank and headed by Lester B. Pearson. The Commission assembled a staff of experts and held regional meetings with some seventy governments to assess the results of twenty years of assistance and offer policies for the future. Its report was published in September, 1969. There is also the report of the U.N. Committee for Development Planning, a group of experts with Professor Jan Tinbergen as chairman, which has been working on guidelines for the Second United Nations Development Decade. Supplementing these over-all reviews is a study of the United Nations Development System carried out by Sir Robert Jackson at the request of the Administrator of the United Nations Development Programme.

Since its initiation, the U.S. program has been reviewed by at least a dozen official groups. The President's General Advisory Committee on Foreign Assistance Problems (James A. Perkins, Chairman) addressed a series of recommendations to the new administration in October, 1968. President Nixon on September 24, 1969, appointed a Presidential Task Force on International Development (Rudolph A. Peterson, Chairman) to develop a "new U.S. approach to aid for the 1970's."

The Peterson Report, as submitted to the President on May 4,

1970 (see also Chapter 2), in general dealt mainly with the way aid is administered by the United States. It recommended that bilateral economic and humanitarian aid be separated from aid designed for security purposes. Economic programs themselves should be administered through four new organizations: (1) an International Development Bank, which would make capital and related technical assistance loans; (2) an International Development Institute to "seek new breakthroughs in the application of science and technology to resources and processes critical to the developing nations"; (3) an Overseas Private Investment Corporation (described below); and (4) an International Development Council designed to increase the emphasis on international development in U.S. efforts on trade, investment, and export promotion. Other major suggestions included the untying of development loans from compulsory purchase of goods in the United States and a greater reliance on multilateral institutions, like the World Bank. Indeed, the bilateral economic-aid effort should be "provided largely within a framework set by the international organizations."

These proposals were essentially the ones submitted by the President in a message on September 15, 1970, and in a presentation to Congress in the spring of 1971. By mid-1972, Congress had still not acted on them.

Finally, the Peterson Task Force called attention to two salient ideas: first, that development assistance is more than aid but also must rely upon trade and private investment; and second, that economic growth itself is not development. On the latter point, it commented:

> Popular participation and the dispersion of the benefits of development among all groups in society are essential to the building of dynamic and healthy nations. U.S. development policies should contribute to this end.

The task force refrained from suggesting any specific level of aid effort for the United States—the needs half a decade in the future simply could not be forecast accurately.

There were still more reports. The Rockefeller Presidential Mission for the Western Hemisphere submitted its report on

August 30, 1969, and it was released to the public on November 10, 1969. This should be read in connection with another report— the Latin American Consensus of Viña del Mar, which discusses Western Hemisphere cooperation.

A number of independent studies were made by private groups in 1969. Perhaps the most comprehensive are those of the National Planning Association, "A New Conception of U.S. Foreign Aid," March, 1969, and by the Committee for Economic Development (CED), "Assisting Development in Low-Income Countries: Priorities for U.S. Government Policy," September, 1969. Each of these reports was the result of initial staff work revised and approved by committees of businessmen and scholars.

These studies vary considerably in emphasis, but they all are reports of progress and agendas of unfinished business. They stress the immense magnitude of the problems of development, the interaction of economic, social, and political change, and the diversity of experience and achievement. Taken out of context, their frank criticisms of past procedure and policies might be regarded as throwing doubt on the whole enterprise, but the authors would be the first to deny any such conclusion. Their deep concern for the needs of the less-developed countries has led them to seek ways of increasing the effectiveness of the efforts of the less-developed countries themselves and of the aid provided by the richer nations. The talk is not of withdrawing but of reorganizing and revitalizing.

## WHY BOTHER WITH FOREIGN AID?

As to why foreign aid should be provided, only the Rockefeller Report gives much weight to cold war considerations. In general, the others present plural objectives, including economic, cultural, social, and moral concerns as well as security interests. The Pearson Commission paraphrases President Kennedy's dictum by declaring "that it is only right for those who have to share with those who have not," and supports the moral argument with a discussion of the increasing interdependence of the world community. "If we wish the world to be secure and prosperous, we must show a common concern for the common problems of all peoples." The rich will benefit from the greater availability of resources, expansion of trade, and more friendly political relationships.

The President's Advisory Committee, in addition to stressing humanitarian considerations, maintains that more rapid material progress in less-developed countries will lower tensions caused by hunger and other misery and reduce the risk that violent political instability will disturb world peace. Development efforts will direct energy to constructive activities rather than international grievances and adventures. Joint efforts by advanced and developing countries provide opportunities for more contact and improved understanding of each other's interests. Finally, the Committee points out the danger of ignoring the frustrations of poverty abroad as well as at home.

All the reports make it clear that rapid growth will not necessarily win friends or ensure peace and stability in the less-developed world. However, profound changes in these countries are inevitable, and, as the CED report puts it, "the long-term political rationale for aid . . . rests on the calculated risk that accelerating the modernization process, and reducing the sacrifice required to achieve it, will enhance the odds in favor of an earlier evolution of responsible and independent states." Creation of a sense of common purpose is an important instrument of foreign policy. And, since foreign policy is a form of national expression, the American image of itself as generous, peace-loving, and all for the underdog requires the demonstration of these characteristics beyond national boundaries.

The reports deal in various ways with specific criticisms by arguing that the domestic cost is small compared with the possible gain in reduced world tension; the effect on the balance of payments is very limited; there is no evidence that economic aid leads to military entanglement; the evolution of procedures has made assistance more and more effective; and the cases of corruption and mismanagement are relatively few. As to the criticism that aid has failed to win friends and influence peoples, all the reviewers agree that assistance should be primarily directed at development and not at short-run political or economic objectives.

Thus, the stated objectives range from the simple purpose of reducing hunger, disease, ignorance, and poverty to economic, cultural and social benefits—the desire to help channel change toward higher living standards, more open and liberal societies, and a stronger world community.

## MEASURING RESULTS

While the reports emphasize difficulties and obstacles, they tend to be basically optimistic about the possibilities; they point out that extraordinary progress is being made by the two-thirds of the world's people who are struggling with postcolonial instability, racial bitterness, ignorance, and massive poverty, and assert that the prospects for their further development are brighter than ever because of the improved performance of both donors and receivers of aid. In fact, the U.N. Committee for Development Planning would step up the economic growth target from the annual rate of 5 per cent set for the 1960's to 6–7 per cent for the 1970's. To be sure, the over-all percentage figure creates too favorable an impression, due to the cases where high growth rates have resulted from circumstances that are not likely to be generalized—Libya, Korea, Taiwan, Israel, Mexico, and Iran. In fact, many unfortunately fell below the 5 per cent rate, and per capita progress was much lower.

The reports discount the use of simple growth rates as a measure of progress, pointing out that development is a matter of quality as well as quantity and involves the building of institutions necessary for the future, such as expanded educational systems. To be sure, they admit that social change is not easy, since it requires altering established traditions and institutions. And political change raises the specter of external interference in the most sensitive area.

While the reports emphasize social needs, especially with respect to population and its growing concentration in cities, they do not give enough weight to the political problems and uncertainties in the less-developed countries. They recognize the key position played by governments and talk about the importance of effective planning, policies, and performance. But they pay little attention to the disintegrating influence on the political structure of tribalism, religion, language, or rigid class distinctions. Likewise, the specter of massive unemployment is kept in the wings.

It is a common criticism that foreign assistance has failed to set social and political objectives, although that was the central idea of the Alliance for Progress, which endorsed not only economic and educational development but agrarian and tax reforms. Probably these sectors have not been stressed because of the problems involved in trying to influence them from the outside. However, foreign aid can contribute readily to economic change through technical assistance and capital flows, and the economy is not isolated from society. Roads and electric power and education are great revolutionary forces. Feudal systems were built on isolation and ignorance. Social and political change is the inevitable consequence of economic expansion.

No one can predict the form of the institutions that will finally emerge, but our ability to influence the patterns of the future depends in large part upon the aid relationship. In the early years of aid, most of the less-developed countries had great expectations but were not ready to plan and carry out a development program. Often, the requirements for infrastructure, such as roads, power, schools, health facilities, and civil service, were so obvious that the problem was less one of planning than one of mobilization. At that time, the international and national agencies played a very active role.

The reports are opposed to any such paternalistic or tutorial position. The word appearing most often is "partnership," although even this is probably too strong. The infancy of the seventy or more new nations is rapidly disappearing into the past. Not only are they capable of assuming greater responsibility for shaping their own development, but it is inevitable that they will do so—a point stressed particularly by the National Planning Association Report. To be sure, they were part of a larger world, and they have important needs that must be supplied from outside, but their social and economic development cannot be imported. It will be the result of their policies and the way they organize and use their own resources. "Assistance" is the right word, for much can be done from outside to help in the process; but the influence and importance of foreign countries are limited. It follows that one must not be surprised when the less-developed countries move in directions contrary to Western experience— and this may be the course of wisdom for them.

This does not mean that the reviewers favor handing over assistance funds nonchalantly. They recommend that each recipient and its suppliers work closely together, so that domestic policies and foreign assistance can be fully coordinated. The U.N. Committee for Development Planning proposes that both developed and less-developed countries make commitments as to what they propose to do, and that a review and evaluation procedure be established to keep track of performance.

## MULTILATERAL INSTITUTIONS

One way of reducing the national element in the aid relationship is to increase the flow through multilateral institutions. This receives universal support, though with a caveat by Jackson as to their present capacity. The Pearson Report calls for 20 per cent of the official flow from donor countries to go to the multilateral agencies, especially urging the expansion of the International Development Association (IDA) because of its soft lending. The Pearson formula for total volume, combined with this recommendation, would increase contributions to international agencies from the $618 million average for 1966–68 to $3.2 billion in 1975. In addition, some of the agencies would raise additional funds in private markets. The President's General Advisory Committee urges increased contributions as rapidly as the managements can expand their competence, but would want other countries also to step up their contributions. Rockefeller urges the shifting of much of the policy responsibility to various regional organizations. In addition to expansion in lending activity, it is generally felt that the World Bank and the International Monetary Fund (IMF) should provide more coordination to the assistance given to individual countries through consortia and consultative groups.

The Jackson Report deals with the capacity of the U.N. Development System. While stressing the importance of the work being done, particularly technical assistance and preinvestment activity, the author suggests that it needs stronger central control, that planning must be focused on the individual country, and that an improved organization could make an exceptional contribution, given substantially more money and sufficient management talent and supporting man power.

## How Should Development Be Carried Out?

The reports show surprising agreement on development strategy. Family-planning programs, while limited in their foreign requirements, would probably top the list, followed closely by agriculture and by education and vocational training. Of special interest is the possible use of aid to backstop a desirable national program, say of tariff reduction or exchange adjustment or land reform, where the local government recognizes the need for action but is dependent on technical help or financial underwriting.

Technical assistance is emphasized, although less is said, except by Jackson, about the problems of man power and effective operation. In early 1969, a report was issued by a task force of the National Association of State Universities and Land-Grant Colleges, drawing on their own experience in developmental assistance and emphasizing the importance of technical assistance in human-resource development and institution building, as well as the need for a much greater research effort.

The reports dwell extensively on the impediments of procedural encumbrances and unrelated policy restrictions, including: requirements for expenditure in the aid-supplying country (tied aid); freight rates and shipping restrictions; unrelated policy positions by the recipient (expropriation, fishing rights, nonrecognition of this or that country); the use of engineers or other specialists from the supplying country; and elaborate inspection procedures. While each requirement may seem reasonable, they often increase the administrative and annoyance costs and make aid appear to be a payment on account. Tying is particularly criticized for reducing the area of choice and increasing the cost of aid programs. On this subject, the Pearson Commission makes an interesting suggestion for parallel untying of aid by donors in such a way as to leave the balance of payments of each virtually unaffected.

There is also considerable criticism of the gradual shift from grants to loans. In 1968, about one-half of the official commitments were either outright grants or loans with payments to be made in local currency, which would be used again in the country for development purposes. The regular loans vary greatly in their terms, but it is estimated that, in total, they are sufficiently below capital-market terms so that they can be regarded as about half grant and half loan. The troublesome debt-service situation is aggravated by the fact that there is a large and growing volume of high-cost export credits and payments related to private-capital flows. To be sure, the resources that the loans provided have been in use and may have added to the foreign exchange available for debt service. Nevertheless, the backflow may create a transfer problem. In general, the experts recommend softer loans and earlier efforts to deal with situations that may require debt relief.

The problem of the wide variety of expanded requirements and payments to outside countries that development requires is never put in its full perspective. To be sure, recommendations for the expansion of trade are common, but they are usually expressed in terms of substituting trade for aid. In fact, added means of payment are required not only for growing debt service but also for increased supplies of nonindigenous raw materials, spare parts, more varied technical advice, increasing representation costs abroad, and growing import demands resulting from rising consumer incomes.

The trade recommendations are directed largely at the richer countries, urging them to reduce, as soon as possible, tariffs and excise taxes on possible imports from less-developed countries. Less-developed countries are also advised to extend tariff concessions to each other. The idea of preferential tariffs for less-developed countries, as distinct from broader most-favored-nation cuts, was put forward most strongly in the Rockefeller Report, where it was recommended that the United States should lower tariffs to the less-developed countries of Latin America if it could not obtain agreement with the European importers to give more general preferences.

## How Much Foreign Aid?

With respect to volume of foreign aid, the most frequent recommendation is for each supplier to bring its aid at least to the U.N. target of 1 per cent of gross national product. Pearson and the CED set 1975 as the goal, while the U.N. Committee for Development Planning prefers 1972. CED remarks "that the proposition that the United States can afford a substantially larger aid program cannot be reasonably doubted." The President's Advisory Committee proposes a goal to be reached in 1973 of 1 per cent of national income, which is about 20 per cent smaller than GNP. The Peterson Task Force, however, rejected any formula.

No one is entirely satisfied with this target, especially since it disregards quality (the proportion of grants) and makes no allowance for the principle of progressive taxation, whereby the richer countries would make a relatively larger contribution. Since it combines official and private flows, Pearson proposes, as a supplemental target, that official aid shall be .70 per cent of GNP by 1975, or at latest 1980.

The Secretariat of the Organization for Economic Cooperation and Development (OECD) has made an estimate of the probable size of this target for official aid. Allowing for growth in GNP, the .70 per cent figure in 1975 would be $16.3 billion. To reach their individual goals, seven countries would merely have to maintain the rate at which their aid was increased from 1964 to 1968 —Canada, Denmark, Italy, Japan, Netherlands, Norway, and Sweden. For the four largest, the annual rate of increase would have to be: United States, 13.8 per cent; United Kingdom, 12.5 per cent; Germany, 12.0 per cent; France, 5.6 per cent.

While recommending "that greater and more assured resources be made available to the U.S. foreign aid agency," the National Planning Association concentrated its thinking on restructuring the aid effort, because it sees little prospect of a substantial increase in appropriations. The Rockefeller Report makes no comment as to the volume of aid but proposes a number of procedural changes to increase its effectiveness.

Suggestions for increasing the official volume other than through direct appropriation include applying part of the new Special-Drawing-Rights (SDR) purchasing power to this purpose, subsidizing interest payments so that high-cost private borrowing can be turned into low-cost lending, and setting up special arrangements for offsetting depressed primary-export earnings. However, the most usual approach is to seek the further expansion of private investments. Its value lies not only in providing capital but in the technical and management skills that are part of the investment process.

While it is recognized that private aid will not replace official aid for infrastructure purposes, and that its distribution among countries is related more to resource availability than to development objectives, the process of growth inevitably opens up increasing opportunities for private foreign investment. The problem is how to do it, since the carrot must be provided by the less-developed country, and private investment depends upon private decisions. The source government can stop private flows but cannot turn them on. The most that can be done by government is to make the process more attractive.

In late 1968, the International Private Investment Advisory Council reported to AID on ways and means to increase the flow of private investment. Its central proposal was the organization of an overseas private-enterprise development corporation funded by the U.S. Government. The President presented the proposal in somewhat limited form to Congress, which has approved an Overseas Private Investment Corporation (OPIC) with a mixed board of public officials and private businessmen—a proposal strongly endorsed also by Rockefeller and Peterson. Established in 1970, it has taken over the existing insurance and guarantee programs and has to invest in private projects.

## ORGANIZING TO HELP

A favorite exercise of American systems analysts is to propose some scheme of reorganization. Rockefeller suggested the transfer of aid programs to the Executive Office and much more cooperative decision-making by the Committee for the Alliance for Progress. The President's General Advisory Committee advocated the replacement of AID by the Development Cooperation Fund, the transfer of military assistance to the Defense Department budget, and an overseas investment corporation to promote private foreign investment. The National Association of State Universities and Land-Grant Colleges proposed the establishment of a quasi-autonomous group for technical assistance. Congress has recently authorized the establishment of an Inter-American Social Development Institute for technical assistance to Latin America through private channels.

So far as the United States is concerned, these organizational rearrangements do not add new functions, although changed and fresh personnel might bring imaginative and energetic activity into old patterns. Actually, most of the suggestions run counter to general expert opinion that closer coordination is needed rather than fragmentation. However, there are two new proposals that may have a considerable positive effect: One is some reduction in the exhaustive procedure of annual authorization legislation; the second is the provision of more of the assistance through funding arrangements not requiring annual appropriations.

Reorganization is not only an American phenomenon. The Pearson Commission calls for strengthening the U.N. machinery for coordination on an individual-country basis and for a centralized means of reviewing development policies in all fields—aid, trade, monetary policy, and private-capital movements. It stresses the need for some means of making reasonably authoritative estimates of development objectives and aid requirements, of assessing regularly the performance of the less-developed countries, and of reviewing donor aid policies and programs. The fact is that, on each subject listed, progress has been made in the last decade. The greatest advance in coordination is being made by the less-developed countries themselves as they strengthen their administrative structures and their civil services. Coordination is an attractive concept, but the learning process is not yet complete, and there is much to be said for multiple participation and responsibility.

## SEEING AID FOR WHAT IT IS

One can find books and articles that are hostile to foreign aid, but most experts on the subject give it strong support. The reports described above generally conclude that, broadly speaking, substantial progress is being made, that the productive capacity of developing countries has increased significantly, that much has been learned so that both developed and less-developed countries have improved their performance, and that the record justifies an even greater effort in the future. To be sure, the experts make many suggestions for improvement, a large number of which are widely recognized and often already are being put into effect. The chief actions recommended for the developed countries are that they regard the objective as development and not immediate economic or political reward, that they increase substantially the flow of technical assistance and financial resources on softer terms, and that they open up their markets to exports from less-developed countries.

In startling contrast to this picture of foreign aid is that painted by the U.S. Congress, where aid is seen as obsolete, outmoded, unrealistic, mindless—a boondoggle, a giveaway by Uncle Santa Claus, and a bureaucratic maze beyond comprehension, consisting of waste, frauds, sham, friends lost, enemies made, and hopes dashed. To be sure, some defend the program with words of praise, but the proof of the matter is that the appropriation for economic assistance, not including amounts for the Food for Freedom program or the Export-Import Bank, reached a post–Marshall Plan high level in the early 1960's but has dropped steadily since 1964–65.

It is important to make some distinction between the attitudes of the executive and legislative branches of the government. While some Presidents have given higher priority to foreign aid than others, they have all declared its significance in messages to Congress. Recently, however, the recommendations by the President have been less year after year until President Nixon, without apology, described his recommendation for 1969–70 as the "lowest proposed since the program began." The shrinking recommendations have been received by Congress without applause, then cut substantially and enacted reluctantly.

## THE CONGRESSMAN VERSUS THE EXPERT

Clearly, there is a wide gap between the judgment of the experts and the action of Congress on foreign aid. There are a number of reasons for this. In the first place, the problem appears to each in quite a different perspective. The concern of the expert is focused on development. He examines it in terms of whether it is going well or badly. He seeks ways of accelerating the process by improving the performance of the less-developed countries and the effectiveness of the aid from the developed countries. He feels that this endeavor is much more important than many items for which public funds are spent, but does not endeavor to establish specific priorities.

To the legislator, priorities are all important. Foreign aid is basically a budgetary problem, competing with all the other claimants. If he looks to the polls for guidance, he finds foreign aid far below such domestic interests as education, roads, and health. But the polls are too simple and represent impressionistic reactions to undefined programs and inadequate information. A decision might be easier if it were possible to say that money saved here would be used there, but the appropriations procedure does not work that way. To be sure, a few members of Congress know a great deal about the subject, and the related committees usually hold several days of hearings. But, in the last analysis, the pressure of immediate domestic needs is paramount. To be sure, the public can influence the situation, as it did in connection with the enactment of President Truman's Point Four; or a President can shift the balance, as Kennedy did in 1961. But, much of the time, so far as Congress is concerned, foreign aid is a political orphan.

The gap between expert and legislator is widened by differences in the source and kind of information to which each is exposed. The expert is most often someone who has had a direct connection with the development process. He knows the complexity of the problem through the diversity of his own experience. Aid matters to him.

The legislator is beset by hundreds of issues affecting government action on which he must record his judgment. He is likely to regard the experts in the executive branch of the government as prejudiced witnesses. He assumes that the proposed program has been padded to allow for congressional cuts. And, as far as public information is concerned, he, like the public at large, is the victim of the general principle that bad news drives out good. The vicissitudes of India's Congress Party are followed much more closely in the news than its extraordinary progress in family planning or agricultural yields. And the misbehavior in Antwerp of four persons on the AID payroll is more newsworthy than the proper performance of all the rest.

Sometimes, the difficulty is that of the incomplete picture. The legislator and the public might be less disturbed by cocktail glasses sent to a Caribbean country if they knew that it was a tourist hotel that was being equipped. In the 1969 debates, several congressmen were upset that the United States had borrowed $135 million from Thailand, Korea, and Taiwan, yet nevertheless was giving them aid. The missing piece in that picture puzzle is that these countries were substituting U.S. bonds for other assets in their monetary reserves—an objective that we have pursued for some years with many countries.

Another form of information that has quite a different impact on the two groups is the comparison of the U.S. program with that of other countries. The expert views development assistance as a common effort, in which all the rich countries should participate. One of his interests is the comparative performance of aid donors as well as that of the recipients. He is impressed that, among the sixteen members of the Development Assistance Committee (DAC), the United States ranked fifteenth in 1970 in terms of its public and private foreign-aid disbursements when measured as a per cent of gross national product (0.61 per cent of GNP, as compared with 0.78 per cent of GNP for all DAC members) and twelfth when only official development assistance was considered. The member of Congress is sure that the United States is really number one. If others seem relatively higher, it is because they have some special selfish interest, or perhaps the statistics are open to challenge. But, in any event, in his view this is a contest not among countries but among interests in, and of, the United States.

The expert and the legislator also have differing attitudes toward foreign relations and foreign policy. The expert sees the aid process as one in which various countries are working together cooperatively and tending to reduce their hostilities in the process. He feels that a proper aid relationship will contribute to the easier handling of the many other unrelated problems involved in foreign relations, and that, in a world of many countries, a nation whose behavior is ungenerous and inward-looking will have increasing difficulty. The legislator is worried about excess foreign commitments that may be implied by, and be the consequence of, foreign aid. Senator J. William Fulbright quotes former Secretary of State Dean Rusk as having said that "one of the reasons justifying our involvement in Vietnam was the aid program; that the aid bill indicated Congress approved of the climate of intervention in that country." The President's Advisory Committee examined this proposition and found no support for it in the evidence, pointing out that Korea and Vietnam had been security problems from the start, aid to the Dominican Republic had been ended before its revolution, and many other armed conflicts had occurred between or within countries where we had substantial economic-assistance programs without our becoming militarily involved.

The congressman, like the public, does not think of foreign aid as an important instrument of foreign policy. He is likely to feel that the richest and strongest country in the world should have no difficulty in dealing with the small, poor, and weak. But national pride is no respecter of size or strength, and international leadership is much more a matter of demonstration, performance, and the effective presentation of one's case than of arm-twisting or the distribution of largesse.

It has clearly been a disappointment to members of Congress that foreign aid has not caused countries to follow the position of the United States in international meetings or to behave with gratitude. They are disturbed by aid recipients engaging in anti-American speeches, expropriating American properties, and refusing to support us in Vietnam. The legislator wants specific results to report back to his constituents. He is under the pressure of the immediate and is looking at a one-year appropriation for a program with no permanent authorizing legislation.

This suggests one of the greatest differences—the time dimension. The expert groups do not expect instant development or current subservience, but they are frightened about the future. They fear that the same strains and stresses may develop internationally, because of poverty, as are now appearng within countries. In the words of the Pearson Report: "Who can now ask where his country will be in a few decades without asking where the world will be?"

# 4

# U.S. Policy in Latin America

## JOHN E. RIELLY

*Of all the regions of the developing world, the only one that has a long historical connection with the United States is Latin America. From the Monroe Doctrine onward, we have assumed special responsibilities for what happens in our hemisphere and placed particular demands on other countries within it. However, our grand design of the 1960's for Latin America—the Alliance for Progress—is now dead. In this chapter, the author takes a broad look at U.S. relations with the countries of South America and with Mexico, and suggests the directions in which we should now proceed.*—THE EDITORS

On many occasions during his short tenure as President, John F. Kennedy described Latin America as the "most critical area in the world" as far as U.S. foreign policy was concerned.* This

* In this essay, I draw a sharp distinction between South American countries and the smaller countries of Central America and the Caribbean. My analysis applies to U.S. relations with South America plus Mexico, since Mexico, though special because of its geographic location, has problems *vis-à-vis* the United States smiliar to those of the larger countries of South America. U.S. relations with the South American countries are historically different from those with the Central American or Caribbean countries and represent relations between viable nation states. Many of the Central American and the Caribbean states continue to function like client states, and their future as appendages to the North American land mass remains undetermined. The U.S. role there is and will remain different.

priority was never fully implemented, but it did reflect his view that Latin America was part of a larger competition with the Soviet Union. Once Lyndon B. Johnson became President and our preoccupation with Southeast Asia grew in the mid-1960's, Latin America soon became a secondary area of interest (with the exception of a brief excursion in the Caribbean in 1965). There is every indication that it is equally low on the list of priorities of the Nixon Administration.

Thus, despite all the grand designs—ranging from the Good Neighbor Policy through the Alliance for Progress to Action for Progress—Latin America today remains a second-level area in U.S. foreign-policy considerations. It figures little in our military concerns, although historically there has been emphasis on arms sales. In terms of U.S. economic assistance, Latin America comes ahead of Africa but well behind Asia. In terms of high-level attention by the President and his principal foreign-policy advisers, Latin America ranks just above Africa. Thus, the Nixon Administration follows the Johnson Administration in its neglect of Latin America. The policies of both contrast with the high priority attached to the area by President Kennedy.

In his report to the President in 1969, Nelson Rockefeller submitted recommendations on U.S. policy that were based on an over-all assumption that the "special relationship" between the United States and Latin America should continue to be nourished. President Nixon has adopted this rhetoric about the "special relationship" with Latin America, but, up to now, his actions have not supported his words.

## U.S. INTERESTS IN LATIN AMERICA

How can we define the essential ingredients of U.S. interests in Latin America? First, as we look ahead in the decade of the 1970's, there appears little reason to believe in the likelihood of a direct attack by a potential aggressor, such as the Soviet Union, on the United States or on any South American country or Mexico. There is less likelihood than in the 1960's that any Latin

This chapter is based on a paper prepared for the Latin American Seminar, Overseas Development Council, May 25, 1971.

American country will be used as a base for an attack on the United States.

Since 1962, the Soviet military arsenal has expanded considerably, with varying implications for the United States in its relations with Latin America. On the one hand, it is generally agreed that the Soviet Union has today achieved parity with the United States, including parity in intercontinental ballistic missiles that can be launched from the Soviet Union and, therefore, do not require a base near the United States. On the other hand, the diversified Soviet military capability, including the swift and dramatic growth of its naval forces, is likely to lead to a Soviet naval presence off the Atlantic and Pacific coasts of North and South America just as there is one in the Mediterranean today.

Latin American countries will probably have to become accustomed to seeing Soviet naval vessels just as European countries are today. But, so long as no important country establishes a military naval base and extends to the Soviet Union the right to use it, this increased presence need not be viewed as a threat to our vital interests. It should be equally clear to both the Latin American countries and the Soviet Union, however, that some aspects of the Monroe Doctrine still apply—in particular, that no superpower competitor can be allowed to establish a military base in this hemisphere. Such a base could provide leverage to disrupt relations between the United States and its neighbors to an unacceptable degree.

There is a special problem in regard to nuclear weapons. In supporting the nonproliferation treaty, the United States demonstrated concern about the possible growth of a nuclear capacity in Japan, India, Israel, or Sweden. By the same token, we cannot ignore the possibility that large countries like Brazil, Argentina, and, to a lesser extent, Mexico may, during the next ten years, achieve a nuclear capability, despite the existence of the Latin American Nuclear-Free Zone (which Brazil has not joined); there is little doubt that they will have the capacity to do so. At present, political and foreign-policy trends in these countries make unlikely a decision to develop a nuclear capability before the early 1980's—and such a capability, if it were developed, would more likely be used to enhance a particular nation's position in international affairs than to harm the United States. This judgment assumes that social anarchy will not become so acute in any of the major countries that a totalitarian government takes over, acquires a nuclear capacity, and then threatens to use it in combination with an external power against the United States.

We cannot exclude the possibility that, in certain countries, social unrest could invite meddling by extracontinental powers. Nor can we rule out direct rivalry and competition with the Soviet Union if major countries fall under the sway of totalitarian governments that seek outside support against us, as did Cuba a decade ago.

Our second vital interest in Latin America is to maintain an economic relationship that permits us to trade, travel, and invest. We cannot ignore the role that the obvious factors of size and population play in influencing this. Brazil alone has a land mass larger than that of the continental United States. Latin America's present population of 270 million is likely to be 390 million in 1980 and 500 million by the year 2000. Even more important, Latin America enjoys a favorable balance between population and land and is rich in natural resources. Among developing areas, Latin America is the most important for U.S. trade and investment, standing midway between Europe, Canada, and Japan, on the one hand, and Africa and Asia (excluding Japan), on the other. Latin America is both a large market for American exports and a principal source of many raw materials imported by the United States. Trade between the United States and Latin America at present amounts to $5,695 billion for U.S. exports and $4,778 billion for imports. Direct U.S. investment is $13.8 billion.* Five hundred thousand U.S. tourists visit Latin America every year. The activity of the multinational corporation increases. All these activities are dependent on a reasonable degree of harmony between the United States and individual Latin American countries and on the prevention of social disintegration.

The third essential ingredient of U.S. interest in Latin America

---

* These figures are for both Central and South America and include the book value of U.S. investments as of December 31, 1969. Data are taken from the "International Investment Position of the United States: Developments in 1969," *Survey of Current Business,* October, 1970.

is correct diplomatic relations with all countries—regardless of the nature of individual governments. If we now apply this standard to Communist China, there is little reason for adopting a different one in this hemisphere. Diplomatic relations can facilitate U.S. economic and security interests through protection of U.S. investments and travelers and through furthering of U.S. competition for commercial contracts. As the balance of economic bargaining power shifts, our political and diplomatic relations will have a greater importance in preserving a U.S. share of the Latin American market. Similarly, U.S. security interests in the Caribbean and elsewhere can be aided by diplomatic cooperation of Latin American states in the Organization of American States (OAS) and the United Nations.

The interests of the United States will dictate a new relationship with Latin America, as will the failure of its intervention in Southeast Asia, its failure to fulfill the exaggerated expectations aroused by the Alliance for Progress, and the coming to power in Peru and Chile of governments that appear to be, in some sense, anti-American.

The changing assumptions of American foreign policy over the course of a decade reinforce the need for a change in the U.S. relationship with Latin America. President Kennedy avidly sought to go beyond the cold war; but the premises of his over-all foreign policy remained largely those of that tense period. The containment of communism was still the overriding consideration, and a Communist threat to any country or continent was seen, in some way, to be a threat to the security interests of the United States. Despite this philosophy, President Kennedy popularized the idea of making the world safe for diversity, confident that the interests of the non-Communist world, including the geopolitical interests of the United States, would come out well in any free choice by the peoples of a given country.

Since the late 1960's, however, the tragic results of implementing a variation of this theory in Vietnam have thoroughly undermined both the continuing validity of the premise itself and the willingness of the U.S. public to continue supporting it. It was clear, by the turn of this decade, that the force of nationalism is now of growing importance, just as earlier we had recognized that the principal Communist governments are motivated mainly by state, as distinct from ideological, interests. Seen in this context, it has become less important to American security interests whether the social, economic, and political systems of Iraq, Ceylon, Chile, or Algeria are socialist or some variant based on a mixed economy.

According to present Administration policy, therefore, what happens in the developing countries is, in most cases, not viewed as critical to the vital interests of the United States, since it would not affect the underlying power relationship with the Soviet Union.

## THE U.S. AND EUROPEAN ROLES

Turning to the subject of a new relationship with South America, it is clear that we should play a less dominant role in the hemisphere. As modernization of Latin American societies increases and as political consciousness spreads, Latin Americans are becoming both restive about the pervasive presence of the United States and intent on curtailing American influence. In many Latin American countries, the security problem is seen as coming *not* from communism, either of the Soviet, Chinese, Cuban, or domestic variety, but from the oppressive presence of the United States. In many countries, anti-Yankeeism is today the cohesive cement binding forces in political life. Yet, to proceed with the modernization that is universally desired by Latin American elites, these nations will require continued assistance from the developed world. However strongly Latin American nationalists may desire development exclusively through their own efforts—however much they reject foreign models—it will be impossible for them to gain the technology, the managerial skills, and the capital that are indispensable to the development of modern societies without continued foreign assistance.

Latin America has a strong interest in remaining involved with the developed world, but these relations need not be centered exclusively on the United States. The United States need not continue to be the preponderant source of outside aid and trade, in view of Latin American ambivalence about relations with their giant neighbor. Rather, the interests of U.S. foreign policy, the internal development and extrahemispheric interests of Latin American countries, and the likelihood that some European countries will seek a role outside their own continent, all argue for a closer association between Europe and Latin America in the coming decade. In the future, the vision of South American and Mexican leaders will increasingly extend beyond the Western Hemisphere.

It is therefore in our mutual interest to promote the strengthening of Latin American ties with Western Europe and to encourage Europe to assume a larger interest in Latin America. (The European countries with the greatest actual or potential influence are Germany, France, Italy, Spain, and the United Kingdom.) Basically, U.S. leaders must come to realize that a larger *political* role for Europe in Latin America is not inconsistent with American national interests. (By "political" I mean European influence on military and diplomatic questions as well as economic and financial matters.) Given the xenophobic anti-Yankeeism in most countries, increased European involvement will decrease the possibility that this nationalism will result in the expulsion of all foreigners and unnecessarily delay Latin American development. A European involvement should also minimize temptations to seek alliances with Socialist states outside the hemisphere as a way of escaping the suffocating dominance of the United States. If national interests are defined as something larger than preserving American hegemony in Latin America, they are not threatened by a greater European involvement.*

The traditional ties between Latin America and Europe, based on a similiar political, religious, cultural, and linguistic inheritance, can be supplemented. Europe today is still far from unity in the West and is divided from the East, but its economic, technological, and military resurgence gives it a considerable capacity to play a role in international affairs *outside* of Europe. If this role will always remain secondary to European interests within

---

* What is said here of Western Europe is to a considerable extent applicable to Canada, notwithstanding Canada's special relationship with Commonwealth countries of the Caribbean. Japan's role in Latin America is likely to expand, and not only in relation to the West Coast countries.

Europe, it is nonetheless potentially important. Certain European countries will continue to concentrate their overseas activities in Africa. But there is no reason why Africa should be the exclusive focus of European attention, especially as the Iberian countries are incorporated into Europe and exert a greater influence on its external involvement.

Many observers are still preoccupied with the "technological gap" between Europe and the United States. Yet, in the coming decade, Europe will be increasingly an exporter of advanced technology and capital. Since many Latin American countries are at an intermediate stage of development, they represent a natural market for Europe's surplus technology. Indeed, the technology and know-how of European countries may be more usable to Latin American countries in their present stage of development than the technology of the North American technetronic era. Despite growing nationalism in Latin America, there would seem to be no reason to anticipate *le défi européen* for at least a decade.

So far, there has been considerable European investment in Latin America, and some interchange in a number of fields involving European nongovernmental groups (political parties, labor unions, foundations, and the churches). The United States has encouraged European governments, banks, and industrialists to provide a greater share of the concessional aid directed toward Latin America through bilateral arrangements or such multilateral institutions as the OECD, the Inter-American Development Bank, and the World Bank—a trend that could be accelerated by membership of European countries in the Inter-American Development Bank.

In the mid-1960's, the United States made a concerted effort to preserve its monopoly in the supply of military equipment to Latin America. The Johnson Administration applied intense pressure on Latin American countries to refrain from buying arms from Europe. However, European aircraft and arms sales to Latin America have blossomed since 1966, when the U.S. Congress prohibited sales of advanced weaponry to Latin America. Today, Brazil, Argentina, Peru, Venezuela, Colombia, and Ecuador all have some modern military equipment provided by European countries. Although Congress continued to limit the amount of

U.S. military aid to $75 million, by mid-1971 European efforts to replace U.S. suppliers had been so successful that the Nixon Administration moved to redress the balance by requesting removal of congressional restrictions on U.S. sales. The need for arms in Latin America is open to question, certainly, but, so long as no one country secures a monopoly in a subregional area, the European sales in themselves should not be viewed as a threat to U.S. interests.

So far, Europeans have been reluctant to involve themselves too deeply in political, security, and social aspects of Latin American affairs, both because of skepticism about the payoff for them and because of a belief that the United States regards the Western Hemisphere as its exclusive preserve—an American "sphere of influence," in which active European involvement would be regarded as an unwarranted intrusion. Europeans have assumed that the Monroe Doctrine still applies with a vigor extending to political as well as military involvements.

There is evidence to support this view. For example, the United States readily acquiesces in West European trade with East European Socialist states or in Latin American trade with Eastern Europe. But we go to extraordinary lengths to hamper European trade with the only Communist state in the hemisphere—Cuba. Moreover, although we have relaxed restrictions on trade with mainland China and are favorably disposed toward the initiatives of some U.S. companies to build factories for the Soviet Union, in 1971 we held up an Export-Import Bank credit for a commercal sale of airplanes to the Chilean Government airlines. In addition, offers of technical assistance made by European labor unions (both Socialist and non-Socialist) in the 1960's to labor groups not affiliated with the AFL-CIO in Latin America were resisted by American labor, usually backed by the U.S. Government. During the 1960's, when France offered Chile the services of two technicians in the intelligence field, a high-level U.S. emissary was sent to protest to President Eduardo Frei. On numerous occasions, high-level U.S. officials have warned their counterparts in Bonn about "meddling" by certain German groups in Latin America, often adding that "what happens in Berlin is more important to Germany than what happens in Bogotá." Indeed, far more than is generally recognized, the record of both the Johnson and the early Nixon administrations during the 1960's was one of constant attempts to discourage European involvement in political, security, and social aspects of Latin America. In the 1965–69 period, the most forceful attempt by Secretary of State Dean Rusk to censor a public speech by Vice President Hubert Humphrey related not to Vietnam but to a proposed statement encouraging a more active European role in Latin America. This policy of opposing European involvement obtained despite the fact that official rhetoric—particularly at OECD meetings—proclaimed the desirability of greater European involvement.

There are indications that some European political programs in Latin America have diminished since the mid-1960's as much as a result of U.S. opposition as of a lack of European interest. By 1972, however, an outsider got the impression that U.S. opposition to European involvement is distinctly less true of the Nixon Administration than of earlier periods. To encourage European involvement, we will have to modify the Monroe Doctrine and the special relationship that has existed between the United States and Latin America in the past. In both their original formulation and the way that they have been defined in past decades, the political and economic assumptions of the Monroe Doctrine are no longer valid. They were once designed to protect against what was considered the nefarious influence of the Old World and to preserve the assumed purity of the New—as well as to preserve the hegemony of the United States. That hegemony is no longer essential, nor can we preserve it in any event. We no longer seek to escape from Europe. Neither does Latin America. We can encourage Europe to seek an international role outside of Europe, not in order to solve the problems of Latin America or of our relations with it, but rather to create a new Western framework within which we can find a more viable and normal relationship with Latin America.

## SIGNIFICANCE OF THE ALLIANCE FOR PROGRESS

If the foregoing perspectives can be translated into specific steps to be taken, we must, to begin with, consider the Alliance for Progress and how, if at all, it relates to future policy.

If only for historical interest, it is worth noting that, as far as the United States is concerned, the Alliance for Progress program was never really tried for any length of time. It was first proclaimed by President Kennedy in March, 1961, and was agreed to by representatives of Latin American governments and the United States at Punta del Este in August of that year. The machinery for implementing the U.S. participation was established in December and only really began to function early in 1962. Twenty-two months later, President Kennedy was dead. Only twenty-two days after that, on December 14, 1963, President Johnson made his first major decision affecting American foreign policy— a decision reversing the policy that Kennedy had followed. In giving responsibility for U.S. policy in Latin America to Assistant Secretary of State Thomas Mann, he handed over U.S.–Latin American relations to an official whose views and record symbolized a rejection of the policy President Kennedy had proposed. As far as U.S. participation in the Alliance for Progress was concerned, this decision killed it. Most officials who had been associated with the Kennedy policy were replaced. From then on, the Alliance for Progress became just another AID program. As Jerome Levinson and Juan de Onis aptly stated in their book, *The Alliance That Lost Its Way: A Critical Report on the Alliance for Progress,* with Kennedy's death the "political theory of the alliance was undone" and technocratic considerations supplanted other objectves.

However, it must be recognized that President Kennedy and his colleagues were overoptimistic in their fundamental assumptions about the Alliance and in their belief that so ambitious a program could be accomplished in ten years. They failed to note that problems that have persisted for two centuries are not likely to be solved in a decade, and probably not even in three or four. They exaggerated the leverage that the United States might exert. With the benefit of hindsight, it is easy to say that aims envisioned in the Alliance for Progress do not provide a wholly adequate base for U.S. policy in the 1970's.

The founders of the Alliance sought to pursue disparate objectives, and, as events after President Kennedy's death revealed a clash between them, political democracy and social equity were generally sacrificed in favor of U.S. security interests, private economic interests, and economic growth.

Do the Alliance goals of political democracy, social equity, and accelerated economic growth have any relevance today? I believe they do. Admittedly, what the United States can do to promote their achievement is more circumscribed than many of us had thought even five years ago. It is much clearer today that the crucial decisions must be made in Latin America by Latin Americans. But we should not forget that Alliance for Progress programs helped train the leaders, managers, planners, and other professionals who now give many Latin American countries a capacity to build and manage modern economies and modernized societies. The Alliance has also left another valuable legacy: the fact that all Latin American governments—even the least progressive—are compelled to subscribe to the goals of accelerated development and social equity. If the Alliance achieved less than was desired, it nevertheless produced some fundamental changes in attitudes that are irreversible.

Despite its shortcomings, the Alliance helped to provide the basis for avoiding social disintegration in Latin America. To this end, development remains an important objective for U.S. policy. Latin American countries may now have a greater capacity to mobilize and manage their own resources, but, as noted, they still need additional external capital, technology, and managerial capacity, and, with the possible exception of Argentina and Venezuela, they will continue to. In many of these countries today, the core population—the population that participates in the money economy—is only 30 per cent of the total. This group generally absorbs 60–70 per cent of total resources and controls the political system. Another 30–70 per cent of the population continues to live at a subsistence level. The relatively well-off minority is generally unwilling to make the sacrifice required in terms of delayed consumption to provide the savings needed to extend the benefits of modernization to the poor majority. Present population, rural migration, and unemployment rates indicate that the problems are going to get worse before they get better, and the "marginal" population will continue to grow in proportion to the core society.

Some observers believe that governments that are disposed to use the instrument of the state to redistribute wealth can successfully integrate the marginal population into the core society—find them jobs, in most cases—without massive external assistance. Others believe that strong authoritarian governments, like that in Brazil, can slow the increase in consumption by the middle sector long enough to provide the capital savings needed to accelerate development and can eventually provide the jobs that will absorb the marginal population. It seems unlikely, however, that either kind of government will be successful unless it receives substantial external resources from abroad. Capital assistance and increased trade revenues (together with technology and management) can help in accelerating the growth rate. But the problem of marginality cannot be dented, unless accelerated growth is accompanied by a redistribution of social and economic gains.

## DEVELOPMENT ASSISTANCE

The development assistance package submitted by President Nixon in 1971 reflected a view that had come to be widely recognized in Congress: namely, that the political liabilities of bilateral assistance for donor and recipient countries alike require a modification of the pattern that prevailed in the 1960's. This means that, in most countries, the large, highly visible bilateral aid missions must be substantially reduced and many of them eliminated. The larger responsibility should be assumed by resident missions of the World Bank, the United Nations, and the Inter-American Development Bank. The IDB should increasingly become the key development institution in Latin America, particularly as its own technical capacities grow after a decade of experience. Under new leadership, the World Bank has become— and the United Nations may become—important factors in Latin America, the latter especially in the field of technical assistance. It would be a mistake for the United States to try converting these multilateral institutions into agencies subservient to the unilateral political fiat of the U.S. Treasury or the White House. There are already disturbing indications that the Nixon Administration is prepared to use its influence in the Inter-American Development

Bank and the World Bank for short-term political purposes by blocking final approval of loans—in regard to Guyana, Bolivia, and Chile. Should this become a trend, the alleged advantages of multilateralism will prove hollow, and we will be back in the mire of bilateral political conflict.

The ability of the United States to channel substantially higher levels of official aid—now down to a net level of $625 million of official development aid for Latin America in 1970—will depend in part on how the Vietnam tragedy ends and whether the President is prepared to use up the political capital required to assure higher priority to Latin American development.

## TRADE

The figures cited before indicate that trade is a far more significant means of resource transfer between the United States and Latin America than is aid. However, the Latin American share of U.S. imports in 1970 was only 12 per cent, compared to 21 per cent in 1960. Only 34 per cent of Latin America's exports go to the United States, while 42 per cent of its imports come from the United States.

At present, the best we can hope for to change this balance is a worldwide preferential trading system that will permit privileged access to the North American market for the products of Latin American countries, along with the other less-developed countries. Enactment by the United States of the necessary legislation today seems unlikely; we will be lucky if we can resist some of the current protectionist pressures to restrict access to the U.S. market even further.

There would be some temporary economic advantages in a preferential trading system based on the Western Hemisphere. But the political disadvantages, both for the United States and for Latin American countries, clearly outweigh any economic benefits. The political effect of this would be to bind the Latin American countries even more closely to the United States; to reinforce our overwhelming domination; and to make it impossible to loosen the U.S. embrace of Latin America gracefully. A hemispheric trading area also runs against the whole idea of opening up Latin America to the outside world, of encouraging Latin America to play a larger role in international affairs, and, finally, of encouraging European countries to take a more active role.*

## ASPIRATIONS FOR THE FUTURE

Even though our aspirations for Latin America are more limited today than they were a decade ago, and our awareness of the difficulties is greater, we can still aspire to use our resources to assist people who are seeking to build a country or continent along lines that correspond to Western traditions. In the process, our trade, aid, monetary, diplomatic, and security policies *vis-à-vis* Latin America can have an important impact. The way we transmit aid will be different; and the relative importance of trade may be significantly greater. But the result will be the same. We will be helping Latin American countries to find necessary markets, thereby helping them to avoid social disintegration, which in the long run could be against our interests as well as theirs.

The realization that U.S. leverage may be more circumscribed than had been supposed is no justification for abandoning certain goals of the Alliance for Progress. In different ways and in a different style, we can continue quietly to support the preservation or restoration of political democracy and civil liberties and the implementation of internal economic and social reform.

Much has been made of the importance of "style" in our relations with Latin America. That it is important cannot be doubted. President Kennedy is still revered for beginning a new era in relations between the United States and Latin America—not primarily by promising material assistance but by conveying an understanding and respect for Latin American people, their culture, and their traditions. He acknowledged that we have as much to learn as to teach. If we are to have good working relations with Latin American countries in the future, we will have to strengthen this attitude of understanding and respect within our leadership and our entire society.

In this regard, the outcome of the war in Southeast Asia may be

* Another problem, relating to the multinational corporation in Latin America, is discussed at length in Chapter 10.

helpful. For there is a possibility that U.S. leaders in the coming decade will approach the problems of other societies and other cultures with a little less certainty, with their messianic spirit tempered, and with a willingness to see that others may have solutions as well as problems. They may be better equipped to resist what contemporary French philosopher Henry Dumery has called the "temptation to do good: the belief that not only must virtue be done but our particular version of virtue in our particular way." If we approach our relationship with Latin America in this spirit, we are more likely to do better in this decade than we did in the last.

# PART II

# PROBLEMS OF THE
# POOR COUNTRIES

# 5

# Violence and Development

## HEDLEY BULL

*One of the most difficult problems in the field of development relates to violence. Is it caused by development, or can it be retarded by policies that bring about political, economic, and social progress in poor countries? Even though there is no universal answer to this question, the author analyzes the major factors involved and evaluates some methods and implications of working to control violence.—THE EDITORS*

The part of the world that is undergoing the series of related processes to which we give the unsatisfactory names "development" and "modernization" is also the scene of a remarkably high degree of political violence. At the outset, there are three sets of questions that invite our attention, and that can lead us to some understanding of this difficult subject:

1. How are political violence and development related to one another? In particular, is lack of development a principal cause of political violence in the Third World, and is development therefore the sovereign solution of the problem of controlling

This chapter is based on a paper presented to the Development Issues Seminar, Overseas Development Council, on November 17, 1970.

Third World violence? Or does the source of this violence lie in the process of development itself? Is the prevalence of political violence a primary obstacle to development of the Third World, or can it also be seen as the midwife of development?

2. To what extent does the developed world need to be concerned about political violence in the Third World? Are the rich countries bound to be affected by violence and tension there, or do they have the prospect of insulating themselves from it?

3. If the developed countries do need to concern themselves about political violence in the Third World, what, if anything, can they do to control it? To what extent is Third World political violence inevitable, and to what extent is it subject to limitation or control? Should the object of the rich countries be to curtail political violence wherever it appears or to limit certain forms of violence while tolerating or even encouraging others?

In order to answer these questions, it is first important to understand two terms that are often used imprecisely or incorrectly: political violence and development. The term "political violence" implies the existence of a conflict between one political group and another. It includes internal or domestic violence as well as that between nations. It embraces violence conducted on behalf of subnational, transnational, or international groups as well as that carried out in the name of the state. It encompasses the whole spectrum of violence from thermonuclear war through biological and chemical war, conventional war, "sublimited" war, and "low-level violence" (such as aircraft hijackings, the taking of hostages, and urban sabotage).

The term "development" causes more problems. It is important to distinguish three forms in which it appears. First, there is economic development, which can be defined as progress made in relation to specific goals, such as the accumulation of adequate amounts of capital, industrialization, the size of per capita income, or over-all economic growth. Second, there is social development, defined as progress made in such fields as education, health, housing, and land tenure. Third, there is political development, which can be defined, following Samuel P. Huntington in *Political Order in Changing Societies,* as the rationalization of authority (*i.e.*, the replacement of traditional authorities by a single, secular, national authority); the differentiation of specialized political functions and structures; and the increase in the number of people playing political roles.

No doubt, there are important connections among these kinds of development. Indeed, these connections enable us to speak loosely of "development" or "modernization" as if it were a single process that extends over these three fields (and others). But it is important to recognize that economic, social, and political development are three distinct processes and not three aspects of the same process. In particular, we must not assume that political or social development is simply a function of economic development. Huntington points out in his incisive study that there has been substantial economic and social development in the Third World in the last twenty years, but that, at the same time, changes taking place in the political life of most poor countries are better described as political decay than as political development. This observation is true inasmuch as traditional forms of political authority in these countries have disintegrated without there having been any significant movement toward modern political forms.

The terms "development" and "modernization" have a number of other implications that it is important to disavow. One such implication is that whatever is more highly developed or modern is always to be preferred to whatever is less developed or less modern. Yet, at a time when development has become a target of widespread attack in the developed world, it should be obvious that this implication is misplaced: Although machine-smashing was considered reactionary at the time of the Luddites, in some circumstances it may now be progressive. Therefore, we should think of development simply as the sum of changes that are taking place, the desirability of which needs to be established in each case.

Another implication that we must disavow is that whatever is less developed or less modern is bound, in the long run, to give way to whatever is more developed or more modern. Depending on the efforts we devote to development, the only question then becomes whether this transition would take place sooner or later.

It is true, no doubt, that those economic, social, and political forms that we call modern have demonstrated a formidable power to destroy primitive and traditional institutions. But we go beyond the evidence if we assume that the world as a whole is bound, in the long run, to conform to the requirements of some particular definition of modernity. In principle, the pursuit of high economic growth rates, the trend toward individualistic and equalitarian social values, and even the displacement of a predominantly religious and authoritarian outlook by one that is secular and scientific could all be reversed. In other words, we could stop thinking of these values as essential to modernity.

## THE RELATIONSHIP OF VIOLENCE TO DEVELOPMENT

It has often been suggested that there is a connection between lack of development and the avoidance of *international* violence or war, and, conversely, that there is a connection between development and peace. In the last century, writers like Auguste Comte and Herbert Spencer, for example, contended that industrial, bourgeois society was essentially unfavorable to war, which was a relic of feudal times. This argument has been restated in relation to our own times by Klaus Knorr in his book *On the Uses of Military Power in the Nuclear Age.* He holds that, on the one hand, among the developed countries war has come to be regarded as of declining utility and increasing cost for reasons of affluence, education, and prevailing economic theory, but that, on the other hand, among the developing countries war remains attractive as an instrument of policy. In fact, however, on the record, developing countries do not seem to be any more prone to violent international conflict than developed ones.

It is rather the high incidence in the poor countries of *domestic* or internal violence that sets them apart from the rich. In 1966, Robert McNamara strongly put forward the view that this violence was caused by lack of development, more particularly by lack of economic development. In his book, *The Essence of Security: Reflections in Office*, he quoted a World Bank study of the 164 internationally significant outbreaks of violence during the period

1958–66. Only fifteen of these were conflicts between states. "What is most significant of all," he said, "is that there is a direct and constant relationship between the incidence of violence and the economic status of the countries afflicted." Only one of the twenty-seven nations classified as "rich" had suffered a major internal upheaval, whereas, among "middle income" nations, 48 per cent had done so; among "poor" nations, 69 per cent; and, among "very poor," 87 per cent. "Given the certain connection between economic stagnation and the incidence of violence, the years that lie ahead for the nations in the southern half of the globe look ominous."

It is now understood fairly widely that this formulation gives a false picture of the actual position. It is true that poor countries are prone to internal violence, and that rich countries are stable. But it is not the poverty of the poor countries that accounts for their instability so much as the processes of development or modernization in which they are now involved. As Huntington puts it, "modernity breeds stability but modernization breeds instability."

Poverty, which has been the lot of man down the ages, has often characterized the most stable and orderly of traditional political systems. At the present time, the point to make about poor countries is that traditional political systems in all of them have disintegrated, and that processes of modernization are under way. It is not merely that economic and social development does not necesarily promote political stability. There are also powerful arguments to the effect that development has a positively destabilizing effect. Rapid economic growth, it has been contended,* disrupts traditional social bonds, such as family and caste groups, that tie individuals to the established order; it produces drastic changes in ways and places of work, distribution of income, and methods of production, and it creates new classes of "winners" and "losers" who become discontented with their place in the system. Meanwhile, social development, in the form of urbanization and the advance of education and literacy, gives rise to increased expectations that, if unsatisfied, lead to political action.

* See, for example, Mancur Olson, Jr., "Rapid Growth as a Destabilizing Force," *The Journal of Economic History,* December, 1963.

Furthermore, although economic development may, in some instances, permit wants to be satisfied, there is no reason to regard it as likely to remove the causes of political violence. Indeed, there is considerable reason to see economic development as a major source of such violence. The argument that economic development dispels political violence is so contrary to the evidence that it is doubtful whether such an argument can any longer be used persuasively to attract support in rich countries for policies of economic aid. For example, it is interesting that the Pearson Commission, in *Partners in Development: Report of the Commission on International Development*, carefully avoided appealing to this argument: "Development is not a guarantee of political stability or an antidote to violence. Change is, in itself, intrinsically disruptive. . . . Nor is development an assurance of peaceful and responsible international behavior."

Of course, socially and politically disruptive processes of economic development are under way in the Third World, irrespective of the attitudes of rich countries toward aid. Responsibility for turmoil in the Third World cannot be laid at the door of the donor countries. Moreover, in some Third World countries—such as India, Singapore, Malaysia, and Chile—stable or "developed" political systems do exist and thus have been able to withstand pressures of economic and social modernization. And, despite the fact that, with regard to controlling political violence, the aid effort does not seem to contain the promise once placed in it, the case for aid may be compelling on other grounds. But it should be recognized that the problem of controlling political violence in the Third World is unlikely to be solved by the indirect route of promoting economic development. To paraphrase a dictum drawn from the discussion of disarmament: The problem of political violence is the problem of political violence; it is not the problem of economic development.

## POLITICAL VIOLENCE AS AN OBSTACLE TO DEVELOPMENT

Just as development is sometimes seen as a means of controlling or eliminating political violence in the Third World, so the control of political violence may be regarded as a necessary condition of development. In the first place, the energies devoted by poor countries to internal and international conflicts may be regarded as a waste of energies and resources urgently needed for the task of economic development. Many poor countries devote a high proportion of their gross national product (GNP) to defense. In 1969, for example, according to the Institute for Strategic Studies in *The Military Balance, 1970–1971*, Nigeria spent 5.9 per cent of its GNP on defense, Cuba 6.1 per cent, Taiwan 9.2 per cent, Iraq 10 per cent, Laos 11 per cent, the then United Arab Republic (Egypt) 13.3 per cent, Syria 14.4 per cent, Jordan 18 per cent, North Vietnam 21.3 per cent, North Korea 24.9 per cent, and Israel 25.1 per cent. Third World countries are also greedy consumers of arms transferred to them by the rich countries (especially by the United States, the Soviet Union, Britain, and France). Simultaneously, the poor countries turn to the rich for economic aid and advocate the latter's disarmament with unflagging zeal. A study by Geoffrey Kemp, "Arms Traffic and Third World Conflicts," published in *International Concilation*, March, 1970, estimates that, during the ten-year period 1955–65, fifty-two Third World countries acquired the following arms from the advanced countries: 7,000 combat aircraft, 1,700 transport aircraft, 2,400 helicopters, 1,500 tanks, 11,800 armored personnel carriers, 6,500 armored cars, 108 warships, 570 patrol craft, and 180 amphibious vessels.

Impressed by statistics like these, the advanced countries often take the view that Third World countries ought to treat economic development as their chief priority and that devoting resources to violent conflict or preparation for it represents waste. It is widely held, for example, that a decision by any poor country to acquire nuclear weapons would be an unwarranted diversion of major resources away from development. Donor countries, it is held, should respond by making an equivalent reduction of economic aid. Indeed, the 1968 U.S. Foreign Assistance Act sought to link the quantity of economic assistance provided to poor countries with their arms expenditures: It required the withholding of economic assistance "in an amount equivalent to the amount spent by any underdeveloped country other than Greece, Turkey, Iran, Israel, the Republic of China, the Philippines and Korea for the purchase of sophisticated weapons systems . . . unless the

President determines that such purchase or acquisition of weapons systems [is] vital to the national security of the United States."

This view that resources devoted to defense are simply waste in terms of development, is, of course, too simple. From their own experience, the developed countries are aware that defense policy can be managed so as to promote economic and social objectives—or at least minimize damage to them. Many Indians argue that an Indian military nuclear industry would serve to stimulate the civilian economy. Likewise, acquisition of "sophisticated" weapons systems may often be accompanied by the transfer of technical skills that are vitally needed for the task of development. In fact, the armed forces in many new states are a conspicuous modernizing force, by virtue of several factors: their national, rather than tribal or sectional, outlook; their commitment to education and technical skills; and their undertaking of a wide range of civilian tasks. Finally, wartime conditions of inflated demand for certain products, along with the difficulty of obtaining foreign supplies, has often stimulated industrial expansion.

In the last analysis, there must be a conflict between the requirements of defense or security and those of economic development. But the advanced countries cannot expect the poor to proceed as though development should always take priority, when they themselves do not operate on this assumption. The issues that divide India and Pakistan, North and South Korea, Israel and the Arab states, China and Taiwan are of vital concern to the countries involved. No doubt, it is regrettable that the world is driven by violent conflicts in this way; but these conflicts do exist, and we in the developed world also play our full part in them. This observation leads to the most significant point about the passage quoted above from the 1968 Foreign Assistance Act: that, in seeking to penalize countries for acquiring sophisticated weapons-systems, it excepts those countries that, in the violent conflicts in which they are engaged, are ranged alongside the United States.

At the same time, attempts by the donor countries to determine the way in which recipient countries divide their resources as between development and other purposes are greeted by the latter with charges of "imperialism." These charges are justified, in the sense that the donor countries are, in fact, using their position of superior strength to influence the way in which weaker countries should manage their affairs. It may be said, in response, that "imperialism," in this sense, is a just and necessary element in the development process. It may be said, furthermore, that the donor countries, in taking advantage of their position to prod the poorer countries into efforts required by development, are being faithful to what was best in the European imperialist tradition. But any sound approach to the development problem must be founded upon the recognition that poor countries have other problems besides that of developing themselves and that they have the right to determine for themselves how to order their priorities. This approach does not mean that the donor countries can, or should, concede to the recipients of aid the right to allocate the resources transferred in any way the latter nations please. It is inevitable that donor countries will attach conditions to the giving of aid. Given the nature of some of the recipient governments, it is also desirable that the donor countries should do so. But they should not seek to apply standards to a recipient country that they cannot meet themselves.

## POLITICAL VIOLENCE AS A MEANS OF DEVELOPMENT

There is a tendency to assume that political violence within and between countries of the Third World inherently works against development and that eliminating or limiting the former would be bound to pave the way for the latter. Scarce resources are consumed by international conflicts like the Indo-Pakistani wars of 1962 and by the civil violence that has engulfed the greater part of the Third World. Development suffers when economic and social dislocation results from fighting, when foreign capital is driven away, when political leadership is subjected to sudden change, or when administrative continuity is disrupted.

Yet, historically, violence has undoubtedly been one of the great instruments of development. The American Revolution, the

French Revolution, and the Russian Revolution all represent the successful use of violence to advance objectives that, good or bad, we now recognize to have been objectives of modernization (among other things). More recently, the Chinese Communist Revolution, the Communist seizure of power in Eastern Europe (except perhaps in Czechoslovakia), the Cuban Revolution, the Chinese seizure of Tibet, and the Indian seizure of Goa, all represent uses of violence that, whatever we might think of them, have resulted in the replacement of political structures less committed (or even opposed) to modernization by regimes more committed to it. It is true that, in many conflicts in the Third World (for example, North versus South Korea, North versus South Vietnam), the issue is best seen as one between two competing paths to modernization, rather than as between modernization and traditionalism. In others (for example, India versus Pakistan), the issue does not, in any sense, concern modernization. But in many countries in the Third World, especially in Latin America, the view that violence provides the surest route to development must seem persuasive.

As in the great revolutions of modern history, it is not merely that violence sometimes may help promote development as its end result. The activity of violence—namely, the processes of internal and external war—also sometimes serves to advance development. One of the great problems of political development or modernization is that of "nation building," of creating a sense of common allegiance or loyalty among contending groups. As among so many of the "early developing countries," so among the "late developing ones," a sense of common allegiance often takes root in conditions of violent struggle. For example, the unity of modern Indonesia was forged in the struggle against the Dutch; the cohesion of Communist China probably owed a great deal to the struggle against the United States in the Korean war; the remarkable progress of nation building in Singapore reflects its people's response to their sense of being surrounded by potentially hostile forces; India's conflicts with China in 1962 and with Pakistan in 1965 and 1971 seem to have strengthened the unifying forces in Indian society over those making for disintegration; and such unity as the Arab peoples have been able to muster derives from their attempts, in 1948, in 1956, and again in 1967, to achieve the victory that would do for them what Bismarck's victory in 1870 did for Germany. If a sense of nationhood does not yet prevail among the Arabs, it is at least partly because they have lost their battle of Sedan each time they have fought it.

## CONTROLLING VIOLENCE AND PROMOTING DEVELOPMENT AS GOALS OF POLICY

Despite the factors presented in the preceding paragraphs, the control or limitation of violent conflict and the promotion of development, in all its senses, may be thought of as the two principal goals agreed upon in the international community. These are the principal objects of policy about which East and West, North and South are agreed at least in principle. And the Third World is the area in which reality is furthest from either of the goals.

In contrast to the rhetoric of the Communist countries and the Third World, which calls for wars of liberation, the official rhetoric of the West presents these two goals as fully compatible with each other. They are seen as compatible, not merely in the ideal world in which, it is hoped, both will ultimately be achieved, but also here and now. Development is presented as a means of checking violence, and the control of violence is regarded as something that will facilitate development. (One expression of this was the naming of the Peace Corps, which is essentially concerned with development activities.) No doubt we should cling to the idea that the two goals of achieving development and halting conflict are ultimately in harmony, and we should strive in the meantime to reconcile one with the other. But there may be some awkward choices along the way.

## THE IMPACT OF THIRD WORLD VIOLENCE ON THE RICH COUNTRIES

Whatever the validity of attitudes concerning violence and development, the rich, industrial areas of the world are at present disenchanted with involvement in the affairs of the Third World.

This mood is reflected in the Communist world as well as in the West, and, within the West, on the Left as well as the Right. Indeed, the left-wing doctrine in the West—that Asians, Africans, and Latin Americans should be allowed to solve their own problems—has converged with the right-wing doctrine that these poor people had better be left to stew in their own juice. Further, the mood of disenchantment is expressed in disillusionment both with military involvement in the affairs of Third World countries and with the enterprise of development assistance.

This mood is also reflected in a reverse form of the doctrine of Lin Piao, formerly China's Defense Minister, namely, that the "cities" of the world should concentrate upon their own advancement to the disregard of the "countryside" that surrounds them. This through-the-looking-glass doctrine was voiced recently in the British Government's Duncan Report on the future of the British diplomatic service. It divides the world into the "inner" (*i.e.*, the developed) and the "outer" areas and proposes that Britain's diplomatic representation be concentrated in the former areas, where the principal task of British representatives will be to promote the sale of British goods. In the latter areas, Britain should maintain only skeleton staffs. Finally, and above all, disenchantment with the Third World is reflected in the historic shift in American public attitudes toward world affairs—a shift that is causing a somewhat reluctant government to disengage from established positions and to relax external efforts in many parts of the globe.

The disenchantment described here springs from several sources —by no means wholly to the discredit of the developed parts of the world. To begin with, in the West, disillusionment with Vietnam and, more generally, with direct involvement in wars of counterinsurgency has caused many people to lose faith in the wider objectives of the United States—namely, resisting aggression, containing communism, and fulfilling treaty commitments. These are objectives associated with the Vietnam war and counterinsurgency, though not an essential part of either. Second, there is disillusionment with the effects of foreign aid, caused by exaggerated expectations, meager gains in terms of economic growth in the Third World, and a feeling of hopelessness induced by the remorseless growth of population. Third, there is the decline of the cold war and, along with it, the ideological struggle for the Third World. This decline has weakened the West's conviction that it must be active in the developed countries in order to check the influence of the Communist powers. Finally, there is a feeling in the developed world generally of exasperation with the aggressive rhetoric of African, Asian, and Latin American countries, their envy and self-pity, their hypersensitivity and self-centeredness, their delusions of grandeur, and their incompetence. This feeling is comparable in some respects to the "white backlash" in the United States.

## WHAT HAVE THE RICH COUNTRIES TO FEAR?

It may be argued that the rich countries, while they will not be able to ignore the poor parts of the world, do have a fair prospect of achieving their essential objectives during the next decade or so while maintaining only a token involvement in Third World affairs. Given the facts of the "widening gap" between developed and developing countries in per capita income, and given the faster development of trade among the former than between them and the latter, the means of sustaining and advancing the prosperity of the developed world may be found essentially within its own boundaries.

Furthermore, in terms of their security, the rich countries do not have as much to fear from Third World hostility as is sometimes claimed—provided, of course, that China is treated as a special case. With the important exception of China, the group of privileged countries—representing one-quarter of the world's population and commanding three-quarters of its wealth—alone possesses the leading instruments of war: not only nuclear weapons and missiles, but also tanks, heavy guns, military aircraft, and warships. The Third World, meanwhile, is dependent chiefly on the advanced countries for the supply of these weapons.

A historical parallel is valuable in illustrating this point. In the 1930's, the main theme of international politics was a contest between a different set of "Have's" and "Have-Not's." The former were represented by Britain, France, and their allies, and the latter by Germany, Italy, and Japan. The issue between them was the control of territory. Today, once again, there is a group of states in the world—now a majority both of states and of the world's population—who see themselves as Have-Not's. Their grievance does not concern the control of territory but their disproportionately small share of the world's wealth. However, by contrast with the Have-Not's of the 1930's, they have neither the power nor enough unity among themselves to make their demands the chief issue on the international agenda and to compel the satisfied states to choose between resistance to their demands and peaceful change—that is, to choose between war and appeasement. Thus, the principal issues of world politics are not those between the Have's and the Have-Not's (again excepting China) but those that arise among the leading Have's. Nor is this situation likely to change. The Have countries do not need to fear any closing of the ranks of the Have-Not countries against them; the prospects of world peace depend essentially on the relations that the United States, the Soviet Union, China, Japan, and the countries of Western Europe have with each other.

Yet, even though the developed countries are not likely to face any powerful coalition of Have-Not's arrayed against them, they are not likely to be able to insulate themselves from political violence taking place *within* the Third World. Nor, even if it were possible, would their interests lie in sealing themselves off from turmoil in the poorer parts of the world. This is so for four reasons:

First, the ease and speed with which persons, goods, and ideas now move about the world, coupled with the interpenetration of societies, mean that the domestic affairs of the advanced countries are bound to interact to a considerable degree with those of the poor countries. Consider, in the case of the United States today, the links between black American groups and African radical movements, between white Americans and white minority regimes in Africa, between student radicals and student movements throughout the world, between Spanish-speaking Americans and the various contending movements in Latin America, and between American Jews and Israel. Consider the way in which techniques such as aircraft hijacking, the taking of hostages, and urban sabotage have been imitated around the world. Considerations of state policy may make desirable a foreign policy of noninvolvement, but the facts of social interaction as between the developed and the developing countries will ensure that conflicts within the latter have their repercussions in the former.

Second, there will be direct effects on citizens of advanced countries who either travel around the world or live in the poorer countries. The world is now familiar with the use of low-level violence against innocent persons by political groups concerned to gain publicity for their cause or bring pressure to bear on governments. The novelty of this development is the use of violence by these political groups not only within their own countries and against their own nationals, but also outside the boundaries of their countries and against foreign nationals. The sovereign state is losing the monopoly of international violence it has enjoyed since the suppression of piracy. This new kind of anarchy clearly could expand both in sophistication of technology and in the number of users. Prospects for controlling the new piracy are necessarily bound up with prospects for the control of conflicts in the Third World.

Third, it is still likely that Third World conflicts will disturb the peace of the great powers by embroiling them on opposite sides. The decline of the cold war may have lessened the danger that a Soviet-American conflict will arise in this way. But the two superpowers are still heavily committed to antagonistic parties in Korea, China, Indochina, and the Middle East. In the world of the 1970's, moreover, the balance of power in Asia and the Pacific is likely to be made up of three and possibly four great powers—the United States, the Soviet Union, China, and Japan—each of which will serve to check the influence of the others.

Finally, relations among the states of the developed world are sensitive to the pattern of relations within the developing world. Many of the central problems of international order remain essentially global in nature. For example, there is the case of arms control. If the spread of nuclear weapons continues in the Third World—for example, as a result of an Indian decision to "go nuclear"—this spread will affect the prospects for proliferation of nuclear weapons in Europe. If chemical or biological weapons are developed and used in Third World conflicts, this occurrence will affect attitudes of advanced countries toward control in this field. And if a state of international animosity is allowed to grow up in particular parts of the Third World, enabling local powers to threaten or attack their weaker neighbors, while the United States and other major powers are concerned only with maintaining a global balance of power, there will be a diminishing of respect for norms of international behavior elsewhere in the world.

Yet, even if it were possible for the rich countries to insulate themselves from violence in the Third World, it would be against their interests to do so. Both the Western and Communist worlds are committed by their values to pursue goals such as the control of violence and the promotion of development on a scale that is worldwide and not limited geographically to themselves. They have an obligation to concern themselves with mankind as a whole, even where they do not have an immediate interest in doing so. And, to the extent that they can achieve integrity and self-respect only by remaining faithful to their values, they have an interest in fulfilling their obligations.

## BACK TO BASICS?

The advanced countries, therefore, cannot afford to ignore violence in the Third World. They should, however, recognize that some violence is an inevitable concomitant of the changes now taking place in the Third World, and that their own ability to control it is limited. They should recognize, also, that violence sometimes serves to promote the interest of Third World peoples— and those objectives of development that the advanced countries themselves espouse. It is not possible or desirable to suppress all violence in the Third World, any more than it is to suppress all change.

In the long run, the control of political violence in the Third World, as elsewhere, depends upon the development of a global sense of community that will permit conflicts to be contained and moderated. The international development effort is of central importance in helping to create that sense of community—not so much because of the results to which it might lead, in terms of increased development, as because of the cooperative effort of international development itself. Along with preventing or limiting war and preserving man's environment, international development assistance is one of the few goals about which all the main political blocs in the world are in principle united, whatever differences of interpretation this unity conceals. The cooperation of all nations in the enterprise of international development assistance expresses, and helps to consolidate, the nascent idea of a world community.

But, as we have seen, development is not in itself a means of controlling political violence. Moreover, it is unhelpful to suggest that the pursuit of political stability, either domestic or international, requires efforts to close the widening gap in per capita income between rich and poor countries. There is no prospect of closing the gap in this century, according even to the most optimistic projections. The problem is therefore not how to close the gap but rather how to achieve political stability, given the existence of a gap.

Economic development appeals to many observers as the remedy for domestic or international political violence in the Third World, because it appears to promise a means of avoiding the intractable political problems of resolving or adjusting conflict. However, it is precisely these political problems that have to be faced. Indeed, the examination of development as a means for controlling violence leads us back to such classic politicostrategic devices as the attempt to maintain a balance among contending local powers, to promote global or regional understandings on arms control, to limit arms transfers to developing countries, to reduce the likelihood of outside involvement in local conflicts, to limit and contain these conflicts, and to facilitate their end. It is beyond the scope of this paper to explore these devices in detail; but it is to this well-trodden territory that we must look for the means of coping with Third World violence.

# 6

# Population Growth, Food Needs, and Environmental Stress

## LESTER R. BROWN

*The rapid growth of the world's population since World War II has brought with it new implications for the way we all live. No longer can we assume that the earth's resources will meet every demand placed upon them, if only they are well managed and carefully used. In particular, despite the success of technical developments like the Green Revolution in new cereal varieties, feeding added billions of people will be a problem. In this chapter, the author brings together information on population growth, the needs of the human family for food, and the stresses that man's agricultural systems are placing on the world's environment. There are warnings here for the poor countries—and for the rest of us.—*THE EDITORS

In order to understand the food-population-environment dilemma of late-twentieth-century man, it is necessary to have a broad perspective. The food problem cannot be viewed solely within the framework of the agricultural sector but must be seen in terms of the global economy and ecosystem. Indeed, the question is no longer simply, "Can we feed the people of the earth?" but, "What

This chapter is based on a paper presented to the Development Issues Seminar, Overseas Development Council, April 14, 1971.

arc the environmental consequences of attempting to produce enough food for the world population?"

We might usefully begin by reminding ourselves what agriculture is in ecological terms. It is, by definition, man's selection for preferential treatment of those species of plants and animals that, in the natural state, best suited his needs. In favoring those species, man has removed the natural cover of grass and forest from some 10 per cent of the earth's land surface, planting it with the crops he domesticated. Wheat, for example, originated in the hills surrounding the Tigris-Euphrates Valley but is now planted on some 600 million acres—roughly the area of India or of the United States east of the Mississippi. Because of man's agricultural efforts, Hereford and Angus cattle today roam the Great Plains, once the home of 30–40 million buffalo. European cattle are displacing the kangaroo on the grazing lands of Australia. The domesticated water buffalo inhabits the river valleys of Asia.

The history of agriculture is one of successive interventions in the natural system, always seeking to alter it to expand the food supply. Technological innovations, such as irrigation, began several thousand years ago. The discovery and widespread use of agricultural chemicals, including both fertilizer and pesticides, constituted massive encroachments on the environment.

These technological intrusions increased the food supply, which, in turn, permitted increases in population. Sometimes, population exceeded the food supply, generating pressure for further innovation. Thus, increases in food production and population have tended to reinforce each other, resulting in an endless upward spiral. Initial interventions were local, but modern agricultural technology often has global consequences. New signs of agricultural stress on the earth's ecosystem appear almost daily as the exponentially rising food demand, fueled by population growth and rising incomes, presses the ecosystem's finite capacities.

## THE PROBLEM OF WATER

One of the first major infringements on nature's processes was the obstruction by man of the flow of streams and rivers, diverting water onto the land he was cultivating. This manipulation of the hydrological cycle, closely associated with the emergence of early civilizations, greatly boosted the productivity of land. It was not long, however, before some of man's technological inventions began to exceed his understanding of them, creating some worrisome consequences. He knew how to divert water onto land, but he did not understand the subterranean dynamics of rising water tables, resulting in the waterlogging and salinity problem that eventually affects most irrigation systems. The remains of civilizations buried in the sands of the Middle East bear witness to man's incomplete comprehension of the consequences of intervening in the hydrological cycle.

Irrigated agriculture has continued uninterrupted now for several thousand years. But it is only within the past few decades, as world population has rapidly increased, that competition for the earth's limited fresh-water supply has become intense and a source of contention in many regions. There have been bitter conflicts over the division of the Jordan's water between Israel and its Arab neighbors. Protracted negotiations were required between the Sudan and what was then the United Arab Republic (Egypt) to divide the Nile's waters. India and Pakistan vied for years for the rights to the Indus' waters. Conflicts over water rights between states in the southwestern United States have become a major political issue in recent years. Russia, forced to import food in several recent years despite its vast agricultural area, is planning to reverse the flow of four rivers now emptying into the Arctic Ocean, diverting them southward, where the water will be used to irrigate the dryland areas. Shutting off this flow of warm water into the Arctic Ocean will undoubtedly alter the climate there; this, in turn, will affect the global climate pattern—exactly how, no one knows, but the Russians are proceeding despite protests by meteorologists, arguing that they need the additional food that this water will make possible.

One way of obtaining more fresh water is to desalt sea water, but it is doubtful whether this will be economical for large-scale food production during this century. Still another way of getting more fresh water for agricultural purposes would be to alter rainfall patterns, shifting some of the rainfall now falling on the oceans over arable land. Firms with headquarters in Washington,

D.C., already are in the business of rainmaking internationally and will contract with national or local governments or groups of farmers to produce rain anywhere in the world.

Unfortunately, there is no supranational institution to regulate such activity, holding out the prospect that nations may one day use advanced weather-modification technologies to compete with each other for potential rainfall in much the same way armies have traditionally fought for control of land. In the continuing absence of global regulatory institutions, one could readily envisage competition between, say, India and Pakistan to shift the life-giving monsoon northward or southward, depending on the particular country's interests.

Like many of man's other interventions in the biosphere, his reshaping of the hydrologic cycle has had unwanted side effects. One of them is a great increase in the incidence of schistosomiasis or "snail fever"—an extremely debilitating disease that is particularly prevalent in the river valleys of Africa and Asia. The disease is produced by the parasitic larvae of a blood fluke, which is harbored by aquatic snails and burrows into the flesh of people standing in water or in water-soaked fields. The snails and the fluke thrive in perennial irrigation systems, where they are close to large human populations. The incidence of the disease is rising rapidly as the world's large rivers are harnessed for irrigation, and today schistosomiasis afflicts an estimated 250 million people. It now surpasses malaria, whose incidence is declining, as the world's most prevalent infectious disease.

## THE ENERGY CYCLE

A thousand years or so after man first learned to irrigate, he discovered a second way of intervening in another natural cycle, this time the energy cycle. The harnessing of draft animals greatly augmented man's own limited muscle power, raising the efficiency of his labor to the point where a segment of the population could be spared from food-producing activities. Even today, perhaps half of the world's cropland is tilled with cattle, water buffalo, and camels.

The harnessing of draft animals affected man's relationship

with nature in two important ways. First, it greatly enhanced his capacity for bringing new land under cultivation: In the New World, for instance, the pre-Columbian Indians limited their farming largely to the rich alluvial soils of the river flood plains, but, with the introduction of draft animals from Europe, and with the use of the steel plow, the tough virgin sods of the Great Plains were opened for crop farming. Second, dependence on animals for draft power as well as for food meant an increase in livestock numbers closely paralleling those in human population, and grazing needs came to exceed the rate of natural replenishment of vegetation, resulting in a gradual denuding of the countryside as livestock populations increased in many of the more densely populated areas of the world.

The next major involvement of man in the energy cycle came much later with the internal combustion engine. These engines, burning fossil fuels, permitted man to tap the solar energy received by the earth eons ago and stored underground in the form of petroleum. The productivity of labor employed in agriculture climbed sharply with this valuable assist, permitting, for the first time in history, a minority of the population to meet the food needs of the majority.

## THE ENVIRONMENTAL IMPACT OF GENETIC ADVANCES AND USE OF CHEMICALS

Man has also greatly expanded his food supply by altering the genetic composition of domesticated species of plants and animals, and by using chemicals for fertilizers and for pest control.

Through selective breeding, man has altered species, gradually improving the productivity of his farmyard animals and fowl. The first domesticated cattle probably did not produce more than 600 pounds of milk per year—barely enough to support a calf to the point where it could forage for itself. The average cow in the United States produced nearly 8,000 pounds of milk last year, and a Maryland cow named Rheinharts Ballad produced a new world record of 42,000 pounds of milk in 1970. (This animal could deliver forty-nine quarts of milk every day, outperforming her early ancestors by a factor of seventy to one!) The early ancestors of our current hen probably did not lay more than fifteen eggs, or one clutch per year. In 1970, the average American hen laid 220 eggs. The world record is held by an industrious Japanese hen that laid 365 eggs in one year.

Advances in animal genetics have environmental consequences, because their new potentials can be realized only through special, highly concentrated diets. These efficient, high-powered producers supply much greater quantities of protein for human consumption than their ancestors but, in turn, require large amounts of concentrated nutrients in the form of cereals and protein-rich commodities, such as soybeans and fish meal, along with their traditional intake of roughage. A large proportion of the earth's agricultural land has been converted from grassland to cropland in order to produce the necessary feedstuffs. Much of the Peruvian fish catch is used to meet the protein needs of modern poultry flocks in the United States.

The use of agricultural chemicals, both to improve soil fertility and to control pests, has enabled man to expand further the earth's food-producing capacity.

As the global food demand curve has sloped sharply upward since World War II, the use of chemical fertilizer has climbed even faster. In 1960, the world's farmers spread 29 million tons of chemical fertilizer—nitrates, phosphates, potash—on their land. In 1971, they poured some 70 million tons of fertilizer into the earth's ecosystem. The use of chemical fertilizer today accounts for easily one-fourth of the world's food supply—the food supply of close to a billion of the world's people. In countries where fertilizer is used intensively, as in the Netherlands and Japan, discontinuing its use could reduce the food supply by half.

Another consequence of man's need to expand his food supply is that he is poisoning or destroying the life support systems of many other species of animals. Little information is available on the effect of DDT on mammals, including man. We do know that the level in a mother's milk in the United States is above the tolerance levels permitted by the Food and Drug Administration in food products entering interstate commerce. This led one ecologist to point out that a mother's milk in any other container would not be permitted to cross state borders.

DDT levels in the environment have reached the point where

they are endangering numerous species of birds and fish, particularly the predatory ones near the top of the food chain. Among those threatened in the United States are the peregrine falcon and the bald eagle, our national emblem. In Denmark, the return of the storks from wintering in North Africa has long been a national event, celebrated by young and old alike. At one time 10,000 storks arrived each year; last year, only seventy pairs came. Pesticides used to protect crops from the locust threat in the Nile Valley are believed responsible. *Pravda* reports the reckless use of chemical pesticides in agriculture is decimating many forms of wildlife in the Soviet Union, causing many species to become "zoological rarities." The duck-hunting season was canceled entirely in 1970 because of the diminishing flocks of wild ducks. *Pravda* sounds as though it is paraphrasing Rachel Carson's *Silent Spring*: "This question (the extinction of species) is worrying us more and more every year. Why do we see almost no flocks of geese and cranes in April? Almost all the partridges are gone. Our woods, gardens, and fields are becoming quieter and quieter."

Thus far during this century, an average of one species per year quietly made its exit somewhere in the world. As the number of human beings goes up, the number of extant species is going down. The Department of the Interior now maintains a list of endangered species within the United States, totaling 79 in early 1970. This list was increased by 22 in October, 1970, adding 3 mammals, 8 birds, and 11 types of fish—an increase of 27 per cent in one year. One worldwide list of endangered species, though obviously far from complete, now includes 275 mammals and 300 species of birds.

Herds of wild elephants in Ceylon now number no more than 2,500—less than half that of twenty years ago. The problem here is not chemicals; their source of subsistence is diminishing steadily as their forest and jungle habitat is cleared to produce food for the island's population, now doubling every twenty-three years. Unfortunately, a large number of the several species threatened may be already doomed to extinction, either because their numbers are already too small to continue the species or because the conditions threatening their survival, such as levels of

DDT circulating in the biosphere or the destruction of forests, cannot be altered in time to save them. The sad thing is that the process is irreversible. A species that becomes extinct is lost not only to us but also to our children and theirs for all time to come.

## EFFECTS OF EXPANDING AGRICULTURAL USE OF LAND

Efforts to intensify agricultural production through the use of irrigation and agricultural chemicals have troublesome and disturbing consequences, but so, too, do efforts to expand the food supply by expanding the area under cultivation. In many parts of the world, man is clearing more and more land for food production while overgrazing by cattle is denuding much of the remaining land of its natural cover. The cutting of forests in the more densely populated, less-developed world is far exceeding the rate of replenishment. As vast areas of the earth's surface are deforested, those living in countries such as India and Pakistan are reduced to using cow dung for fuel (although statistics are not available, it is entirely possible that the number of people now using cow dung as fuel for preparing their meals exceeds that using natural gas.)

As man's efforts to alter the earth's composition of flora and fauna continue, an expanding area of the earth's land surface is deprived of its original cover of grass and trees, leaving soil to be severely eroded by wind and water. Millions of acres are abandoned each year in the poor countries, forcing rural people into already overcrowded cities. Nature requires centuries to create an inch of topsoil, but man can destroy it in a matter of years. The thin mantle of life-sustaining topsoil, measured in inches over most of the earth's surface, is being slowly destroyed in many areas. A historic example of the effects of man's abuse of the soil is all too plainly visible in North Africa, which once was the fertile granary of the Roman Empire and now is largely a desert, or near-desert, whose people are fed with the aid of food imports from the United States.

A study undertaken several years ago to examine the feasibiity of constructing the Mangla Reservoir in West Pakistan based its favorable recommendations on a life expectancy for the reservoir of 100 years. It now appears that the $600 million reservoir, completed in 1968, will be completely filled with silt within fifty years, as a result of accelerating soil erosion. The exploding populations of people, cattle, and goats in the Mangla watershed have denuded large areas of natural cover, permitting wholesale erosion to occur. Gullies in the region, some of them only a short drive outside of Rawalpindi, are so deep they are becoming minor tourist attractions.

Not only is the removal of natural cover associated with man's quest for food resulting in the removal of topsoil, but also, in many areas, dustbowls are being created. The result is a rise in the particulate matter in the atmosphere. Some scientists feel that this increase in particulate matter, which may be reducing the amount of solar energy reaching the earth, is partly responsible for the decline in average temperature at the earth's surface of nearly one-half degree Fahrenheit over the past twenty-five years. Dr. Gordon MacDonald, a member of the President's Council on Environmental Quality, points to an associated southward shift in the frost boundaries and heavy ice in the North Atlantic, hindering the activities of Icelandic fishermen, and warns that a cooling trend of only a few degrees in the earth's fragile and delicately balanced climatic system could initiate another Ice Age. We must reckon with the prospect that man's efforts to expand his food supply may also be altering the earth's climate in a way that will affect human economic activity.

Efforts to intensify agricultural production also have adverse environmental consequences beyond the eroding of land surface. If the effect of chemical fertilizer could be confined to agriculture, it would be fine, but unfortunately it cannot. The water runoff from agricultural land carries large quantities of nutrients with it, raising the nutrient content of streams and lakes throughout the world. As the nutrient content rises, the algae population literally explodes. Its decomposition, in turn, uses more and more oxygen, reducing the oxygen content to the point where fish can no longer survive. This process, known as eutrophication, converts fresh-water bodies into putrid, algae-laden swamps.

Lake Erie, the best-known victim of eutrophication, has received nutrients from both agricultural and industrial sources. It would require an estimated $50 billion, equivalent to the Department of Interior budget for the next twenty-two years at the current level, to restore Lake Erie to its original state as a fresh-water body. Thousands of fresh-water lakes are threatened throughout North America, Europe, the Soviet Union, Japan, and, now increasingly, the poor countries, too, where fertilizer use is beginning to climb. No one has calculated the cost to mankind of losing these fresh-water lakes, but it is staggering.

Damming the Nile at Aswan expanded the irrigated area for producing cereals but shut off the flow of rich alluvial silt to the Nile estuary, causing a precipitous drop in the fish catch there. This type of activity, along with eutrophication and pollution of lakes, streams, and estuaries, is affecting the fish catch in many localities. The world fish catch climbed steadily higher each successive year from 1950 through 1968 as world protein demand climbed and fishing technologics advanced, then suddenly declined without warning in 1969. Coming at a time when world demand for protein was rising, this forced prices of many types of fish sharply upward. Some marine biologists now feel that we are very close to the maximum world sustainable catch of table-grade fish, although there is an opportunity for a severalfold increase in the catch of fish suitable for grinding into fish meal.

## FOOD AND MORE FOOD

Signs of stress on the agricutural ecosystem are becoming universal, occurring with increasing frequency even at existing levels of food production. If the projected world population of 6.5 billion at the end of the twentieth century materializes, food production will have nearly to double present levels merely to maintain the current decidedly inadequate consumption levels. If allowance is made for achieving nutritionally adequate diets, food requirements will nearly triple by the century's end. Such an increase in the earth's food-producing capacity over the next three decades would equal that achieved from the time agriculture was invented to the present.

Increased production of food can come either from expanding

the area under cultivation or from raising yields of land already under the plow. Throughout most of the 10,000 years or so since the beginning of agriculture, increases in production have come largely from expanding the area. Only over the past twenty years, roughly since 1950, has most of the increase come from raising production on the existing cultivated area. Intensifying cultivation on the existing cultivated area translates into a sharp increase in the use of agricultural chemicals, especially fertilizer, perhaps tripling by the end of the century. Within many densely populated poor countries, the increase in food needs translates into additional marginal land brought under cultivation. In either event, the result of the projected increase in food needs is a steadily growing stress on the earth's ecosystem.

Although mankind is paying dearly for efforts to expand the food supply, the hunger probem is far from solved. Despite the fact that the earth's food-producing capacity has been increased several hundredfold since the introduction of agriculture, hunger is still the common lot of most people. For this hungry majority, the quality of life is influenced more by the lack of food than by any other single factor. For them, daily existence is largely circumscribed by the quest for food, reducing life to very fundamental biological terms. These facts should dispel once and for all the notion that expanding food production alone is likely to eradicate hunger.

The 2 billion people living in the poor countries consume an average of about 360 pounds of grain per year, or about a pound per day. With only one pound per day, nearly all must be consumed directly to meet minimal energy requirements; little remains for feeding to livestock, which may convert only a tenth of their feed intake into meat or other edible human food. The average American, in contrast, requires nearly one ton of grain per year. He eats only about 150 pounds of this directly in the form of bread, breakfast cereal, and so on; the rest is consumed indirectly in the form of meat, milk, and eggs. In short, he enjoys the luxury of the highly inefficient animal conversion of grain into tastier and somewhat more nutritious proteins. Thus, the average North American currently makes about four times as great a demand on the earth's agricultural ecosystem as someone living in one of the poor countries. As the income levels in these countries rise, so will their demand for a richer diet of animal products.

The latest world food budget compiled by the U.S. Department of Agriculture indicates that the average caloric intake in countries containing close to two-thirds of the world's people is less than the nutritional minimum required for normal growth and activity. A large part of this group suffers from chronic protein malnutrition, as well.

The geography of hunger closely coincides with those regions where incomes average less than $400 per year—essentially, most of Africa, Asia, and Latin America. Where death certificates are issued for preschool infants in the poor countries, death is generally attributed to measles, pneumonia, dysentery, or some other disease. In fact, these children are more likely the victims of malnutrition. Severely malnourished infants or children with low resistance frequently die of routine childhood diseases.

Protein is as crucial for children's mental development as for their physical development—as was strikingly shown in a study made over several years in Mexico. Youngsters who had been severely undernourished before the age of five were found to average thirteen points lower in I.Q. tests than a carefully selected control group that had not experienced severe malnutrition. Protein shortages in the early years of life impair development of the brain and central nervous system, permanently reducing learning capacity. Furthermore, this damage is irreversible. Protein shortages today are depreciating the stock of human resources for at least a generation to come.

Malnutrition has many costs, both economic and social. The effect of low levels of energy intake on the productivity of labor is easy to see. American construction firms operating in developing countries and employing local labor often find that they get high returns in worker output by investing in a good company cafeteria that serves employees three free meals a day.

The young people of Japan today are visible examples of the change that can be brought about by improved diets. Well-nourished from infancy as a result of Japan's new affluence, Japanese teenagers on the streets of Tokyo are perhaps an average of two inches taller than their elders.

Unfortunately, as Americans know, producing an abundance of food within a country does not necessarily mean that everyone will be adequately fed. The state of nutrition in a society is also determined by such things as food costs, the levels and distribution of income, levels of education, availability of food technologies, the commercial marketing system, and government-sponsored food distribution programs. Eradicating hunger and malnutrition is a complex undertaking for even a wealthy society. The principal factor preventing better distribution of food in the poor countries is the lack of purchasing power among a large share of the population. Increasingly, this problem is being aggravated by the steadily rising levels of unemployment characterizing all but a small handful of these countries.

## A GLOBAL STRATEGY TO ELIMINATE HUNGER AND MALNUTRITION

The effort to eliminate hunger is a complex undertaking, extending far beyond agriculture and the capacity to produce food. It must be global in scope and fully supported by the rich countries. Otherwise, decades will pass and hunger will still be the common lot of most of mankind.

A principal component of such an effort, given the demonstrated close relationship between nutrition and poverty, must be a massive effort to raise incomes to a level required to obtain the basic food nutrients for an adequate diet. There is no possible way of eliminating caloric-protein hunger in Bolivia, Ethiopia, or India while incomes average only $80 per year.

A world that is seriously interested in eradicating hunger and malnutrition must be prepared to support a sharp acceleration in economic growth rates in the poor countries in the years immediately ahead. This, in turn, requires a much greater transfer of resources from rich countries to poor than occurs at present. A share of the needed resources can be earned by the poor countries themselves, if the rich ones will simply permit competitive access to their internal markets for such things as sugar and textiles. Beyond this, the financial assistance from the rich must also expand.

On their side, poor countries must step up their efforts to accelerate growth as well as reform their internal systems so that this growth will provide the means for most, if not all, people to buy the food that can be produced. Growth must mean improved income for the many rather than just for the few.

A second critical component of a global strategy must be a crash effort to reduce birth rates everywhere, significantly slowing global population growth during this decade. Stabilizing population growth is essential not only to eliminate hunger but also, over the longer run, to preserve the ecosystem and protect the future food supply for mankind as a whole.

Efforts to eliminate poverty and reduce birth rates must proceed hand in hand. A sizable segment of the population in the poor countries will lower its birth rate, provided there is access to family-planning services and some encouragement regarding the benefits of limiting family size. But the great bulk of the population in the poorest countries must be raised above the socio-economic threshold below which birth rates will not be reduced voluntarily.

## Changing Dietary Habits to Help Save the Ecosystem

As we attempt to eliminate hunger and malnutrition, stresses on the earth's ecosystem are now such that we must also begin placing some upper limits on consumption of certain kinds of food. One way to reduce agricultural pressure on the earth's ecosystem is to use vegetable-derived, livestock-product substitutes. Some consumption trends within the United States are already moving in this direction. Both milk and egg consumption have declined more than 20 per cent since 1950 as Americans have made the transition to a more sedentary way of life. Vegetable oils are being substituted for animal fat. In 1940, the average American consumed seventeen pounds of butter and two pounds of margarine. By 1968, butter had dropped to six pounds and margarine had climbed to eleven pounds. This was closely paralleled by a decline in lard consumption, as lard was nearly pushed off the supermarket shelf by the hydrogenated vegetable shortenings. Recent data indicate that 65 per cent of the whipped toppings and 35 per cent of the coffee whiteners purchased by U.S. consumers are now of nondairy origin.

Countering these trends, however, is an increase in beef consumption within the United States—from fifty-five pounds per person yearly in 1940 to 110 pounds in 1968. On balance, this may have more than offset the reduction in agricultural pressure on the ecosystem by the reduction in milk and egg consumption and the substitution of vegetable oils for animal fats. If pressures on the earth's agricultural ecosystem become too severe, we may eventually be forced into using soybean-derived and other substitutes for livestock products. Perhaps the first significant breakthrough in the process of substituting vegetable-derived imitation products for meat is the successful commercialization by General Mills of a soybean-derived, bacon-like product marketed under the trade name "Bacos." A plant devoted entirely to the production of Bacos has just been constructed in Cedar Rapids, Iowa; it buys soybeans grown in the surrounding countryside and converts them into Bacos, bypassing the livestock phase of the cycle. The new vegetable protein is marketed in direct competition with the bacon produced by farmers adjacent to the plant site, who still rely on hogs to combine soybeans and corn to produce meat. Once vegetable-derived meat substitutes are perfected, the extent of substitution for meat could increase steadily.

New seeds are helping to overcome calorie deficits, but they are not contributing as significantly to alleviating protein malnutrition. Historically, diets in the richer countries improved when cereal supplies began to exceed direct consumption needs, leaving large quantities to be converted into high-protein livestock products. But this conventional path to achieving high-quality diets is a costly one. If cereals could be re-engineered or fortified so that their protein quality approached that of livestock protein, the cost of achieving high-quality diets could be greatly reduced. Corn, for example, is deficient in lysine and, to a lesser extent, tryptophane—both essential to human nutrition. Corn-consuming populations, therefore, suffer from a shortage of these amino acids in their diet. These deficiencies can be overcome either genetically or biochemically through fortification of the corn itself. The discovery of a high-lysine gene, Opaque-2, opened a new front in man's efforts to combat malnutrition on a global scale. From this breakthrough, Rockefeller Foundation scientists in Colombia developed commercial corn varieties with a high lysine content—varieties that were released for general use in 1969.

To the extent that both high-yield and high-protein content can be incorporated in the same varieties, the prospects for expanding protein supplies are exciting, indeed. Seeds that give double yields and raise protein content by one-fourth increase protein output per acre by 250 per cent. Interestingly, nearly all nutritional shortcuts that reduce the cost of attaining an adequate diet also reduce pressure on the ecosystem.

## ALLEVIATING AGRICULTURAL STRESSES IN THE ECOSYSTEM

While striving to reduce the pressure of the growing demand for food on the earth's ecosystem, man must also seek to reduce the destructive nature of his agricultural efforts. One way of reducing the adverse impact of pesticides is to substitute "selective" for "broad-range" pesticides. Another is to devise more biological controls, a few of which have been used quite successfully on minor pests. Among the more successful is the "sterile-male" technique, which involves sterilizing large numbers of males of a given insect species.

The first large-scale use of this technique was on the screwworm fly, a pest of cattle. A large number of male screwworm flies were sterilized by irradiation and then released. These bred with local females, which laid eggs that were infertile. When a high ratio of sterile males is maintained, population of the screwworm fly decreases. Within the United States, the population of this pest has been held to negligible levels by releasing 125 million sterile flies weekly wherever the flies reappear, including particularly a 300-mile zone along the Mexican border. The cost of this control program is estimated at one-fifteenth that of the annual losses that would result from the screwworm fly in the absence of control. The U.S. Department of Agriculture and the Mexican Government are now considering whether to push the control zone southward to the Isthmus of Panama in order virtually to eradicate the screwworm fly from North America. Efforts are now under way in California to control the Mexican fruit fly and the pink cotton bollworm using this technique.

Another approach is the breeding of pest-resistant strains. An example of this is the Hessian fly pest of wheat. In areas where resistant strains of wheat have been used, the population of the Hessian fly has been reduced to the point where it is no longer a problem. Strains of corn resistant to the corn borer and to the corn earworm have also been released. Work is now under way on a strain of alfalfa that is resistant to both the alfalfa aphid and the leafhopper.

Action must also be taken to affect the adverse consequences of overextending areas under cultivation. The only possible way to stabilize the relationship between man and the land on which he lives in the densely populated poor countries is to introduce techniques to conserve the soil by reducing wind and water erosion. The dustbowl era of the 1930's in the United States did not end until the formation of the Soil Conservation Service and the widespread adoption of conservation practices by farmers. Then, an estimated 20 million acres of land were left fallow with strips of wheat (strip cropping) to reduce the blowing of soil on the idle land, and thousands of miles of tree windbreaks were planted across the Great Plains perpendicular to the prevailing winds. The relationship between man and the land on which he depends for his food supply in the Great Plains has now been stabilized; erosion is negligible, and yields are good.

The world's more densely populated regions, however, are in no position to adopt such tactics. Their food needs are so pressing that they cannot afford to take large areas out of cultivation. Nor do they yet have the financial resources, or technical skills, for the vast projects—in reforesting, contour farming, terracing, regulated grazing of cattle, and systematic managing of watersheds—that are required to preserve their soil. If these soil-erosion trends continue to accelerate, and particularly if it should be determined that rising levels of particulate matter in the atmosphere are adversely affecting the earth's climate, it would be in the interest of the rich countries to provide massive capital and technical assistance to the poor countries, joining with them in confronting this common threat.

## THE COSTS OF PRODUCING MORE FOOD

One of the great difficulties at the moment is that there is no complete inventory of the costs associated with efforts to expand continually the world food supply to meet pressing and ever increasing needs. There is no way to calculate the trade-off between increases in population and improvements in the quality of life— a choice we must now make as we press against the finite limits of our ecosystem. The earth cannot both feed an ever expanding number of people and feed them better. What is the rule of thumb for converting the current annual global increase in population of 70 million into extinct species of mammals, birds, and fish? Does such an increase cost an average of three species per year? Or ten? And what about ten years from now? What changes will occur in the earth's climate between now and the end of the century? Will the concentration of dust particles in the upper atmosphere continue to reinforce the worldwide cooling trend in evidence since 1940?

These are some of the complex questions we must ask. The world's wise men do not have the answers. But we do have enough information now to know that the costs of continually expanding the earth's food-producing capacity is high.

As more information becomes available concerning the costs of trying indefinitely to expand our food supply in the decades ahead, it is certain to raise the level of public concern both within this country and abroad. We can hope that this increasing awareness will bring changes in our attitudes toward, among other things, child-bearing and our relationship with nature.

A global effort to eradicate hunger must be viewed as part of a total effort to cope with the complex of problems confronting mankind. It cannot be considered apart from global poverty, uncontrolled human fertility, high and rising levels of unemployment in the poor countries, and the signs of growing agricultural stresses on the ecosystem. Hunger now affects more than half of mankind and probably diminishes the quality of life of more people than any other single factor. If it is to be eliminated, a massive global re-allocation of resources will be required; far more must be devoted to the attack on global poverty than is currently in sight. New information must be translated into changes in attitudes; in turn, these attitudes must be translated into a more rational order of national and global priorities.

# 7

# Jobs and Justice: Economic Growth Alone Is Not Enough

## JAMES P. GRANT

*Relations between the United States and the poor countries will depend on many factors, as discussed throughout this book. As important as these relations is the nature of policies adopted by poor countries themselves to advance their own development. For a variety of reasons, yesterday's emphasis on economic growth has proved to be insufficient. Today and tomorrow, poor countries will need to adopt a wide variety of supplementary policies if the impact of growth is to be beneficial. At the same time, policies adopted by the rich countries must also reflect an awareness that growth alone is not enough. In this chapter, the author advances ideas for a new strategy for development that could help to meet the problems confronting the poor countries.—THE EDITORS*

A growing crisis in development progress is threatening the survival of many governments in Asia, Africa, and Latin America in the 1970's. Quite simply, the substantial achievements of the development strategy followed by most developing countries—a strategy dominated by economic growth—fall seriously short of the minimum those countries need to cope with their problems. Their unemployment levels continue to increase, in some countries, exceeding those of the Great Depression in the United States; the income gap is widening between the poorest half of their work forces and those relatively well off (who are benefiting from unprecedented increases in output); their population explosions remain out of control; and they face serious, still largely unforeseen, environmental problems.

There is a partial analogy between this situation and the years leading up to 1848 in Europe, when forces for change culminated in revolutions that toppled many European thrones. Robert McNamara, President of the World Bank, has underscored the crisis being created by the widening rich-poor gap in most developing countries. In his address to the Third U.N. Conference on Trade and Development (UNCTAD III) in Santiago, Chile, in 1972, he emphasized that "the state of development in most of the developing world is unacceptable—and growing more so." Already the stresses are contributing to shifts in governments, generally toward either of two extremes: the Left, in response to pressures from the dissatisfied, as in Ceylon, Peru, and Chile; or the Right, in an attempt to contain these pressures, as in Brazil and Ghana.

Why is this crisis occurring? What possible solutions are there? And how do these solutions affect the runaway problems of population and environment? These urgent questions must be answered. Fortunately, some useful lessons were learned in the 1960's and there are some hopeful signs indicating that, if rich and poor countries alike act with foresight and introduce social justice measures to increase jobs and reduce income disparities, they will thereby also *accelerate*—not slow down—economic progress.

## BEYOND ECONOMIC GROWTH

In view of development progress made during the 1960's, many observers are surprised by warnings of impending crisis. When Development Decade I (DD-I) was proclaimed in 1961—for the first time setting as a goal of global policy the bringing of progress to all mankind—the single major quantified goal was the achievement of an ambitious 5 per cent annual growth in output by the developing countries during the decade. This goal—unmatched by the Western countries in their comparable stage of development—was in fact accomplished in the 1960's. It was accompanied by an unprecedented annual growth in trade of over 6 per cent.

And in specific areas of development, including the Green Revolution, new agricultural technologies swept countries like India and Pakistan faster than any technology ever swept the American farm belt.

Despite these successes, it has now become clear that the definition of development as economic growth alone is grossly inadequate. Asia, Latin America, and Africa certainly need even more rapid growth than in the past. But they need other things as well. In fact, the "trickle-down" theory of development—whereby the poor supposedly benefit from over-all economic growth or policies benefiting the rich—is proving utterly inadequate to the needs of the poorer halves of populations in developing countries.

The limitations of traditional development concepts for the developing world are most evident in Latin America, where the population explosion started early. Even though this region has had a 5 per cent growth in output each year for more than a decade, open unemployment has risen over the past twenty years. The number of people unemployed has probably quadrupled to over 12 per cent of Latin America's work force. Many are "marginal men"—people who have reached adulthood with no useful role to play in their society. Largely the product of an unprecedented "baby survival" boom, these individuals now find a dearth of jobs, of the means to provide for themselves and take part in life around them. The impact of the population explosion on employment has been aggravated in Latin America, as elsewhere in the developing world, by the unprecedented migration from the countryside to the cities, by the spread of increasingly capital-intensive technology, and by financial policies favoring use of capital over labor.

## The Example of Mexico

Mexico provides a good example of the need for a development strategy that is much broader than the pursuit of growth alone. Most observers see Mexico as a success—which, by traditional standards, it is. Mexico has had a 6–7 per cent annual rate of growth for the past fifteen years. Its per capita income is now above $600, and it has what most observers call a reformist government. But, despite this achievement, Mexico's development problems remain grave.

First, Mexico needs to make better use of its labor force,

much of which remains idle. New entrants into the labor market have risen from 300,000 a year in 1960 to 600,000 a year in 1970, and their ranks will increase to 850,000 by 1980, as babies already born reach working age. Not surprisingly, underemployment is growing in Mexico at a rapid rate despite the country's economic growth. The number of landless laborers, for example, increased from 2.3 million in 1950 to more than 3.3 million ten years later. At the same time, the average number of days each laborer worked dropped from 194 per year to only 100, and his real income dropped from $68 to $56 a year.

Second, Mexico needs to slow its excessive rate of population growth. Its population has doubled in the past twenty-five years to 50 million, and will double again in only twenty years.

Third, Mexico needs a development plan that will at least stop —if not reverse—the widening of the present income gap between the well-off and the poor. Some simple comparisons show the trend. In the early 1950's there was a 10 to 1 ratio between the income controlled by the *top* 20 per cent and the *bottom* 20 per cent of income recipients. By the late 1960's, this ratio had shifted to 16 to 1, and the national income share of the poorest 20 per cent had dropped from 6 to 4 per cent. The income of landless laborers fell by 15 per cent in ten years, while the income for factory workers went up about 70 per cent in the same period. Thus, in Mexico, as in most of Latin America (and Asia, too), the people for whom the system has been working so far —a sizable group that includes civil servants and industrial workers—are doing very well. But for a sizable and growing portion of the population at the bottom, there has been little progress and in many cases their situation is getting even worse.

Fourth, Mexico needs a development model that will provide a significantly higher return for funds spent on education and health, and greater benefit for the poor half of its population, particularly in rural areas. Malnutrition is still very widespread, and the health-care system reaches only a small fraction of the people, most of whom live in cities. It is little wonder that in Mexico, as in most developing countries, the rate of migration from rural to urban areas is so high. Rural areas have high unemployment and underemployment, poorly paid jobs, and few social services. Cities offer the promise of something better, even if that promise is often not fulfilled.

If Mexico, a relative success, faces the problems described above, it is obviously much more urgent to create a development model more beneficial to the "little guy" for the very poor countries, such as India, Bangladesh, and Indonesia, whose per capita incomes are only one-sixth or one-seventh that of Mexico. These countries will not reach Mexico's present per capita income until well into the twenty-first century—when their poor will doubtless need to be far better off than Mexico's poor are today. The very poor need a development model that will give them, within a generation, and at a per capita income no higher than $200, the minimum requirements for human dignity—namely, food, jobs, health, and shelter. A development model that can provide human dignity for the great majority of people at a national income level of $200–300 per person would offer much more hope for our environment than does the present model, which assumes that social justice for most people becomes a reality only at a per capita income well above Mexico's present $600.

## Successful Models?

Difficulties and dilemmas like Mexico's are not limited to countries in the so-called Third World. Developing Communist countries that are experiencing unprecedented population growth are also having to struggle with unemployment problems. Yugoslavia did nòt revise its policies to increase employment, but did allow large-scale emigration. As a result; some 20 per cent of its adult work force has now left Yugoslavia. Cuba, by contrast, has adopted policies to make full use of its rapidly expanding labor force, but so far this new approach has led to stagnation in output, despite massive Soviet aid.

In general, country after country reveals the same pattern of relatively high growth rates, combined both with a failure to meet other major needs and with dramatic inequities in the distribution of economic and social benefits. Yet it is feasible to achieve economic growth *while* overcoming several of these newly defined problems—even where there is a high rate of population growth.

The possibility is best illustrated in East Asia, by countries with very different political and economic systems—China and North Korea on one side of the ideological barrier, and South Korea, Taiwan, and the city-states of Hong Kong and Singapore on the other. Elsewhere, countries as different as Israel, Cuba, Ceylon, Egypt, Yugoslavia, and Barbados have dealt effectively with some of these newly perceived problems.

It is significant that China, after considerable experimentation, now appears to have found a pattern that combines increasing national output with full employment (at least in the rural areas), with falling birth rates, and with comprehensive, low-cost social services. This new pattern, about which we still know far too little, emerges at a time when there is both the coming global job crisis and Peking's new legitimacy on the world scene. As a result, the Maoist model will attract many people in the developing countries—and not just because of acupuncture and "barefoot doctors" disseminating birth-control information.

Some analysts suggest, in fact, that the Maoist model, which includes turning away from the outside world, is the only realistic alternative for large countries such as India, Indonesia, and Pakistan. Only with this model, they contend, can these countries combine economic growth with progress for most of their people.

I do not agree. It can be amply demonstrated that in the 1960's there were successes and failures in dealing with particular development problems under a variety of ideological labels: "capitalist," "socialist," and "mixed." Many of the problems of the 1970's—such as the consequences of an unprecedented population explosion—are too serious and important for their solutions to be straitjacketed by any one ideological model. The "barefoot doctors" of China and the "pharmacists" and "midwives" of Ceylon—really skilled paramedics—have more in common with each other than they do with the medical-care system of either the United States or the Soviet Union. Developing countries do need to change the structures of their societies. But in doing so, they need to, and can, draw on experience from both sides of the ideological barrier.

For example, four small East Asian countries—South Korea, Hong Kong, Singapore, and Taiwan—had much higher rates of increase in their work forces during the 1960's than did China, yet they achieved rapid growth and drastically reduced unemployment while improving income distribution and dramatically reducing birth rates. In Taiwan, the gap in income distribution decreased by more than 50 per cent in the same twenty-year period during which it increased in Mexico by 60 per cent. The reason is clear: these four East Asian countries have successfully combined the right national policies with substantial foreign investment, access to rich country markets, and (in the case of Taiwan and Korea) significant foreign aid.

Of course, there are limits in applying the formulas for these successful experiences to the problems of the larger poor countries. The successes were, after all, achieved in relatively small countries. Even though South Korea, for example, has more people today than Mexico or Turkey less than a generation ago, the development approach adopted by the four East Asian countries should be viewed more as a "working model" than as a demonstration of what is possible in India or Indonesia.

The success of these outward-looking Asian countries also raises an important issue concerning developed countries. Will the developed countries provide the larger poor countries an equally helpful mixture of aid, trade, and investment? Even if the answer is no—if the developed countries withdraw behind their walls of affluence—the large developing countries can profit from the experience of the small East Asian countries and city-states in such matters as land reform, rural credit, financial policies favoring use of labor over machines, urban redevelopment, and the provision of effective low-cost health and education services to most of the population.

One should never underestimate the importance of adopting the right policies for the progress of developing countries. It bears remembering that many countries have had even more outside income than Taiwan or Korea *without* achieving the same improvements in livelihood for the poorer half of their people. The $150 per capita of economic aid for Taiwan from 1950 to 1965 is equal to Venezuela's per capita earnings from only seven months of petroleum exports, and equal to Chile's per capita earnings from just eighteen months of mineral exports. Yet Taiwan—like Korea in the early 1960's, Puerto Rico in the 1950's, and the two Punjabs of South Asia in the mid-1960's—did not begin its spectacular performance until it had made a series of highly important policy changes: changes for its rural areas in the early 1950's, and for its industrial export sector in about 1960.

## Developing Country Initiatives

There are several initiatives that most developing countries could take to make their growth far more labor-intensive and equitable, thus helping to reduce unemployment and narrowing the gap between rich and poor people in society.

Most poor countries need to begin by reducing the persistent imbalances in the prices of capital, labor, and foreign exchange, which favor the use of equipment rather than labor. (It is nonsensical, to give one example, that until recently farmers in labor-surplus Pakistan and India paid much less for a 35-horsepower tractor than do farmers in labor-scarce Iowa.) By ending subsidies on plant and equipment, lowering their exchange rates, and raising interest rates, poor countries could make the price of capital more realistic. In Korea and Taiwan, where this lesson has been learned, the scarcity of capital has been reflected in interest rates as high as 30 per cent. Raising interest rates while broadening access to savings institutions could also lead to increased rates of saving— especially among farmers and small-scale entrepreneurs. Most poor countries should probably also extend less protection to industries making products that will substitute for imports, exposing those industries instead to the winds of competition. At the same time, they should encourage industries that make the best use of available labor, and they should assure more equitable distribution of income through revision of existing tax structures and through holding down wage increases in industry and government. Establishing this general economic framework would both foster labor-intensive industry (such as textiles, electronic components, toys, and furniture), and inspire businessmen to expand and make innovations with fewer capital-intensive methods of production.

The application of measures such as these has had a significant impact on employment in Korea and Taiwan, as is clearly illustrated in an International Labor Office (ILO) study that compares the rubber-products industry in those countries with that in the Philippines and India. During the mid–1960's, investment per worker was $1,272 in India and $2,645 in the Philippines (where policies were even more favorable to the use of equipment rather than labor). At the same time, the figures for Taiwan and Korea were $756 and $626, respectively. Thus, while the products of all four countries appeared to be equal in quality and profitability, the rubber industry in Taiwan and Korea provided far more employment for a given amount of investment.

If the jobs crisis is to be met, action also needs to be taken to improve income distribution and rural development.

Inequality of income distribution contributes to the slow rate of growth in employment. Raising the incomes of the poor in developing countries should create more jobs than would an equivalent rise in the incomes of the wealthy, since production of the goods bought by well-off people in poor countries tends to use relatively large amounts of capital, whereas the goods poor people buy tend to require more local labor than capital. For example, producing an automobile in a developing country requires large amounts of capital but relatively little labor, whereas producing bicycles, shirts, or food depends much more on use of local labor. Luxury products also generally require more foreign exchange reserves, either because the goods themselves are imported or because their manufacture demands more complex, imported machinery than does a labor-intensive product.

Rural development—and in many cases land reform—must also be actively pursued, since two-thirds of the people in poor countries live in rural areas, and their absolute numbers will increase considerably by the end of the century. Land reform in Egypt, as in Korea and Taiwan (where no one may hold more than seven and one-half acres), has led to great increases in employment and productivity when it has been supported by an effective credit and extension system. It is also significant that the use of labor in these three countries is far more intensive than in either India or Mexico, averaging two and six times as much per acre, respectively. (Interestingly, their food grain yields per acre nearly triple those of India and Mexico.)

Finally, poor countries need to tailor their social services, such as health and education, to reach the great majority of their people and not just the privileged. For example, infant mortality is still very high in some poor countries with relatively high per capita income. This category includes Mexico, Brazil, and Chile (with 68, 94, and 92 infant deaths per 1,000 births, respectively). By contrast, in poorer countries that rely heavily on the use of paramedics and other new approaches to mass medical care, better results have been achieved. This category includes Ceylon, Korea, Taiwan (with 50, 41, and 19 infant deaths per 1,000 births, respectively). Apparently, China has also reduced its infant mortality rate by similar means.

The same contrast is seen in education. Korea and Taiwan devote the bulk of their public education budgets to the lower grades and charge heavily for higher education. By contrast, Mexico, Brazil, and Chile devote a lion's share of their budgets to subsidizing the costs of the higher grades and college, which are attended free or at little cost by students who are overwhelmingly from relatively well-off families. As a result, not enough funds are available for educating the rural poor in these Latin American countries.

## LESSONS OF EXPERIENCE

One lesson to be learned is that the rural and urban poor can save. For too long, it has been a premise of Western economics that poorer people save little because they spend their money first on consumer goods and services. Hence, government policies designed to increase savings and investment have been aimed chiefly at the higher income groups. We are now learning a different lesson from the urban working poor in such cities as Singapore and Izmir, and from the small farmers of such diverse countries as Taiwan, Egypt, Korea, and Japan. The evidence provided in these countries is that the savings rates of the poor on increased income can be very high if they own or rent their own economic facilities and if governments create a nationwide network of financial institutions and economic incentives to support them. In other words, with the right system, the working poor can become a major source of savings. Their improved livelihood can accelerate, rather than be achieved at the cost of, over-all growth.

The effect of the right policies on the poorer half of a developing country's population is best illustrated for urban areas by Singapore, and for rural areas by Taiwan. Singapore today has full employment and high rates of literacy and life expectancy. It also has surprisingly good housing conditions for the poor. Forty per cent of Singapore's people now live in public housing for low-income families, and the most recently built units compare favorably with low-income housing being built in Europe. Most of Singapore's public housing is being financed by the workers themselves through the use of an ingenious device. All workers—household, service, and industrial—contribute 12 per cent of their salaries, matched by their employers, to a National Provident Fund. Workers generally are enthusiastic about this high rate of withholding, because it can be used to cover the down payments for their flats and to finance mortgage installments. Thus, the benefits of these savings are not deferred until some remote retirement date. Through largely self-financing devices such as this, 80 per cent of Singapore's slum dwellers have had their living conditions dramatically improved in the past ten years.

Like their counterparts in other poor countries where circumstances are comparable, Taiwanese farmers with relatively small holdings are also confounding traditional economic analysis. They are showing a high propensity to save and invest out of their small incomes whenever it is clearly made profitable for them to do so. As a result, the average rural Taiwanese householder has more than trebled his real income since 1950 to well over $1,000. In addition, his children now get more than six years of education and have a life expectancy close to that of rural Americans.

The Taiwanese farmer's home, built from masonry and with a tiled roof, is electrified. He owns at least one bicycle and radio, and—as part of a sizable and increasing part of the population —he may own a television set and refrigerator. His multipurpose farmers' association, in which he has an active say, is his principal source of credit and technical advice. It owns the village rice mill and provides him with a major cooperative marketing outlet.

The Taiwanese farmer's use of agricultural research and technology has helped him more than double his agricultural output over the past twenty years. He has the latest in high-yielding seed varieties and hog breeds, and also a whole range of small farm implements developed for his tiny farm with its relatively ample supply of labor. He probably uses more capital per acre than does the average Midwestern farmer in the United States, but this capital increases the productivity of the labor force on his farm rather than displaces workers.

It is significant that Taiwan's rural progress in the 1950's and the 1960's has not resulted from government subsidies based on taxes levied on the urban and industrial sectors of the economy. Rather, this progress has been paid for primarily out of land reform and the farmers' increased production.

The East Asian experience provides two other heartening lessons. One is that a development strategy that provides social justice through making it possible for a farmer or laborer to work more effectively for his own advancement can actually accelerate growth. In other words, the right kinds of social-justice policies can increase production rather than cause its stagnation. Even though this conclusion runs counter to most current thinking by economists, it should not be surprising. Unemployed labor is a developing country's most plentiful asset. If 20 per cent of a poor country's labor force is idle, simply putting the unemployed to work accelerates growth. Moreover, the income earned by these workers stimulates demand for local products, particularly for labor-intensive goods such as food and textiles. Thus, the gross domestic products (GDP) of Taiwan and Korea grew annually at 9.9 and 9.2 per cent, respectively, during the 1960's, while exports grew at the phenomenal annual rates of 34 and 69 per cent, respectively.

The other important lesson is that it may now be possible to attack several problems simultaneously. For example, a comprehensive land reform program, backed up by an effective credit system, simultaneously increases savings, output, farm employment, and demand for labor-intensive products, while improving income distribution and attitudes toward family planning.

Possibly most encouraging, the combination of full employment, income growth, and greatly improved health and education services has led to declining birth rates even *before* the attainment

of a $200 per capita income level, and *before* the introduction
of large-scale family planning programs. In Taiwan, for example,
birth rates dropped from 46 per 1,000 in 1952 to 32 per 1,000
in 1963—at which time a vigorous family planning program was
introduced and helped continue the birth rate's decline to 26
per 1,000 in 1970. China, Barbados, Hong Kong, South Korea,
parts of India, and the Chinese, Indian, and Malay populations
of Singapore also illustrate the effect on birth rates of the right
pattern of social and economic progress.

## STRUCTURAL REFORM BY POOR COUNTRIES

There remain great difficulties for most poor countries that
seek to apply the policies we have been discussing. To meet the
problems of poverty, unemployment, and the dearth of such social
services as health care and education, there must be a series of
structural reforms—not just little projects here and there that
get at the symptoms of what is wrong with society, but basic, far-
reaching reforms to make social, political, and economic structures responsive to needs.

A land tenure reform program, for example, requires a shift
in the balance of economic power from landlords to tenants. A
decent health system in a poor country requires changes in doctors' professional attitudes and standards, which have been set
by the developed countries, to allow the use of less costly paramedics. Wage increases of factory workers may have to be slowed,
to ensure that some of the economic benefits from increased
productivity go to the families of nonfactory labor, who constitute
the bulk of society. And these wage increases may have to be
slowed to reduce themselves for use of costly labor-saving machinery at a time when much surplus labor is available. The prices
farmers get for their products must be improved, despite protests
from city dwellers. Of course, making these changes will be
difficult. Even in a wealthy, modern society like the United States,
we are still debating full employment and full health care. This
debate is even more intense, and the solutions even more difficult
to achieve, in poor societies.

The issue of structural change in societies has yet another

dimension. It is correctly believed that development will contribute to conditions of lasting peace. However, many commentators have distorted this idea, interpreting it to mean that development can only be ensured by stability, i.e., no disturbance to existing political, economic, and social structures. Yet such a requirement ultimately leads to greater instability. As the American experience of growth during the past century demonstrates, comprehensive development is not possible without constant change in these structures. The growth of one sector leads inevitably to forces for change elsewhere, and this change either occurs in increments or is bottled up. If the latter happens, change ultimately may be explosive, as it was in Russia in 1917 and in Cuba in 1959. Extreme violence perhaps can be avoided, however, if political leaders come to view development and structural change as mutually sustaining and reinforcing.

## THE ROLE OF DEVELOPED COUNTRIES

The initiative for change and development rests with the poor countries themselves. Yet in many cases outsiders can play major and useful roles.

First, as in the food crisis of the mid-1960's, they can help to identify a world problem. Second, they can aid the search for new techniques, as was done, for example, by the Rockefeller and Ford foundations in developing the new high-yielding seeds. Third, when a developing country is actually ready to move, there is a valuable opportunity to provide support—such as the U.S. AID-financed fertilizers, tube wells, and pesticides that were needed in the food program. Fourth, there is a need for a major increase in the general flow of resources from rich countries to poor to help the latter achieve higher growth rates.

Although it is now clear that economic growth alone will not solve all the problems of the poor countries, neither will these problems be solved by denying higher rates of growth. Quite simply, higher rates of growth are required if necessary reforms are to be carried out without major violence or extreme authoritarianism. And achieving higher rates of growth requires more foreign exchange for machinery, for raw materials, and for other things required for growth.

It is no accident that the development "successes" have taken place in societies with broad access to aid, investment, and trade. Furthermore, restructuring an economy that is growing is clearly much easier than restructuring one that is stagnating. We Americans see in our own society how much more difficult it is to move people out of depressed industries during a period of recession than it is in a period of growth, when employment alternatives are available. The same is even more true for developing countries.

Some increase in foreign exchange can result if more poor countries adopt outward-looking economic policies. However, the international economic environment is not congenial to their development. Policies followed by rich countries and the structure of international institutions often discriminate against poor countries in such matters as trade and finance. Therefore, there must be major changes in the ways rich countries relate to the poor countries if there is to be anything like the needed increase in the transfer of resources in the 1970's. Additional sources of foreign exchange must come from trade, investment, aid, and, possibly, from such new global sources as the raw materials of the seabed and the foreign exchange made available by the International Monetary Fund (IMF) through the Special Drawing Rights (SDR) mechanism.

Changes required on the part of rich countries will not be easy to achieve. For example, a major increase in U.S. aid through direct appropriations is not likely soon. Nor will trade be increased easily. At UNCTAD III on April 14, 1972, Robert McNamara estimated that, to meet the needs of the developing countries, the manufactured exports of these countries would have to increase from $7 billion today to $28 billion in 1980. Will developed countries accept this increase in labor-intensive imports?

Of course, it takes two to trade. In the longer term, both rich and poor countries would gain if workers in the former concentrated on products requiring high levels of skills and capital while workers in the latter concentrated on products with a high labor content, at least as long as labor remains their most abundant resource. Unfortunately, the rich countries usually follow opposite policies to those recommended here. In the face of competition from cheaper labor abroad, they allow the principal financial burden of adjustment to fall on workers producing the same goods that the poor countries are trying to export. Moreover, success in exporting by the poor countries is breeding restrictive reactions by rich countries. The cotton textile worker in South Carolina, the shoemaker in Maine, the French sugar-beet farmer, the Japanese rice farmer belong to groups that usually are disadvantaged. They receive low wages, and they have little skill or training. Not surprisingly, they protest—politically. As a result of such political pressures, President Nixon on his own initiative in late 1971 imposed new restrictions on textiles from Korea, Hong Kong, and Taiwan. And the AFL-CIO, long a free trade supporter, in 1972 sponsored the highly protectionist Burke-Hartke Bill in the U.S. Congress.

Social justice at home in the United States and social justice abroad are integrally related. We cannot afford to fulfill the demands in the poor countries at the expense of our own poor here at home. Such a moral travesty could not long survive as policy. But a far more effective set of domestic employment and adjustment assistance policies than we now have must be devised. The two are not mutually exclusive—they can in fact reinforce each other. Combined with a fairer trade policy, such measures can benefit labor and the consumer in the United States while also helping to alleviate the jobs and foreign exchange crises of the Third World.

Today's rich countries originally designed the present international economic system primarily with their own needs in mind. This system, in effect, provides less than equal treatment for the more than two-thirds of the world's people who are poor. Consequently, reforms of the *international* economic system are just as imperative as those required within the poor countries, and within the United States and other developed countries.

Attempts to foster such international structural adjustments in the 1960's were flagrantly inadequate. The Kennedy Round of tariff negotiations reduced tariffs by half on the goods traded between the rich countries. But it did almost nothing to the tariffs on goods from poor countries, and thus left these countries relatively worse off than before. This situation has been further aggravated during the past decade—to the detriment of the

American consumer as well as the poor abroad—by the great increase in nontariff barriers on products from poor countries. Subsequently, the non-Communist world also created its so-called paper gold—the IMF's SDR's—in the amount of about $3 billion a year. Under the distribution formula that was established, however, three-quarters of these assets were made available to the rich countries—since these countries again set up the system and determined how SDR's would be allocated.

If our prosperity depends on our standing in the way of development for millions of people in the poor countries, and if we thereby become a threat to their existence, we shall be forever insecure. A system of national security, in its broadest sense, can only be viable in the late twentieth century if social justice at home does not mean injustice to the people in the Third World, and if social justice in the Third World does not mean injustice for poor people in the rich countries. At the international level, too, the policy alternatives exist to promote social justice and accelerate the progress and well-being of the majority in both developed and developing countries. What is needed is the political will to implement them.

It should be possible to mount comprehensive, coordinated efforts to ameliorate, if not solve, the mammoth problems faced by poor countries—problems of jobs, income distribution, social services, and population growth. These efforts can also accelerate economic growth, and not be at its expense. But strategies capable of coping with these problems require major, difficult internal changes by most developing countries, including a greater sharing of economic and social power within their countries. And these strategies also require cooperation on an unprecedented scale from the rich countries.

Reforms within developing countries, as well as changes in trade, monetary, and investment patterns between rich and poor countries, are now becoming more than requirements of social justice; they are becoming requirements for survival of a world economic system.

# PART III

# FOREIGN TRADE, INVESTMENT, AND THE MULTINATIONAL CORPORATION

# 8

# Trade and Development

## HARALD B. MALMGREN

*In the past, the debate about transferring resources to poor countries has centered on foreign aid. Yet, there is compelling evidence that trade has more of an influence on the prospects poor countries have for development, if only because the volume of exports from these countries is vastly greater than the aid they receive. In this chapter, the author surveys the particular problems—including tariffs and nontariff barriers—poor countries face as they try to trade and makes some specific recommendations for change.—THE EDITORS*

The management of economic policy toward the developing countries is becoming increasingly more complex and politically treacherous. The question is no longer simply one of promoting direct investment and maintaining reasonable aid and trade relations. Direct investment in manufacturing in low-wage countries is now under heavy fire from the American organized-labor movement. The aid program is in deep trouble with Congress. And the executive branch has added to the problems with abortive proposals for aid reform; on August 15, 1971, it also announced

This chapter is based on a paper presented to the Development Issues Seminar, Overseas Development Council, on January 12, 1971. For an elaboration of these arguments, see H. B. Malmgren, *International Economic Peacekeeping in Phase II.*

cuts in aid expenditures as a part of the President's New Economic Policy (NEP).

In trade, the problems are even more basic. In the late 1960's, it became increasingly evident to the governments of the rich, industrialized nations that trade was an essential part of development. For most developing countries, improvement of export performance was necessary to help finance imports of machinery and raw materials and to help the process of industrialization and the modernization of agriculture. Moreover, it was increasingly understood that trade was the biggest item in the economic relations between rich and poor countries. Aid, investment, and other financial flows from the developed to the developing nations amounted to about $13.6 billion gross in 1969. (Governmental aid was about one-half of this.) As against this flow, exports from these countries totaled $48.3 billion in 1969. Trade thus accounted for nearly four-fifths of the total resource flow. This ratio has held for several years. Trade, in other words, is responsible for the lion's share of the total flow of foreign exchange to poor countries. For them, each percentage point increase in trade is worth over 7 percentage points increase in foreign aid, or about 3.5 percentage points increase in aid and private investment combined.

## THE SLOW GROWTH OF POOR COUNTRIES' EXPORTS

In the 1960's, the exports of developing countries grew by about 7 per cent per year, compared with about 4 per cent in the previous decade. This improvement was a direct consequence of the more rapid growth in income in the developed countries in the 1960's as compared with the 1950's. Indeed, trade growth is dominated by, and highly sensitive to, income growth, inflation, and other internal conditions in the wealthiest countries, because their share of total world income is so large. However, as world income and trade grow, world market demand for exports of the developing nations increases less rapidly than it does for the exports of the developed countries. For example, in 1969 the value of total world trade grew by 14 per cent, but the exports of developing nations grew by only about 9 per cent. Even in their best years, the developing countries have been losing ground in terms of their share of total world trade. In 1950, their share was nearly one-third; but by 1969 the share had fallen below 18 per cent, and it has fallen in almost every year since 1950.

A major reason for the poor relative performance of developing nations relates to the composition of their trade. To begin with, the pull exerted on world trade by growing demand in the industrialized nations varies in strength from product to product. For example, an increase of income in the developed countries by 1 per cent normally will raise their imports of foodstuffs from developing countries by 0.6 per cent and of agricultural raw materials by 0.5 per cent, while their imports of manufactured goods from developing countries go up by 1.9 per cent. Thus, demand for poor-country manufactured goods tends to go up faster than income growth, but demand for primary products (other than fuels) by much less than the growth in income. Of course, the developing nations rely on exports of primary products for the major part of their export earnings—still over four-fifths of total exports. Therefore, the declining position of the poorer nations relative to the rich in recent decades is a consequence of their heavy reliance on exports of primary products.

This continuous weakening of their position is abetted by other forces. In the developed countries, for example, progress in technology results in less use of raw materials per unit of output. Similarly, services are rising as a share of gross national product, but they do not require raw materials. Finally, the world agricultural picture is now different from what it was a decade or two ago. On the one hand, since incomes are high in the industrialized countries, very little of any increase in income gets spent on foodstuffs, as compared with a high proportion of income spent on food in poorer countries. On the other hand, some developed countries are relatively efficient in agricultural production themselves (particularly the United States, Canada, and Australia), and technological improvements have reduced the influence of natural factors on farm production. Furthermore, all rich countries have major farming sectors that they protect for reasons of social policy toward their own rural areas, thereby making their markets very difficult to penetrate and generating inefficiently produced surpluses. These surpluses, in turn, are exported with government subsidies, artificially depressing the international market. On top of all this, natural commodities like cotton and rubber are being displaced by synthetics and other man-made substitutes.

When the developing countries do manage to shift some resources into generating exports of manufactured goods, they find that, with few exceptions, producing consumer staples like textiles is not necessarily a way out of the quicksand. The proportion of income spent on manufactured consumer staples like clothing also tends to decline with income growth. Moreover, these manufactured consumer staples tend to be made, in the developed countries, with large amounts of low-skilled labor in regions where low wages prevail. Competition is keen from these producers. When imports, nonetheless, make significant inroads, there is a tendency for importing countries to erect trade restrictions in order to moderate what is feared to be employment-displacing import growth.

The outlook is even more depressing for those countries that will face rising levels of unemployment in coming years. The average growth rate of developing nations in the 1960's was about 5 per cent per year, which was better than most experts had expected just a few years earlier. However, the prospect of rising unemployment adds enough political pressure to require significantly higher growth rates in the 1970's and 1980's. Such increases cannot occur unless the internal productivity of agriculture and industry rises more rapidly in the poor countries, and unless the flow of resources from outside is dramatically stepped up. In this context, trade assumes even greater importance in the 1970's and beyond.

## Reducing Imports

Since the trade balance, as a whole, is important, some means must be found to improve it. One means is to reduce imports into the poorer countries. If this reduction is accomplished by increasing import restrictions, the opportunity is created for development of "infant industries" within the protected market. In many cases, the developing nations have made a headlong plunge into the substitution of domestic production for imports. It is now increasingly recognized among trade experts that this process has got out of hand. Today, poor-country industries that are potential exporters face extremely high costs of production, because essential imports are high priced or home production of materials is costly relative to world standards. In other words, protectionism has begot patently inefficient as well as potentially efficient industries. In most developing nations, there is little room for further reduction of imports through increased protection, because the substitution of domestic production for imports has already been pushed to its limits.

Where import protection has been resorted to heavily, it is often true that a wide-ranging array of complex trade barriers are used. Most of these devices lend themselves to bad administrative practices and bribery and often amount to little more than devices for harassment. As a result, their effects cannot be easily measured, and they are therefore not readily usable as selective instruments of a conscious development policy. Compounding these problems, the developing nations frequently maintain exchange rates that are unrealistic.

If the developing countries are to improve their internal efficiency and their competitiveness in the world market place, they must first put their own houses in order. They cannot easily adjust their exchange rates with every vicissitude in world commodity markets, or too frequently with regard to internal inflation. Therefore, they will probably have to be allowed to continue using selective tariffs and subsidies for exports to offset the disadvantages of structural costs suffered by selected industries. Nonetheless, the measures used to regulate imports and exports should be simple, measurable, and adjustable to the changing needs of their industrial sectors. A major effort at simplification would be valuable for most of these countries, with heavy reliance on tariffs in place of the present array of administrative controls and other nontariff barriers. The use of tariffs would bring several benefits. Impediments to trade could be measured and manipulated as instruments of development policy. And tariffs would provide revenue for governments, in place of high administrative costs now borne in the administration of complex procedures, and in place of the bribery that is a natural partner of complexity.

Too often, this protectionist aspect of the trade problems of developing countries is overlooked or given low priority in policy analysis. Moving in the direction suggested here, however, can only provide a basis for breaking into the highly competitive world markets. At the other end of the transaction between exporter and importer lies a formidable array of protective devices maintained by importing countries, developed and developing alike. In addition, in some product areas the developing country must cope with the export-subsidization practices of some wealthy countries, which create artificial conditions of competition.

It is sometimes recommended that developing countries should make a greater effort to trade with each other. It can be argued that their quality standards, somewhat relaxed delivery schedules, and unsophisticated marketing techniques need not provide as many difficulties in trade with each other as might be the case in trying to export to developed countries. True enough, but the trade barriers maintained by the developing countries themselves are often so difficult to penetrate that all these potential advantages are offset. Thus, the recommendation made above concerning the simplification of protective measures in developing countries becomes even more important in promoting trade expansion among them, and it holds true with respect to trade either among all developing nations or simply between a few of them within the framework of regional trading arrangements.

## TRADE POLICIES OF THE DEVELOPED COUNTRIES

Turning, then, to the trade policies of the developed countries, it must be said quite candidly that the outlook is not good for more liberal access to rich-country markets for poor-country goods. The developing countries have concentrated their diplomatic and negotiating effort, almost to the point of obsession, on the scheme of general tariff preferences that was finally hammered out and agreed to by the industrialized countries in the Organization for Economic Cooperation and Development (OECD) and the U.N. Conference on Trade and Development (UNCTAD). The idea is to allow imports of manufactured goods from developing countries to enter free of duty into the markets of the rich countries, giving poor-country exporters preferential terms of access.

For a long time, the U.S. Government opposed the idea of granting tariff preferences for developing countries. It was concerned that such a move would damage the principle of nondiscrimination in international trade. That principle had proved again and again to be an important defense against lapses into protectionism and discriminatory bilateralism, and it has helped governments to resist special pressures from within their countries as well as from closely allied nations.

In the end, President Lyndon B. Johnson shifted U.S. policy and agreed to the *principle* of generalized preferences on export of manufactures and semimanufactured goods from all poor countries to all developed ones. This change in policy was directly related to three fundamental objectives:

1. Ending the growth and spread of special, preferential arrangements on a discriminatory basis, being negotiated by European countries. These would be subsumed in a global approach to preferences.

2. Ending the practice of "reverse preferences," by which recipients of special preferences, in turn, granted special access to their markets for some exports from developed countries granting the special preferences. These were harmful to poor countries and discriminated among the rich.

3. Providing truly better conditions for the trade of developing countries generally.

However, although President Johnson agreed, in principle, to a scheme of preferences, during international discussions on its shape the United States failed to persuade Europeans to give up their special preference arrangements with Africa and the Mediterranean, or even to hold up on new arrangements. Nor was Europe prepared to give up "reverse preferences" on a fixed, agreed timetable.

Finally, it was eventually conceded that there could be no agreement on a single common scheme to be implemented in the same way by all developed countries. National schemes involved different kinds of safeguard mechanisms, which were designed to protect against unusual and disruptive increases in the imports of particular products. The United States, for example, intends to implement a scheme that would leave aside certain sensitive-product areas (shoes, textiles, and oil). As for other problems that might arise in the future, the United States intends to use the standard escape-clause mechanism that exists in today's trade legislation, whereby firms or workers in the United States who are troubled by increased imports in a preferred-product area might apply for tariff relief. This relief might be granted if the Tariff Commission found that injury to U.S. industry resulted from increased imports deriving from the elimination of tariffs.

Understandably, therefore, the developing countries were not wholly convinced that the U.S. approach was as liberal as it was said to be. Europeans and Japanese also argued that the American system was not practical, because it would lead to a spate of escape-clause cases based in part on political considerations. These, in turn, would lead to continuous diplomatic friction between the United States and developing countries. Europeans pointed out that a handful of developing countries were already highly competitive in many kinds of manufactured goods, and that there had to'be some way to ensure that they did not receive all the benefits, with nothing for others. Moreover, the exports of some of these competitive developing countries were in competition with exports from countries like Italy and Japan. If they were to receive preferences on competitive products, the exports of developed countries would be directly hurt.

To meet such problems, the Europeans proposed a different system based on tariff quotas, with almost no exceptions for sensitive products. Under this system, no duties would be imposed on imports of manufactured goods up to an over-all limit on trade volume for each product entering each country granting a preference. Once the limit was reached, the products would be placed under surveillance. Alternatively, the normal tariff rate would be reimposed. For products under surveillance, rapid increases would tend to lead to reimposition of tariffs. No administrative judgment would be required regarding injury or disruption. Wherever possible, political decisions would be avoided on the question of continuing or suspending preferential treatment. Being fairly automatic, the process would be nonpolitical. Furthermore, countries already competitive in one or more products might not receive benefits for those products, thus making room for the less-developed countries and ensuring that one or a few countries do not take all the benefits of preferences for themselves.

In principle, the arguments made by the Europeans make a great deal of sense. In practice, the European system was initially designed to give little benefit to potential exporters. The levels of the tariff quotas were set very low, with a small allowance for growth. Yet, the *normal* growth in exports from these countries will rapidly overtake, and in many cases has already overtaken, the stipulated import levels for duty-free access.* The political decision of the European Community to go forward in 1971 with a general-preference scheme was partially countered by the ingenuity of trade technicians in creating a complex system designed to deter rapid growth of imports from low-wage developing nations. While Community officials claim that tariff quotas would often not be formally invoked, uncertainty about administrative discretion will tend to spoil the incentive effect of preferences. Since Japan has adopted this scheme, too, and Britain must do the same on entry into the Common Market, its implications are very broad.

Nonetheless, aside from the question of deciding when protection would be triggered, there is much to be said for the basic concept of having automatic safeguards, with provision for keeping a handful of relatively competitive developing countries from taking all the benefits. Further American thinking on the right kinds of safeguards is desirable. Moreover, if the United States relies solely on the escape clause, this will tend to increase protectionist pressures, which are already intense, to make the escape clause more readily usable and more restrictive in character. In practice, the escape-clause procedure has already changed somewhat. The Tariff Commission finds injury more readily under less strict criteria or interpretations than had traditionally been used.

Another element in this mix of politics and economics should

* Professor Richard Cooper has analyzed the European scheme in an unpublished paper, "The European Community's System of Generalized Tariff Preferences," Royal Institute of International Affairs, Spring, 1971.

also be borne in mind: namely, that future improvements in terms of access may be desirable, once the general preference scheme is under way. These can be brought about by periodic negotiations. Of course, it would be difficult to negotiate internationally over such abstract questions as the method of reaching judgments on injury, or on administrative procedures. The developing countries would have difficulty concentrating their diplomatic efforts in international talks on matters subject to the interpretation of sophisticated bureaucracies in developed countries. By contrast, tariff quotas can be measured, and the volume of trade that would trigger protection can be more easily negotiated upward over time. In setting up any such scheme to improve the trade prospects for developing countries, therefore, we should always bear in mind that there would need to be future negotiations on the nature of the scheme and on continuing improvement in its terms.

## WHAT POOR COUNTRIES SHOULD BE ASKED TO DO

In principle, general preferences would be granted without any requirement that developing countries grant reciprocal preferences. Traditionally, however, U.S. trade legislation has required some form of reciprocity in return for concessions. Therefore, as a substitute for the traditional legislative notion of reciprocity, and as a way of making the tariff-preference scheme seem genuinely useful as a part of an over-all global economic policy, developing countries might be required to take some actions of their own in order to qualify as beneficiaries. For example, most developing countries are unlikely to secure significant benefits from preferences unless they rationalize their own relationship with the international market along the lines discussed earlier. The price advantage that might be obtained through preferences would not be sufficiently big in most cases to revolutionize the problems they now have with gaining access for their goods.

Consequently, it might be proposed that developing countries undertake steps to put their own houses in order and adopt export-oriented policies, as a condition of receiving general preferences. Toward this end, an international panel or committee might be established to review the performance of developing countries under the general-preference scheme. The panel should be composed of a select group of people from both developed and developing countries. The panel's purpose would be to encourage developing countries to adopt policies that would promote exports: there might be periodic review of exchange rates, foreign exchange controls, tax policies, investment policies, their own nontariff barriers, and any other factors that potentially would affect export performance. Pressure of this type, coming especially from a panel that included developing as well as developed countries, might prove useful to politicians in poor countries in helping them to take desirable options that would otherwise be politically difficult.

Finally, it should be recognized that the trade benefits of preferences are likely to be modest. Most expert estimates, both official and unofficial, put trade expansion in the neighborhood of $0.5–$2 billion. As against current exports of nearly $50 billion from these developing countries, the figure is not very encouraging; it would be on the low side of this range if many products are excepted because of their "sensitivity." By contrast, to some extent preferences may encourage investors in developed countries to build new plants in developing countries. But this could cause some labor unions, especially in the United States, to become increasingly concerned about the direction of international trade policy, out of fear of "runaway mills." This labor concern must be figured as a strong political influence working against an effective preference system that really stimulates new investment.

## The Problem of Nontariff Barriers

The really big problem, however, lies with nontariff barriers, particularly import quotas, that are maintained by developed countries. Not only are these barriers already serving as effective deterrents to would-be exporters; but, in addition, there is a tendency by developed countries to impose new restrictions when developing countries do manage to gain significant access for their goods or threaten to do so. Success breeds restrictive reaction.

Why is this? In part, it is a simple matter of the threat that labor-intensive imports will displace labor-intensive domestic production in the rich countries—usually in labor-surplus, low-wage regions. When gains and losses are added together, there is no evidence that a developed nation loses jobs on a national basis as the consequence of rising imports. On the contrary, the evidence seems to point to a neutral, or even positive, effect as domestic jobs and jobs that produce exports rise to counterbalance the displacement from imports.* However, the problem does not usually arise politically in relation to a nation as a whole. In the United States, a labor-union leader facing a decline in the employment of his union's membership is not especially interested in whether the displaced workers are picked up by other firms in other industries, thus joining other unions. Instead, the union leader seeks to preserve membership and employment for his members, without regard to alternatives. Textile workers dropped from employment in New England as the mills move to the Carolinas and Georgia may—and usually do—end up in other industries; but the union leader nonetheless makes a plea to save jobs in textiles by reducing the pressure of imports, however marginal the import problem may be. This political calculus is sometimes difficult for the layman to understand, although, to a member of Congress or to the president of a confederation of labor unions, it is all too clear.

Most generally, the recent rise in congressional sentiment for import quotas does not augur well for the prospects of liberalizing restrictions against trade in products of interest to developing countries. Of course, all major developed countries maintain import quotas on at least some products. Sometimes these quotas are set on a global basis, and sometimes they are assigned country by country. Sometimes they take the form of export restrictions maintained by developing countries pursuant to bilateral agreements with rich countries. Sometimes the quotas are set informally, or are agreed to on a "voluntary" basis, in face of the threat of formal, legislative restrictions that might be exceptionally hampering.

* See the statement of George P. Shultz, *Tariff and Trade Proposals: Hearings before the Committee on Ways and Means*, U.S. House of Representatives, 1970; and I. Little, T. Scitovsky, and M. Scott, *Industry and Trade in Some Developing Countries*, Oxford, 1970, especially pages 285–89 and Appendix, pages 459–66.

The reasons for quantitative import limitations vary widely among countries and even among products. Some of these limitations were originally established to protect the balance of payments during past periods of crisis. They often then remained long after the crisis had disappeared, because the protected industries or workers became accustomed to them, or because removal would have required new domestic policies for economic adjustment, which might be costly. Import quotas can be set for alleged national-security reasons, as is the case for American quotas on oil and oil products. In these instances, domestic production is given special protection to ensure viability of the domestic industry and self-sufficiency in times of international trouble. The industry is declared to be essential to national security, and a tolerable level of imports is then established through quotas.

Import quotas can also be aimed at keeping imports from "disrupting" domestic markets. This concept, for example, is behind present American quotas on imports of cotton textiles.

The concept of *market disruption* is different from criteria used in past years to test injury. It is used increasingly by political lobbyists in arguing for new quantitative import restrictions. Many industry and labor representatives argue that import levels must be kept within certain specific limits, in order to prevent dislocation in the economy of the importing country or to slow the rate of domestic adjustment to changing world market conditions. The argument is that tariffs, even when very high, are not an effective limit on imports from very-low-wage countries or on imports of products sold at cut-rate prices in order to clear inventories or avoid storage. In its more sophisticated form, the argument is that we should allow a "reasonable" level of imports and even allow imports to share in the growth of the domestic market. Yet, their growth rate should be less than, or at least no more than, domestic market growth for the product in question. This standard ensures that production, employment, sales, and profits can continue to grow in the domestic economy. If labor productivity is rising rapidly, layoffs can be avoided by ensuring sufficiently rapid expansion of home production. And so on.

Some years ago, imports were thought to be creating *injury* if, among other things, domestic employment, sales, profits, and investment were falling off. The new concept of *disruption* is related to market expansion rather than contraction.

Disruption in the new sense is also sometimes thought of in terms of price behavior. For example, an import is considered to be "dumped" if its price is lower than the price at which the same product is sold in the country of origin. Although the developed countries have dumping laws aimed at impeding sales at dumped prices, remedies under the dumping laws depend upon a finding of injury. Since injury is often difficult to demonstrate, and since the issue really involves limiting the rate of import growth in order to ensure growth of domestic production and sales, these laws are not satisfactory to the seekers of quota protection.

To sum up, the desire for import quotas is a desire to limit the quantity of imports to a specific level or growth rate. Such a rate ends the market uncertainty for domestic producers, which is created by unseen, uncontrolled foreign exporters, and it often allows tacit or explicit "arrangement" of domestic prices at levels satisfactory to domestic producers.

The types of import restrictions imposed on industrial products do not normally apply to trade among developed countries themselves. The ostensible reason is that the import problem arises only in connection with low-priced imports from low-wage countries. The real reason, usually, is that developed countries have enormous power to retaliate against each other and therefore avoid restricting each other. The leverage of developing nations in such situations is very modest, indeed. Consequently, it is possible for an American official to assure Europeans that textile-import restrictions would not be applied against them, and that the only problem is with Asians. This was, in fact, done in the early 1960's in regard to cotton textiles and in 1969 and 1970 in regard to wool and man-made fiber textiles. (Japan's own import restrictions put her in the embarrassing position of being unable to argue strongly against restrictions placed on her exports.)

## What Rich Countries Should Be Asked to Do

There are two problems to be dealt with in any search for measures to liberalize access for the exports of developing nations. First, international formulas are needed for the liberalization of existing restrictions. Second, principles are needed to protect the interests of developing nations when new restrictions are sought by the rich countries, particularly new restrictions of the voluntary-agreement type.

These two problems cannot be dealt with effectively on a bilateral basis. Here, too, developing countries have little negotiating leverage. (This is always true, unless critical military-base rights or some other major policy issue is involved in relations with that country; but, even then, most countries are reluctant to link security issues explicitly with trade issues). In a bilateral context, developing nations are little more than beggars. Consequently, it would be in the interests of the developing countries themselves to join together in the search for *multilateral* solutions.

A beginning could be made by a multilateral effort to regulate the administration of national import quotas and to keep under review the conditions under which new quotas are introduced. By drawing up some principles and rules on procedures, together with provision for a consultative mechanism, the bilateral restrictions would become "multilateralized" insofar as they conformed to the multilateral rules.

Guidelines might limit the more unreasonable practices of governments and provide a sensible basis for *liberalization*. In addition, however, some way should be found to curb the use of import restrictions solely for permanent protection. The aim of restrictions that are imposed should be to provide for an orderly transition or adjustment to new, unrestricted circumstances. It might be possible to reach agreement that countries imposing new special import controls should also take on certain commitments. They might agree to embark upon a *government-assisted program of domestic adjustments*. This adjustment program should be subject to multilateral surveillance.

Within the developed country itself, it would seem desirable to find some mechanism for ensuring that an industry given the benefit of special relief from competition uses that temporary relief for the benefit of its workers. A simple procedure would be to require an industry that requests protection to provide a modernization plan along with its statement of injury. It should be required to accept adjustment assistance from the government. During the period of protection, the industry would have to submit an annual report on the progress it has made in modernizing (or on the nature of difficulties it has encountered), on its progress in dismantling its less efficient sectors of production, and on its employment progress. The government body concerned could then recommend new measures to be taken by the industry, perhaps with improved government programs of adjustment assistance, which would have to be implemented by the industry in order for protection to continue. General information on prices, investment, productivity, and employment—especially employment of disadvantaged workers—should be published by the government body so that public scrutiny would be possible. In turn, governments would be obliged to file a report on progress to the international surveillance body. Such procedures would ensure more effective programs of modernization, better protection of consumers, and *less political pressure* on congressmen, cabinet members, and heads of state.

Many other kinds of nontariff barriers exist in the developed countries. Some of these barriers are simply manifestations of domestic social policies that incidentally have trade effects. Others are deliberate devices to discriminate against imports or to pass some of the costs of domestic programs on to foreign interests. Troublesome nontariff barriers include health, safety, and quality standards; discriminatory taxes; government procurement practices; agreements to guarantee import prices; procedures for imposing countervailing duties on subsidized imports; uncertain procedures of customs classification and valuation; and so on. Added to these impediments to trade are the array of government aids to domestic production and transport, as well as aids to exports, all of which create further distortions in world market conditions.

These nontariff barriers affect both developed and developing countries. However, their impact is often much more severe on the poorer countries. Manufacturers in developed countries are accustomed to producing for different markets with different standards, labeling requirements, customs formalities, and administrative procedures. And where the nontariff barriers are particularly troublesome, these manufacturers often can jump them by investing in production facilities in the protected country.

Developing countries are not yet fully aware of how difficult some of these problems can be, since they are not yet significant exporters of manufactured goods or processed foods. Nonetheless, looking to the future, we can see that poorer countries should have an even greater interest than the rich in multilateral liberalization, simplification, and harmonization of nontariff barriers. However, sorting out nontariff barriers does not lend itself to giving preferential treatment for developing countries. On the contrary, the problem more often than not is one of drawing up principles or codes of conduct—together with establishing consultative procedures—in order to moderate the effects of conflicting national economic and social policies. Harmonization of practices would be important for all traders, whatever their countries' stage of development. The key objective would be to limit the passing on to other countries of the costs of domestic policies and—where costs are passed on—to provide for compensatory adjustments on the part of importing or exporting countries.

The developed countries have been examining many of these problems in the General Agreement on Tariffs and Trade (GATT) and in the OECD during the last few years, with a view to holding new trade negotiations. Although developing countries have sat in on GATT meetings that discussed these questions, they have not taken an active interest in nontariff barriers. Only recently, in UNCTAD, has there been a modest awakening of interest.

However, representatives of developing countries have been mesmerized by the question of tariff preferences. As a result, there is real prospect for implementing a modest but restricted global preference scheme. Yet, it would be circumscribed by import quotas and other nontariff barriers that may well turn out to be far more important to trade prospects than tariffs. Of course, the developing countries need not suffer such an outcome. They can play an important and constructive role in pressing for multilateral negotiations on nontariff barriers. In this field, their negotiating leverage as a group is considerable. However, negotiating leverage on many of these questions is not crucial. After all, reciprocity—in the traditional sense of horse-trading one measurable tariff concession for another—cannot readily be applied to immeasurable nontariff barriers. Instead, the question is one of reaching international consensus on sensible codes of conduct and on consultative procedures.

## AGRICULTURAL TRADE

In analyses about the trade outlook for developing nations, the main ingredients are often the prospects for agricultural trade and primary commodities. Problems here have been covered by many authors, and little that is fresh can be said at this juncture. One comment, however, is necessary. Some developing nations are now embarked upon programs to stimulate agricultural production, and the Green Revolution in the technology of food production has given some of these countries hopes of new export markets. Yet, thus far the outlook for the world market does not support such hopes. Grain production in most developing countries is supported at high domestic prices, roughly double world market prices at current rates of exchange. This means that the poor countries are emulating the costly agricultural programs of the rich. Moreover, as agricultural productivity goes up in a number of countries—leading to self-sufficiency—prospects for trade between countries goes down. Compounding these difficulties are the merchantilist agricultural policies of many developed countries, which restrict imports, artificially stimulate home production, and subsidize exports. Since all countries, developed and developing alike, freely use nontariff barriers and export subsidies as complements to their rural and farm-income policies, the future will depend upon success or failure in finding a multilateral way out of today's chaotic conditions of trade. Progress in agricultural trade will require essentially the same type of approach to negotiating as that described above with regard to nontariff barriers. In fact, remaining problems in agriculture and industry are very much alike, with tariffs being the least important element in the over-all picture.

## PROBLEMS OF SOPHISTICATION

During the last few years, exports of manufactured goods have been gaining as a proportion of total exports from developing countries: The growth rate for manufactured goods is roughly double that of commodity exports. Can this improvement be sustained—much less accelerated? The answer to this question depends upon adequate handling of the problems posed in this chapter. However, one final problem remains to be aired. The exportation of manufactured goods to developed countries requires sophisticated quality control, production scheduling, and marketing techniques. Producers in developing countries are often unable to cope with these requirements and prefer, instead, to produce for sale within their sheltered, comfortable home markets.

Some of the most successful programs of export to the United States have involved American retail chains and importers reaching out to developing countries. Some of the successes have been the result of American investment in production facilities abroad, in order to produce parts or to assemble goods for export to the United States.

The international companies and the large retail chains in the developed countries provide channels of distribution, marketing know-how, designs that are tailored to current tastes, and so on. Thus, when companies in the developed countries reach backward into the production system of developing countries with firm orders and designs, the companies sharply reduce the uncertainties of entering the export market, while guaranteeing a fixed volume of sales.

Viewed from the developing countries, there is need for fundamental rethinking of government policies in many of them. In some, for example, there has been increasing resistance to multinational corporate activity. Yet, in face of the developing countries' need to step up exports, and in face of general industrialization that is at least partially oriented toward exports, the role of large international businesses may often be crucial in bringing the appropriate technology to produce for world quality standards. It may also be crucial in providing the necessary international marketing channels. After all, the development of markets is expensive, both in terms of costs and foreign exchange outlays and in terms of sending out into the field some of the scarce engineering and administrative talent needed at home to manage production. Selling manufactures in world markets requires much more than an old-fashioned traveling salesman. Quality and marketing are at least as important as production efficiency for the prospects of developing countries.

## NEW POLICIES

In the future, with an increasing trend toward internationalization of production within companies and among countries, those developing countries which are flexible in their attitudes to outside economic interests will probably fare best in their own export performance. The success of Eastern Asia provides a good example.

Taking all these problems together, and facing the increasingly protectionist mood in the United States and elsewhere, we can see that developing countries need to reassess their policies and the aim of their diplomatic pressures. From the American point of view, there is need for a more broadly conceived development policy that comprehends all trade and investment relations.

Too much concentration on trade preferences in the early 1970's, to the exclusion of other matters, will lead to long-term disappointments and short-term risks that there will be new restrictive trade measures contained in legislation as "riders" to preferential authority. A new policy design that would provide real benefits—rather than illusory ones—would have several elements. As regards new trade policy initiatives, the implementation of tariff preferences should be accompanied by a new series of multilateral discussions, on a global basis, about import quotas and nontariff barriers. Without work on the latter front, preferences will have only modest value and may even be totally negated. At first, the multilateral work could be initiated on selected problems, with priority attention given to the need for international guidelines and consultative procedures on import quotas. The United States could easily begin this process by moving the discussion of its own proposals for textile import quotas into a multilateral context. (U.S. problems with textiles are not as exceptional as is sometimes argued, and similar difficulties will arise in the case of exports of other labor-intensive manufactured goods.)

International work on nontariff barriers and on preferences should be linked with the need for developing countries themselves to put their own houses in order. In this regard, developed countries could call for reform of the trade policies of developing countries as part of the necessary combination of international measures needed to make trade preferences meaningful. They could call for the forming of an international panel to keep under surveillance the import safeguard systems of developed countries—safeguards that are allied to national preference schemes—and keep under surveillance the measures taken by developing countries to put their own trade policy houses in order.

The developing countries themselves must complement the efforts made by rich countries in trade liberalization with new measures of their own, in order to capitalize on the opportunities. In addition to modernizing their own trade policies, they will need to review their own attitudes toward foreign companies. They will need to come up with more imaginative and sophisticated solutions to the political problems presented by foreign entities.

In addition, developing countries must do more homework and undertake better coordination among themselves, leading to more active and constructive participation in multilateral discussions on the liberalization of trade. They should press hard for an international effort on nontariff barriers, which will help them even more than it will help the developed countries.

As regards their diplomatic pressures, the developing nations have not spread their pressures evenly or equitably. The United States has been subjected to much pressure and criticism, while the European countries have been let off with much less. The East European nonmarket economies have done very little to provide trade opportunities for the developing countries. This is unconscionable, because that group of countries has repeatedly said that its contribution to world development must primarily take the form of improved trade access. At the present time, only Egypt, India, and Yugoslavia have good export performance with the East European countries, for obvious political reasons. This sorry record deserves to be illuminated with as much heated rhetoric as has been applied to Europe and to the United States during the last decade.

More generally, the developing nations should ensure that their diplomatic efforts are applied, and are seen to be applied, to all the developed countries without unjust pressure on any one or even on a few. In this regard, governments in developed countries are extremely sensitive to an equitable distribution of the industrial burdens of adjusting to increased imports among the various national markets. Unless pressures on issues like import quotas are distributed more evenly, some developed countries will continue being able to point to restrictions in other countries as the excuse for imposing new restrictions of their own.

To make all this even more concrete for U.S. policy, we should note that the benefits of U.S. legislation that implements tariff preferences would probably be more than offset by legislation like the abortive Trade Bill of 1970. What would be given with one hand would be taken away with the other—with interest. Can we now get hold of this set of problems and devise a genuine development policy to meet the needs of the 1970's and 1980's? If we cannot, then the lack of trade opportunity, combined with festering unemployment in the developing nations, will result, before too long, in major stresses on our foreign policy.

# 9

# The Multinational Corporation and Economic Development

## PETER P. GABRIEL

*During recent years, there has been a rapid and widespread growth of business firms that operate in more than one country— the so-called multinational corporations. Naturally enough, these firms have become involved in dozens of poor countries, where they have necessarily assumed major roles in national economies and plans for development. At the same time, they have become the subject of much controversy, leading to charges of "imperialism." In this chapter the author analyzes the relationship of multinational corporations and host countries and sets forth rules to govern a mutually advantageous relationship.*—THE EDITORS

Few developments have played as critical a role in the extraordinary growth of international trade and investment during the last twenty-five years as the rise of the multinational corporation, with its far-flung networks of subsidiaries in different countries, all marching to the drum of centrally determined strategies. The resource needs of these corporations are being supplied from common pools of capital, management, and technology. Although precise data on the scale of their operations are nonexistent or

This chapter is based on a paper presented to the Development Issues Seminar, Overseas Development Council, February 23, 1971.

quite out of date, some rough orders of magnitude can be pieced together from what statistics are available. These figures relate to foreign direct investments—not all of them made by multinational corporations, to be sure.

The statistics that can be found show that the distribution of investments has been rather skewed, both at their source and at their destination. As far as the source is concerned, almost two-thirds of all foreign direct investments have come from American firms (whose overseas assets reached a book value of $71 billion in 1969, having increased tenfold since 1946). A similar dispro-portion is evident in the destination of direct capital flows. In 1966, the most recent year for which global estimates are available, more than two-thirds of the world total of foreign direct investment—then $91 billion—was in industrialized countries. Barely $30 billion had gone to the poor countries, almost half of it concentrated in the petroleum and mining industries.

The multinational corporations' massive investments in the in-dustrialized countries have given currency to such slogans as the "American invasion of Europe" (and of Canada, for that matter). But their relative neglect of the poor countries has created con-cerns of a different sort.

The flagging interest of multinational corporations in the poor countries is seen by many people as depriving these countries of the stimulative role that commitments of foreign corporate re-sources can perform in economic development. The official ex-hortations and diverse incentives, which were the cornerstones of the development decade of the 1960's, have fallen far short of producing the hoped-for escalation of direct-investment flows to the Third World. In fact, many foreign corporate investors in the poor countries are retrenching. Others are pulling out. What lies behind this reluctance to capitalize on investment opportunities in the less-developed countries? What does it presage for the role of the multinational corporation in their economic development?

There are, of course, good reasons for the failure of these coun-tries to attract a larger share of investments by the multinational corporations. Throughout the Third World, investment climates have deteriorated steadily. More and more countries in Latin America, Africa, and Asia are either proscribing foreign direct investment in its traditional form altogether or are severely limiting the industrial sectors it is allowed to enter. Other countries are relentlessly tightening the reins on the multinational corporations they once welcomed with open arms. Almost all of the countries that still are comparatively hospitable today—including Brazil, some Central American republics, a few new African states—are ruled by regimes without, or with unstable, popular constituencies. Time and again, apparent harmony between the interests of the multinational corporation and those in power in the host country has turned out to be merely a prelude to ultimate confrontation.

## A NONCHARITABLE MISSION

Under these circumstances, what is the role of the multinational corporation in economic development—the role on which its advocates have traditionally based their case for private direct investment in the poor countries? To begin with, we can agree on what it is not. No one would argue that the mutinational corporation is either a charitable institution or a foreign-aid agency—if, by foreign aid, one means outright resource grants or commitments at concessional rates of return. As a wholly private institution, the multinational corporation cannot realistically be expected to make more than a token commitment of corporate resources to "public-interest" (that is, non–profit-making) purposes. Since it must compete for money and man power in private markets, the private firm cannot offer its shareholders competitive rates of return on their investment, if it commits substantial resources to purposes, however worthy, that do not offer rewards commensurate with the opportunity costs of the resources deployed (that is, the profit obtainable from alternative uses).

This is not to deny the place for support by the multinational corporation to the local community in areas such as education, vocational training, medical care, and the like. But the cost of these resource diversions must ultimately be offset by sufficiently attractive returns from the company's normal business operations. Surely, this is the rationale that governs the willingness of many foreign companies in the poor countries to support, with more than token gifts and commitments, projects unrelated to their own operations. Claims to pure altruism, moreover, are likely to backfire. At best, they risk the charge of hypocrisy. At worst, they build host-country expectations of future corporate largesse—and generate subsequent ire when the company fails to deliver.

This reasoning essentially rejects the public-interest (or "good-neighbor," or "corporate-citizenship") dimension as a central part of the multinational corporation's role in economic development. I am obviously not arguing that the multinational corporation can afford to be insensitive to the environment in which it operates: In setting corporate objectives and formulating strategies for their attainment, such insensitivity is plainly incompatible with sound business policy. My contention is that one should not impute to the multinational corporation's role in economic development any functions that detract from its central mission as a private enterprise. This mission is to allocate the firm's resources —capital, man power, technology, management skills, and other corporate capabilities—so as to maximize economic return. Unless the multinational corporation elects to become partly government funded (a possibility we will discuss later), any extended departure from this principle will gradually erode the firm's ability to attract in private markets the resources and capabilities that it seeks to apply in the less-developed countries.

## THE INSTANT PRODUCTION PACKAGE

If we grant the controlling need of the multinational corporation as a private firm to maximize economic returns on major resource commitments (in terms of current earnings as well as asset appreciation), what specific role does it perform in economic development?

The classic answer centers on the distinctive resources that foreign direct investment transmits across national borders—resources distinctive not so much in their substance as in their aggregation. The multinational corporation not only supplies financial assets, it also makes available the entrepreneurship, management skills, technical knowledge, and organization required to put these assets to effective use.

This ability to assemble "factors of production" for specific and sustained application cannot easily be duplicated by national and multilateral foreign-aid agencies and technical assistance programs. Securing capital alone, without the complementary capabilities required for its efficient use, is a very different matter from securing a complete "package" of productive factors tailored specifically to the needs of a given project. Similarly, there is a decisive difference between the deployment of individual experts and technicians through official technical-assistance missions and the commitment of an established organization through the direct investment of a corporation. In contrast to experts and technicians—who typically embody all the relevant skills and know-how the sponsoring institution can field and are otherwise on their own—the managers sent out by a multinational corporation can draw on the technical and administrative arsenal of the corporate parent. In fact, the unique contribution and strength of the multinational corporation is represented by this immediate link to the corporate parent, the availability of back-stopping services by head-office staffs and laboratories (of inestimable importance in an age of ever accelerating change in technologies and management methods), access to procurement channels and marketing outlets, and the capacity for global mobilization and deployment of all the other resources of a large corporation.

In principle, all the foregoing is fairly noncontroversial. It is when we consider the terms on which the multinational corporation's contribution has been forthcoming that controversy sets in.

## What Price Industrialization?

The resources of the multinational corporation obviously exact a price from the receiving country. The commercial return on the resources committed through conventional direct investment is only part of that price. Increasingly, other costs are being associated with foreign direct investment. Imports of foreign capital, a typical argument runs, are offset by demands on local savings, as the superior credit of the multinational corporation competes with local enterprise for the scarce funds of indigenous financial institutions. Another charge is that the multinational corporation pre-empts whole industrial sectors (usually those of most rapid growth), thereby discouraging the development of local entrepreneurship, innovation, and initiative generally. This disadvantage, it is reasoned, more than counterbalances the acknowledged effectiveness of the multinational corporation in rapidly introducing new technologies and management methods, establishing new work disciplines, and changing popular consumption patterns. Increasingly, too, poor countries echo the current outcry in the advanced countries against the environmental ravages of industrialization: the depletion of natural resources once thought to be in infinite supply; the suffocation of cities through pollution, noise, congestion, and refuse; and the social, cultural, and psychological debris behind the glitter of technological advance. Inevitably, popular attacks in the advanced nations on big business or the "Establishment" are more than matched in the poor countries by strident polemics against the most conspicuous agent of change—foreign enterprise.

Arching over all these concerns is the issue of control. As abundantly shown by the experience of multinational corporations in Europe, Japan, and Canada (to say nothing of the poor countries themselves), few nations today are immune to anxiety over the perceived or potential threats to national autonomy posed by foreign ownership of local industry. It is arguable whether, in any given situation, the operations of the multinational corporation in fact support or subvert, on balance, the politicoeconomic objectives and policies of the host government. What most abrades host-country sensitivities and catalyzes suspicion is the shadow of foreign control over local institutions that determine or significantly influence the pace and direction of economic development.

Not surprisingly, this cacophony of alarms in host countries has drowned out objective analysis of the "real" costs and benefits of foreign investment. But objective analysis, even where heeded, has not usually proved sufficient. Juxtaposition of costs and benefits is no more than a necessary prelude to trade-off choices that are largely subjective. Only the multinational corporation itself can assess expected gains against perceived risks in actual or contemplated overseas commitments. For both gains and risks are a function of the needs, opportunities, and options within the corporation's total system.

By the same token, only the host country concerned can assess benefits realized against costs incurred. Both benefits and costs are a function of host-country goals, priorities, and time horizons. Where these are in conflict with the interests of the multinational corporation, what the multinational corporation views as a net benefit to the host country the country itself will view as a net cost. Thus, the so-called benefits of foreign infusions of capital, for example, come to be considered liabilities on the future of receiving countries that have to service that capital in terms of dividend payouts and other remittances. The presumably beneficial demonstration effects of foreign know-how become costs if the superior efficiency of the corporation's overseas subsidiaries is believed to frustrate or retard development of local capabilities. The benefits of the corporation's international division of labor become costs if emerging countries believe that this division permanently condemns their workers to be hewers of wood and drawers of water.

The catalog of arguments and counterarguments is endless. They can be reversed and they can be read backward. The result is the same: The issues are identified and sharpened, but the argument remains unresolved. If people cannot agree on objectives, because their most basic interests are in conflict, they cannot agree on means. The core problem of the corporation's role in the less-developed countries, one must conclude, is primarily a problem of inherent conflict and only secondarily one of mutual misunderstanding.

The conventional cost-benefit line of reasoning might remove misunderstandings, but it cannot resolve inherent conflicts of interest—any more than, for example, objective analysis of issues can resolve a basic difference between a militant labor union and an obdurate company management. Neither side will abandon its demands, regardless of how unreasonable the other may represent them to be, until its true power is tested by a strike or the threat of a strike—in other words, by a confrontation. And resolution of the issues at stake is a function less of the fairness, equity, or logic of the demands and counterproposals made by the parties to the dispute than of their relative bargaining power. The same situation, fundamentally, applies to confrontations between foreign enterprises and the countries in which they operate.

## BARGAINING POWER TO THE PEOPLE

If attempts at mutual persuasion on the basis of the conventional arguments just discussed cannot bridge the gulf between the two sides in the conflict, attention must turn to the prospects for institutional adjustment or adaptation. Reduced to fundamentals, adaptation will take one of two forms, or compromise between the two. One possibility is to expect the institutional arrangements according to which the multinational corporation has traditionally operated (*i.e.*, the framework of direct investment) to remain essentially intact. In this case, the host country will have to adapt its policies to these arrangements. The other possibility is to look for change in these arrangements where they conflict with the way the host country chooses to exercise its sovereignty as a nation-state. Which of the two sides will have to yield more than the other in a given conflict will depend on their respective bargaining positions.

A steady shift in these bargaining positions has been the most notable feature in the evolution of the relationships between the multinational corporation and its host countries—as amply evidenced by the wholesale abrogation of oil and mining concessions in producing countries, the divestiture forced on multinational banks in many African and Latin American countries, the nationalization of foreign-owned utilities, and the "phase-out" program being implemented by the Andean Group (to name only a few examples). In every case, the foreign company has had to relinquish substantial revenues, if not assets, as well as important rights to the host government or other local interests.

The accretion of bargaining power on the side of host countries has resulted from a variety of factors. The success of the early waves of foreign direct investment attracted additional firms in large numbers to the countries where investment opportunities had proved so profitable. At least some of the imitators would perceive smaller risks than the pioneers and therefore were willing to enter on less favorable terms. Quick to seize the advantage of increased competition for investment opportunities, access to which they controlled, host governments did not usually find it difficult to dictate to the early investors the conditions accepted by those coming later. For the very success of the original investments had created captive financial assets, physical plant, marketing outlets, or sources of supply that the host government could use, so to speak, as "hostages" in pressing the foreign corporation to agree to more onerous terms. In turn, the success of some countries in bargaining with the multinational corporation for more taxes or royalties, or for greater subordination to national-development plans, or for acceptance of more severe restrictions on financial and operating policies, inevitably encouraged other countries to insist on similar conditions—and strengthened their hand in doing so. The ripple effect throughout the Organization of Petroleum Exporting Countries caused by Libya's renegotiation of its oil-concession agreements furnishes a recent illustration of this point.

Another cause of the continuing erosion of the multinational corporation's bargaining position in the less-developed countries is the largely self-liquidating role of foreign enterprise in economic development. As previously noted, this role essentially consists of the transfer of certain corporate resources and capabilities (such as money, man power, know-how, and access to markets). To the extent that this transfer is accomplished—to the extent that the foreign corporation in response to host-government insistence dismantles local enclaves of foreign operations and integrates them into the host economy, trains local personnel, develops local sources of supply, builds local markets, and diversifies overseas outlets for locally produced materials and manufacturers—the uniqueness and importance of the foreign investor's contribution will diminish. And so will his bargaining position.

At the same time, the pressures on host governments to make aggressive use of their gains in bargaining power will mount. These pressures come from a number of sources. The most apparent ones are financial. Economic- and social-development plans have to be funded. Military establishments want to be maintained. The additional taxes required are more easily levied on foreign enter-

prises than on local business and individuals. Similarly, in times
of foreign-exchange crises, host governments find it easier to suspend profit remittances of foreign companies than to curtail imports of essential goods—even if this means reneging on as-
surances given or agreements made at the time the foreign
investor entered the country.

Equally powerful are the pressures brought to bear by the host
government's several constituencies. Local businessmen, whose
loyalty to the concept of private enterprise does not ordinarily
extend to unqualified support of foreign companies, are often the
first to clamor for protection against supposedly unfair competition by the more powerful foreign firm. The military, traditionally
supportive of business interests, have veered sharply to the left
in many countries and become advocates of the radical reforms
they once left their barracks to suppress.

But by far the most important pressures causing host governments in poor countries, whatever their ideological persuasion, to
inveigh against foreign investors on their soil derive from the
social turmoil that accompanies not only failure but also success
in economic development. Contrary to the confident expectations
of early development programs, the experience of the past decade
has shown that social conflict and political tensions not only are
endemic to economic stagnation but attend rapid growth—indeed,
are often aggravated by it. If stagnation makes people revolt in
despair, growth raises their expectations—and their impatience
for having them met. A doubling of annual per capita real income
from $200 to $400 in, say, ten years would be an extraordinary
achievement. It would require national income to rise at the extraordinary rate of 10 per cent a year for ten years, assuming that
population expands at the rate of about 3 per cent (as it does in
most poor countries). But, even so, it would not remove abject
poverty. However difficult it may be to accept the notion, no
realistically conceivable growth rate could effectively cope with the
population explosion of the past ten to twenty years in the poor
countries, the massive migration from rural to urban areas, and
the vast armies of unemployed bred by these trends.

If the outlook for social peace and political stability under
these conditions is bleak, so are the prospects for maintenance or
establishment of "favorable investment climates," as conventionally

defined. There is, in fact, a fundamental contradiction in the explicit urgings of many policy-makers in the advanced nations that less-developed countries move toward representative government and social reforms, while at the same time maintaining "investment climates" hospitable to foreign investors. To the extent that the first part of the advice is heeded, rising popular expectations assume political force and frustrate compliance with the second part. Nationalism and its twin, xenophobia, cause agitation and government action against established social structures and traditional patterns of wealth and income distribution to be focused, in the first instance, upon the foreign investor's position, privileges, and prerogatives.

The convulsions shaking most of the poor countries today are powerful portents that this trend will gain force for essentially unalterable reasons of both economics and internal politics. Indeed, if we look at the ever more precarious position of foreign-owned companies in the Third World—whether in the deeply troubled countries of the Andean Group, the newly emerging nations in Africa, strife-torn Asia, or even the oil-rich lands of the Middle East—the conclusion is difficult to resist that the era of the multinational corporation as a direct investor along traditional lines is coming to an end in the less-developed countries. So is the role of the multinational corporation in economic development, unless the multinational corporation can bring itself to abandon some of the institutional arrangements that proved so profitable in the past—specifically, to abandon complete or controlling ownership through conventional direct investment.

## ALTERNATIVES TO DIRECT INVESTMENT

What alternative arrangements might prove more viable? From the standpoint of the multinational corporation, any alternative must compare favorably with other opportunities of committing the same resources. As I contended earlier, it is unrealistic to expect private firms to make more than token commitments to public-interest projects, whether at home or abroad. If the multinational corporation is to perform any significant role in economic development, this role must be a profitable one.

From the standpoint of the host country, any acceptable alternative method of importing foreign corporate resources must avoid the major disadvantages perceived in conventional direct investment. Almost all of these disadvantages relate to the ownership issue—more specifically, to the special rights derived from ownership that theoretically extend to perpetuity. These rights are the essence of the direct-investment concept. They are of concern to the investment-receiving country because they perpetuate both foreign control over local industry and foreign claims on a steadily expanding stock of foreign-owned capital, with correspondingly rising foreign-exchange liabilities.

The crux of the problem is the basis on which resources are forthcoming. No country objects to the inflow of private capital as such. Even less does it object to the inflow of new technologies, management know-how, and other corporate capabilities. The point at issue is the host country's need to dissociate the boon of the resources that accompany direct investment from the bane of foreign ownership inherent in such investment. One might generalize that, while the foreign corporation is no longer wanted in the poor countries as a *direct investor*, it will continue to be welcome as a *supplier of services*.

Such a shift will involve a major change in the very concept of corporate investment. Whereas traditionally the capital element was held to be primary, alternative arrangements of committing corporate resources will have to assign first place to the so-called intangibles—managerial, administrative, and technological capabilities, as well as all the other institutional resources mentioned earlier as characteristic of large-scale enterprise. Accordingly, under such new arrangements, management of the overseas venture will no longer be a right vested in ownership of theoretically indefinite duration, but rather an obligation assumed by agreement for a specified period of time. And the managing firm's reward will no longer be an entrepreneurial one for risks taken, but a managerial one for services rendered.

There is growing evidence that such alternative arrangements to replace the traditional direct-investment approach can, in fact, be worked out on terms satisfactory to both the resource-importing country and the resource-supplying firm. Variously called "service contracts," "management contracts," "coproduction agreements," "contractual joint ventures," and the like, some of these arrangements make the foreign firm responsible for the entire operation of the project or venture. Others limit the firm's involvement to certain functions for which no capability exists. Some of the arrangements include the provision of capital funds by the foreign firm. In other cases, the firm's contribution is limited to management and technology, overseas marketing, and other services. Compensation may be fixed or variable (for example, linked to performance), or it may be in cash or in kind (for example, materials or manufactures produced by the venture being managed). In many cases, the benefits to the foreign firm include sales of parent-company products or the strengthening of a multinational corporation's international network (for example, airlines, hotels, banking).

Common to all these arrangements are various combinations of the following features: (1) Ownership is left, in whole or in controlling part, in national hands. (2) The duration of the foreign company's presence is limited. (3) Explicit provision is made for renegotiation of terms at specified intervals. The most widely known examples of these contractual devices are to be found in the petroleum, mining, steel, chemical, public-utility, airline, and hotel industries.

But do these alternatives to traditional foreign direct investment represent only isolated responses to special situations? Or are they the beginnings of a more general reconciliation of host-country with foreign-corporate interests? If it is true that the curtain is being rung down on the era of the multinational corporation as a direct investor in the less-developed countries, will contractual devices prove to be a mutually acceptable basis for continuing the multinational corporation's unique contribution to the economic development of these countries?

Several requirements will have to be met if contractual arrangements are to become a viable alternative to direct investment. The first is to relieve the foreign corporation of the need to put major capital assets at risk in poor countries. One of the main reasons why private direct-investment flows have favored industrialized countries is that the risks there are primarily commercial rather than political or environmental.* Because of the prominence of environmental risks, direct investors in the poor countries quite understandably make their entry conditional on the promise of commensurately high returns. Usually, this promise takes the form of sharp reductions in the commercial risks of the investment—as, for example, by tax exemptions or tariff protection. In the event, however, the investor's insistence on high rates of return often proves to be self-defeating. For, as soon as the anticipated returns materialize, charges of "foreign exploitation" gain force and bring into play the very risks that had made the investor hesitate at the beginning. In short, the greater the profitability of the investment, the more likely the threat of host-government curbs on the foreigner's bonanza. And the earlier the high rates of profitability are achieved the sooner the host government will impose measures to curtail the investor's profits.

Under these circumstances, it is neither realistic nor reasonable to expect the foreign corporation to invest major capital funds in the poor countries. The problem has been recognized for some time. The U.S. Agency for International Development (AID) and its predecessor agencies have been writing investment insurance against political risks since the early 1950's. These functions have now been taken over by the recently established Overseas Private Investment Corporation (OPIC). Whether OPIC will be more successful than AID in stimulating private corporate resource commitments in the less-developed countries remains to be seen. In my view, investment insurance on *equity* investments does not go to the root of the problem. It is still predicated on the traditional direct-investment concept that confers on foreign corporations certain property rights that are now acceptable in the poor countries only on a highly restricted basis, if at all. Even if governments in the advanced nations were prepared to *give* to their

* A comparison of U.S. direct investments in Europe and Latin America is telling:

BOOK VALUE
(*in billions of dollars*)

|  | 1946 | 1960 | 1969 |
|---|---|---|---|
| *Europe* | 1.0 | 6.6 | 21.6 |
| *Latin America* | 3.1 | 8.4 | 11.7 |

SOURCE: U.S. Department of Commerce, *Survey of Current Business.*

private corporations the capital funds they now insure, the direct investments in question would not, therefore, become any more acceptable to the host countries—probably the contrary.

The solution is more likely to lie in a different direction. National and multilateral foreign-aid funds must be made available not to foreign corporations as such, but rather to the projects or ventures that have been identified as worthwhile investment opportunities. The debtors would be governments or public or private enterprises in the host countries. Loan agreements would specify the kinds of involvements and nonfinancial resource commitments, as well as the compensation of the foreign corporation concerned. The agreements could cover projects owned entirely by local interests, as well as joint ventures (in which the foreigner's equity might consist of either a capital contribution of his own, if he elects to make one, or the capitalization of intangibles supplied to the local enterprise).

## ILLUSIONS AND REALITIES

The point is that continued commitment of a foreign corporation's unique capabilities in the poor countries becomes illusory where it is contingent on a degree of foreign ownership that the host country regards as intolerable. By the same token, foreign corporations cannot be expected to incur capital risks justifiable only by rates of return that host countries are bound to resent and, sooner or later, take action to reduce.

Another basic requirement must be met if the multinational corporation is to continue to perform its role in economic development. Here, the burden lies squarely on the governments of the poor countries. Once the foreign firm, for its part, has made reasonable and effective institutional responses of the kind just discussed to objections made by host countries to the traditional terms of foreign direct investment, host governments must keep their commitments to protect the foreign corporation's interests on the new terms agreed upon. Experience has shown that the multinational corporation is not usually turned away by tough bargaining on the part of host governments. What makes an investment climate unbearable is uncertainty about the stability of the legal and regulatory framework under which the company is asked to commit its resources or about the host government's willingness to honor not only its own contracts and agreements but also those that foreign firms entered into, in good faith, with predecessor governments. Clearly, one of the most urgent imperatives for many poor countries is to achieve and maintain the reputation for absolute reliability in contract compliance that, for example, has been established by the governments of the Eastern bloc as well as by mainland China.*

Alas, the best intentions of an incumbent government are only as good as its own stability. In the cauldron of coups and upheavals characteristic of so many of the poor countries, will the suggested new arrangements with the multinational corporation fare any better than traditional foreign investments? I believe they will.

The self-interest of the host government will be the multinational corporation's protection. Consider the difference. If direct investments can be nationalized or expropriated, or such measures threatened in order to extract greater benefits from the foreign corporation, the prospect of immediate gain to the poor country tends to outweigh the possibility of future loss (as from a decline, if not cessation, of future capital inflows). The actions of Peru, Chile, Algeria, and Zambia show that governments in the poor countries are quite prepared to "go over the brink" in this sense. It seems reasonable to assume, however, that even a revolutionary government is less likely to renege on its contractual obligations if a highly advantageous agreement has already been negotiated with a foreign firm; if controlling ownership is no longer an issue; if the possibility of wresting still better terms from the foreigner is uncertain; if no significant foreign assets can be taken over; if an already arranged loan and the future willingness to lend of a public institution like the World Bank are at stake; and if, finally, the contract in question is foreseeably up for renegotiation in any case. There is, of course, no absolute guarantee for the multinational corporation in the new arrangements here proposed. But certainly far better odds. No more can be asked.

* See Samuel Pisar, *Coexistence and Commerce*, pages 283–87.

## REASSESSMENT AND ADAPTATION

The foregoing analysis necessarily contains oversimplifications that must be qualified. On both the side of the multinational corporation and the side of host countries, vast differences exist in essential nature, historical experience, and current perceptions, attitudes, and aspirations. Still, members of each side show certain characteristics sufficiently common to permit some basic conclusions that can be adapted to specific situations.

In this sense, the points brought out in this chapter might serve to divert attention from the self-conscious debate that both sides have been conducting about the reasonableness or justice (or lack thereof) of traditional investment arrangements—and to focus instead on the need for examining more practicable alternatives. We have ignored too long the need to reassess, in light of current international relations, the institutional framework within which the multinational corporation operates in the less-developed countries.

To be sure, not all of its supporters would comfortably go along with the panegyric that Courtney Brown, editor of the *Columbia Journal of World Business,* showers on multinational corporations. Likening these firms to a "new world symphony," he looks to them as "the hoped-for force that will ultimately provide a means of unifying and reconciling the aspirations of mankind." Still, the view seems fairly common that the traditional concept of foreign direct investment has been vindicated by the multinational corporation's manifest achievements: its growth in sheer size; its successful penetration of one overseas market after another; its "rationalization" of investment, production, and distribution across borders and oceans; and its efficiency in discovering new resources and technologies and in combining and transmitting them all over the world. According to this view, the problem does not lie with the operations of the multinational corporation. These, as Courtney Brown avers, reduce international conflict through promoting understanding among nations and spreading economic benefits worldwide. By this reasoning, it is the nation-state, as an obstacle to the multinational corporation's drive toward creation of a world economy, whose viability is under question.

Such may be the case in theory. In point of fact, however, recent history and current developments show rather conclusively that it is the multinational corporation, not national sovereignty, that is at bay. As we have seen, the rise of the multinational corporation has not made the institutional framework that has sheltered its growth more acceptable to host countries. On the contrary, resistance to the expansion of foreign direct investment (at least to its expansion within individual countries) has steadily spread and intensified. There is almost no historical or current evidence to deny, and a great deal of evidence to support, the proposition that the multinational corporation will continue to grow only if it can adapt its operations to the host country's exercise of its sovereignty. This exercise, at least in the less-developed countries, will surely continue to be guided primarily by national goals and nationally perceived priorities. It will only secondarily, if at all, be sensitive to the global scope of the multinational corporation's interests and needs.

The task before multinational firms, then, is to adapt their interests and needs, as well as their strategies and operations, to the limited control and finite-time horizons to which future commitments of corporate resources in the poor countries will almost certainly be subjected. In response to these adaptations on the part of the multinational corporation, host countries, for their part, will finally have to bury the hatchet, acknowledge the vital role that the multinational corporation's resources can and do perform in the development of their economies, and commit themselves to abide by the new terms on which these resources are being made available.

What are the probabilities of such a dénouement based on mutual accommodation? The increasing overtures of the Eastern bloc countries toward Western private corporations are instructive. Not on account of any latent love for capitalist enterprise do these countries seek to import foreign corporate technology, management capabilities, and market outlets. They are anxious to import these resources because they are acknowledged to be essential to national-development plans. The willingness of multinational firms to compete for these opportunities is a matter of record. So is the success of the Eastern European countries in negotiating terms that are compatible with their sociopolitical systems. Do the less-developed countries really evince the kind of irrationality that would make them recoil from doing the same?

# 10

# The Multinational Corporation in Latin America

## JACK N. BEHRMAN

*Chapter 9 looked at multinational corporations in general. The author of this chapter presents his own definition of the new beast and then analyzes its role in a single region—Latin America. He spells out the ways in which the corporation can be a help or a hindrance to development plans and stresses the possible conflict between "efficiency" and "equity" in judging the corporation's role.*—THE EDITORS

The multinational corporation is more than a group of companies tied together through foreign direct investment. It is most usefully characterized as a group of corporations, located in several countries and owned by a single (parent) company, whose operations are integrated with each other under a single strategy and controlled from the center. Such enterprises are found largely in manufacturing—as distinct from mining and service industries. By this definition, there are no multinational corporations headquartered in Latin America. Nor are there any operating among Latin American countries in ways that would integrate two or more economies. And none are significantly tying Latin American

This chapter is based on a paper presented to the Latin American Seminar, Overseas Development Council, June 22, 1971.

operations to those in the rest of the free world. Almost all foreign operations in Latin America represent the more historical pattern of direct investment for production and sale within the host country or for export back to the home country. With the exception of the mining industries, there is little export to the world market by foreign-owned affiliates of multinational corporations. The minor exceptions arise from the increasing interest that foreign-owned affiliates have in taking advantage of opportunities for trade within Latin America that result from possible regional integration.*

This raises a real question in Latin American minds: Are the gains from integration likely to accrue mainly to foreigners—a result Latin Americans wish to avoid? The problem is how the multinational enterprise might be used effectively to accelerate industrial integration both within Latin America and between that region and the advanced countries. However, few concrete steps toward these objectives have been taken in the past few years. The only new initiative is the European Community's offer to extend preferences to all poor countries—that is, to permit import of their goods at tariff rates lower than those applied to goods from rich countries. And even this benefit might redound greatly to the advantage of foreign-owned affiliates.

The trick will be to let existing foreign-owned affiliates become integrated into the growing worldwide multinational corporations, so that they can tie Latin American industries together and, in turn, tie them to the more advanced countries. The obstacle, of course, is the matter of control: Who decides what will be produced, and where? How much? Where will it be sold? And how will the benefits be distributed? In order to answer these interrelated questions, we must begin by describing the multinational corporation, emphasizing its capabilities. After that, we need to analyze the effect that governmental restrictions in Latin America have on the multinational corporation's operations there, then analyze the problems of using the corporation for regional industrial integration, and, lastly, assess the different approaches

---

* This trade is increasing not only in goods for which duties have been lowered but also, and significantly, in goods not given any tariff concessions.

governments may take to use the corporation in promoting industrial development.

## WHAT IS THE MULTINATIONAL CORPORATION?

The special characteristics of the multinational corporation can be seen in comparison with other forms of direct investment—notably, the colonial form and the international holding company. The colonial type of corporation served mainly the metropolitan market or that of the colony and was largely unrelated to other activities of the same company elsewhere in the world. In Latin America today, there are many examples of the same colonial type of investment—United Fruit (now United Brands), Bethlehem's iron-ore mine in Venezuela, the copper companies and other mining firms, and the few remaining public-utility investments. In essence, they give rise to problems that have been written about for over half a century. Many problems remain, but they are not new ones, and it is likely that this kind of investment will be treated more harshly than investments of multinational manufacturing corporations. In the case of colonial companies, after all, Latin American governments will see themselves as able to dispense with foreign ownership and still retain almost all the benefits of the investment.

The "international holding company" type of investment is illustrated by the widespread operations of Casa Grace in Latin America. Each operation was more or less independent of the parent and all were independent of each other (except in the transport services supplied by shipping and airline affiliates to manufacturing affiliates). Grace made little or no effort to integrate these operations into a unified family, operating under an interlocked strategy. And, indeed, Grace's present acquisitions in Europe follow this loosely structured pattern, which does not create a multinational corporation.

It is true that governments have some problems with the affiliates of an international holding company, and that some of these same problems arise with the multinational corporation. Yet, the latter creates even more problems. This observation can be illustrated by a shift that took place in International Telephone and Telegraph (ITT) in the 1960's.

Before Harold Geneen became its president, ITT held nationally oriented affiliates in communication equipment in each major European country; these affiliates were considered almost "national" companies, since each had a national name and local personnel as managers. The only contact of each affiliate with the parent company was through the payment of dividends and through some exchange of technology. But President Geneen decided to integrate the company's operations. He had affiliates in different countries specialize in the production of various components and equipment and then exchange these products among the affiliates. Before, each nation that housed an ITT affiliate held within its boundaries a company making a complete communications system; local governments could, if necessary, control the entire process. But, after integration took place among the affiliates, each one became dependent on supplies from another country, and the ability of local governments to control the affiliate (if necessary) was reduced. In addition, important decisions shifted to ITT's center of operations in New York.

## THE CONTRIBUTIONS OF THE MULTINATIONAL CORPORATION

As this illustration makes clear, the multinational corporation poses real problems for most countries. Unfortunately, its specific characteristics are not well understood. As a result, there is much confusion in talk about its growth, contributions, and tensions with governments.* A variety of suggestions have also been made to alter the behavior of multinational corporations— suggestions that are, in fact, requests that the multinational corporation change its basic nature. For example, there are proposals that it give up equity ownership and substitute management contracts or licensing arrangements. Proposals to form joint ventures would effectively reduce the ability of the parent to integrate its affiliates; they amount to asking the corporation to "die a little."

But the corporation brings specific contributions, which will

* For a detailed examination of the special characteristics of the multinational corporation, see also my research paper "Some Patterns in the Rise of the Multinational Enterprise," University of North Carolina School of Business.

cease if these (and other) proposals are put into effect. Contributions include the meshing of marketing strategies throughout the free-world economy, the ready transfer of technology without lengthy negotiations or regard for "fair remuneration," the rapid transfer of capital to capital-scarce areas, the husbanding of scarce managerial talent, the ready mobility of production, the introduction of new products, and the achievement of economies of scale —both in production and in research and development—that would otherwise not be so readily attainable. Each of these contributions must be traded off against any desire to reverse the pattern of building up multinational corporations.

## PROBLEMS WITH GOVERNMENTS

The multinational corporation faces special problems with both host and home governments, because of power based on the fact that it has a variety of options. The ability of the multinational corporation to shift the location of production, as well as funds, to transfer technology and technicians, and to change the revenue base in any host country can alter (for good or ill) the country's financial situation, tax revenues, employment level and characteristics, and balance-of-payments position. Tensions thus arise over the power of the corporation to alter the host country's economic situation. It does not matter that the corporation may not act against the interests of the host government. It could do so, and the decision could be taken in a far-distant city by individuals hardly familiar with local conditions. Even worse, there is not only ignorance at the center of the corporation and concern in the host government; there are also either no channels of communication between them, or, if there are, such channels are sporadic and fractured.

Actually, as noted earlier, the multinational corporation, as I have defined it, does not yet operate in Latin America. Local affiliates are controlled by the parent, but a single strategy cannot be developed because of policies adopted by the Latin American governments to prevent corporations from operating within the region in an integrated fashion. Moreover, these governments lack adequate communication with international companies, especially about the kinds of contributions the latter could make if they were permitted to operate their affiliates as part of multinational corporations.

## GOVERNMENT ATTITUDES AND POLICIES

Since World War II, Latin American attitudes toward economic development have induced a flow of private direct investment. First, much *manufacturing* investment has been induced by protectionist policies of national governments, which have required direct investment in order for the market to be served at all by U.S. companies—that is, to leap over tariff walls. Second, investment in *mining* industries has been induced mostly by the existence of resources at relatively low cost compared to their cost in the United States. Third, investment in *agriculture and rubber* has been induced by the favorable climate and the existence of resources not readily available in the United States (the political climate was also stable enough to permit exploitation and development of these resources).

The Latin American governments did establish tariff barriers and exchange restrictions, but these were not sufficient in some industries (such as autos) to induce local production, because the costs of producing locally were high as well. Therefore, protectionist policies in Latin America have also taken more extreme forms. These include quotas and requirements for a sizable proportion of local content in finished products. Furthermore, these protectionist policies have been oriented wholly toward the national market; if there has been any "industrial policy" within Latin America as a whole, it has been a series of national policies to build up a nationally diversified industrial base as rapidly as possible. There has been no regional industrial policy as such, although each nation is building industrial strength against the day when regional integration may require a merging or trading-off of specific industrial sectors. This approach is clearly wasteful.

Therefore, the national orientation of Latin American protectionist policy has meant that foreign direct investment in manufacturing has had to be almost wholly oriented toward the national market. Many companies have invested in one country with the objective of exporting to others in Latin America, but few of them have been able to invest in one Latin American country with the *express* purpose of integrating facilities with those in another: IBM and Toyota are the only well-known examples of this practice. In the case of IBM, three countries signed an agreement to permit specialization in the production of calculating machines and cards, which are then sold within the three markets. Toyota has been trying to put together an auto package among several countries and seems to be succeeding. Other companies have tried for several years to reach agreements that would permit specialized production and regional trade among affiliates—but without success.

The protectionist policies in Latin America have had yet another effect: They have fostered high-cost industry, oriented toward the national market and frequently unable to compete on the world market. There have been efforts to integrate Latin American industry through reduction of duties across the board under the Latin American Free Trade Association (LAFTA), but these efforts have failed. Attention now is centered on the reduction of duties within specific industrial sectors. A dozen agreements to create preferential or free-trade sectors have been negotiated, and another twenty-five or so are under consideration. In the main, these agreements are confined to specific products within an industry sector, and each agreement is limited to only a few countries.

These agreements might be the basis for regional industrial integration. However, the existence of foreign-owned affiliates is an obstacle to their effective use, since (it is argued) these affiliates will get the major benefit from the agreements. There is little doubt that local affiliates of large U.S. manufacturing companies would be in a better position to meld their operations than would independent companies in the different countries of Latin America. The U.S. firms would, in fact, make integration work more quickly. Thus, the multinational corporation could be a means of speeding up integration in Latin America, but it is also a serious obstacle to some efforts that local countries would make on their own behalf.

As defined above, however, multinational corporations do not yet exist in Latin America, and their formation faces serious problems. In the auto industry, for example, there is a requirement that final products have a high degree of local (national) content. In addition, the assemblying companies (U.S., European, and Japanese) can produce only certain key elements of the auto, such as the engine; all the rest must be farmed out to local enterprises. This rather diverse and widespread pattern of local suppliers creates a serious obstacle to integration, since no government wishes to see any of its suppliers replaced by those in another country. In addition, the integration that might be accomplished by the affiliates of assemblying companies among themselves would mean other changes. Either the assembly of particular types of vehicles would have to be relocated—heavy trucks in Brazil, light trucks in Argentina, passenger cars in Mexico—or production of various types of engines would have to be specialized among the countries. Neither type of change is acceptable to governments and particularly to the military. Indeed, the military appear to be among the most serious obstacles to integration in the auto industry, for they insist on having the capability within the country of producing the various vehicles they need.

A different industrial structure in petrochemicals has created an equally serious obstacle to integration in Latin America. Basic chemicals are produced largely by state-owned enterprises, which have a monopoly on feedstocks. Yet, the high cost of these basic chemicals prevents the export of intermediate or final products. Furthermore, governments are unwilling to permit different operations within the industry to be integrated by affiliates of foreign chemical companies. This prevents the kinds of cost reductions that are available in the United States and in Europe. And governments are unwilling to merge state-owned enterprises in petroleum and basic petrochemicals, thus making it impossible to achieve economies of scale.

Other major industries, such as heavy machinery, iron and steel, and electronics, also face obstacles to integration that prevent governments from making the major adjustments that are necessary. In many of these industries, large foreign direct investment is the major problem. After all, relying on the affiliates of foreign investors to carry out integration would create multinational corporations within Latin America. As a result, control would slip away—first to the regional group and then to the multinational corporation. Decisions would be seen as oriented to the interests of the Latin American countries even less than they now are.

In other words, the concerns of Latin American governments over foreign direct investment are magnified in the multinational corporation. It is subject to all the complaints listed above, plus those related to its centralized strategy and integrated operations. Still, as argued earlier, it remains a potentially useful means of achieving industrial integration.

## THE MULTINATIONAL CORPORATION IN REGIONAL INDUSTRIAL INTEGRATION

Both the economic benefits of, and obstacles to, industrial integration in Latin America can be summarized in two concepts: efficiency and equity. On the one hand, as stated in the LAFTA agreement and the many discussions concerning its modification, the benefits to be sought from integration emphasize the greater efficiency to be gained—both to lower the cost of goods within the region and to make its products more competitive internationally. On the other hand, emphasis is placed on the equitable balancing of benefits among the participating countries—so-called reciprocity —so that the poorer countries do not make sacrifices on behalf of more rapid growth in the region's advanced countries. However, trying to gain the two benefits simultaneously—efficiency and equity—*may* prevent the attaining of an acceptable level of either. A careful analysis has to be made of the ways to achieve acceptable levels of both at the same time. The multinational corporation could help do so, but then the political objective of (national) autonomy and control would arise to complicate the problem.

Undoubtedly, the multinational corporation can achieve high levels of efficiency and of market competitiveness. Although it generally operates in markets with few sellers (oligopoly), it can provide international competitiveness for the countries in which it operates. But there is no assurance that the structure of industrial production and trade that is determined by the multinational corporation will match that dictated by the criterion of the "most efficient use of free-world resources." The multinational corporation is not likely to achieve the desired goal of economists: the "first-best" allocation of resources in order to make international economic welfare as large as possible. The corporation is not concerned with comparative advantage (that is, producing a good in that country where it can be done most efficiently), but rather with company advantage; the two are not the same.* In view of the multinational corporation's historical development, it is virtually impossible for it to take into account all the alternative uses of the world's resources—or even those within a region—and to decide to use them in accordance with criteria of comparative advantage.

More important, comparative advantage itself is being eroded as a useful economic concept because of the increasing mobility of factors of production—namely, labor, capital, management, and technology. Not only is labor more physically mobile, but it is being made technologically mobile through the transfer of know-how. Even land and natural resources are being made mobile—in the economic sense—through long-term purchase contracts that effectively tie output to an industrial complex in another country. And, of course, synthetic substitutes are still being found for natural resources. As a consequence, there is little basis, in the concept of comparative advantage, on which to determine which specific economic activities should take place in any one country as opposed to another. Where differences remain in the availability of factors of production, conscious policy can remove them. Of course, there is some cost involved, though possibly only in the short-run, but this is a cost that is acceptable to the nation concerned.

Therefore, the effective limitation on a nation's ability to pursue any given activity has been greatly narrowed. Some industries, in fact, show no natural comparative disadvantages for any nation. This is true, for example, with airlines, for the neces-

* Limitations on relying on the multinational corporation itself to achieve integration are presented more fully in Jack N. Behrman, "Multinational Enterprise: The Way to Economic Internationalism?" *Journal of Canadian Studies*, May–June, 1969.

sary factors of production are as readily available to one country as to any other. The real limits on a nation's ability to move into various industrial sectors will henceforth be only the over-all capacity of a nation; it will simply not be large enough to go into every sector, even to produce specialized products in each. It must choose among the various opportunities. But what is to guide the choice? It is unacceptable to leave the choice to the multinational corporation, even if maximum efficiency were achieved. And it is doubtful that it would be.

## EQUITY IN ECONOMIC GROWTH

However, if acceptable levels of efficiency can be achieved, then the objective of equity in economic growth will come to the fore. The poorer nations are increasingly concerned with achieving equity between themselves and richer countries. They see equity not merely as just distribution of the benefits of industrial advance, but also as participation by the country itself in the process of industrial and agricultural growth. This means a diversity of employment, along with adequate levels. It means a role in the development and design of industrial processes and products. It means sharing in technological advances, and sharing in decision-making. In many instances, it also means that there should be no significant drain on foreign-exchange resources of the country. That is, the poor nation wishes to make and earn its own way through local production and international trade—not just through contributing a small portion to total economic growth and then receiving some of the benefits as largesse from the advanced countries.

Enter, once again, the multinational corporation. It is an excellent mechanism for making the adjustments in equity among participating countries. One company spent several man-years of research in determining how to set up an integrated operation throughout Latin America. Its solution showed each government how it would benefit reciprocally under the arrangement. The multinational corporation was able to do this because of the intra-company transfers of goods and funds that would be possible. It could allocate profits equitably among the countries, diversify employment, and spread the technology. Yet, it failed to convince the governments. They considered that, if the multinational corporation could do all this in their favor, it could also do it in a way that would maximize its own benefits, thus reducing benefits accruing to governments by hiding its actions. The governments distrusted the corporation as the controlling mechanism.

How, therefore, can the multinational corporation be used effectively in regional integration for Latin America? It can be useful, but it will not be used unless it is somehow fitted into the over-all objectives of Latin American countries in industrial development. To date, industrial policies have been largely nationalistic; but there are alternatives that should be examined to determine whether new initiatives are desirable.

## Alternative Industrial Policies

Latin America faces three major alternative policies in fostering industrial development: one is oriented to national markets; a second is oriented to a regional market; and a third is oriented to the international market. Of course, not all Latin American nations have to choose the same alternative; nor does any one nation have to choose the same alternative for all its industry. At present, Latin American countries are relying mostly on nationally oriented policies, but they are mixing these, on occasion, with arrangements within the region in some industry sectors, while attempting in others to become internationally competitive.

Few Latin American countries, however, have anything resembling a thought-out industrial policy that would establish what sectors they should specialize in; which they should stimulate or phase out; where they should locate specific activities; and what levels of efficiency they should seek. Yet, each of them has sought to entice industry into the country. As a result, so many companies have entered (as in the auto industry) that overcapacity has resulted and produced inefficiencies. New efforts have therefore been required to rationalize the industry, by inducing mergers or permitting failures. In the Argentine auto industry, for example, the number of companies has been reduced from 22 to 9 and may now be reduced to 4.

Despite the difficulties of doing so, almost all countries remain dedicated to achieving efficiency through industries that are oriented wholly to the national market. Mexico and Brazil are economically large enough to sustain diversified industries on efficient scales. But even they will have to specialize within individual industries; they will not be able to produce a full line within all the major industries.

These two countries, plus Argentina and Venezuela, have adopted a policy of building strength against the day when negotiations will be needed on the division of industrial activity among countries—whether negotiations take place under LAFTA or directly with multinational corporations. Venezuela appears to have cast its lot with Mexico and Brazil; and Argentina seemed to be going it alone until its announcement in late 1971 that it would seek membership in the Andean Pact. But its motives for bidding to join the Western countries are not yet clear, and the success of its bid is in doubt.

The Andean countries—Colombia, Ecuador, Peru, Bolivia, and Chile—have decided that they are economically unable to support sufficiently diverse and efficient industry on a national basis. They have therefore agreed to open their markets to each other. One critical element in this decision, however, relates to the method of allocating industrial activity. Another relates to the need to do something about foreign-owned affiliates, which permeate their economies. They could attempt to use these affiliates as a way of allocating industrial activity among them. This could have been done in the auto, rubber, and petrochemical industries. Instead, they have announced procedures for forcing the divestment of these affiliates by the parent companies. This agreed tactic toward foreign investment was proposed by Raul Prebisch in a paper presented to the Inter-American Economic and Social Council, and by some North American advisers to these governments.* However, it undercuts directly the very objectives that Prebisch has enunciated for Latin America, by reducing or eliminating con-

---

* See Albert O. Hirschman, "How to Divest in Latin America and Why," *Essays in International Finance,* Princeton University, November, 1969. Paul Rosenstein-Rodan has also written in a similar vein, as have Raymond Vernon and Raymond Mikesell.

tributions of foreign capital and technology, which he also asserts are necessary if Latin American industry is to be internationally competitive.

## THE PROBLEM OF DIVESTMENT

Apart from what divestment will do to the continued flow of capital, technology, and management into the Andean countries, it will prevent even those corporations that are willing to come in under these conditions from tying the activities of their affiliates in these countries with those of affiliates elsewhere. That is, divestment effectively prevents the formation of multinational corporations throughout Latin America or between that region and advanced countries. No U.S. or European multinational corporation will integrate an affiliate in the Andean Group fully into its worldwide operations, if it must divest ownership of the affiliate within seven to fifteen years. However, divestment might induce the formation of private Andean corporations if there are not enough national purchasers of divested companies. Alternatively, governments might have to set up a regional public company to buy the divested enterprises.

Of course, the divestment agreement contemplates that an outside investor can retain an affiliate for a longer period than fifteen years and possibly indefinitely, if it exports a sufficient volume of its production. A multinational corporation would be better able to guarantee a specific volume of exports than would other foreign investors, apart from some investors in mining industries. This is true because the multinational corporation could direct sales either to other affiliates or through them. The multinational corporation, therefore, could meet the export requirement, but the prospect of future divestment reduces its willingness to meld its Andean affiliate into its worldwide marketing operations.

Multinational corporations are likely to respond to the Andean initiative by staying out. Entry will probably be limited to Japanese companies, which are not yet imbued with the concept of the multinational corporation, and some European and American companies that are interested only in gaining returns from licensing and management contracts. Only certain types of companies fit this category, however. Their number is further limited by the availability of opportunities elsewhere to build long-term operations in more stable and attractive economies.

## RATIONAL INTEGRATION

Still, there are ways of using the multinational corporation to help reach the objectives of regional integration—rather than rejecting it—both within the Andean Group and throughout Latin America. It would be necessary to establish appropriate rules of behavior under an agreed industrial policy, and to set up an intergovernmental body to oversee the agreement's implementation. The auto industry, for example, could be integrated throughout LAFTA or within the Andean Group. In either event, the integration would have to rely heavily on the multinational corporations that own the assembly and some production operations in these countries. What form would the integration take? How could each be assured of reciprocal benefits? Could such an integration scheme be accomplished without interference from U.S. and European governments?

To begin with, it is likely that any effort by the Latin American governments to rationalize the auto industry—in a way that forces U.S. and European companies together—would be opposed by the U.S. Justice Department. Yet, this opposition might be overcome, provided that Latin American officials took a strong stand. Furthermore, if the alternative were wide-scale divestment or expropriation, official U.S. opposition could be turned to acceptance, if not support. Equally, little opposition is likely to arise from the multinational corporations themselves, provided they can be shown that the result will be greater efficiency and larger-scale operations, plus fewer headaches. They would not even have to anticipate larger profits, since they would benefit from the greater certainty of the new arrangements.

How could such an arrangement be set up? The model starts with industrial complementation agreements,* which are now

---

* Complementation agreements are provided for in the treaty creating LAFTA. They may provide for reduction of duties on a reciprocal basis covering a given list of products in an industry or, in addition, allocate production among the parties to the agreement.

urged by officials of LAFTA, by company officials in a variety of industries, and by advisers such as Sr. Prebisch. It borrows from experience gained from NATO's coproduction projects, plus that derived from other cooperative arrangements among nations, such as *Concorde*, the European Scientific Research Organization (ESRO), the European Launcher Development Organization (ELDO), Satellite Communication (Satcom), European System of Air Traffic Control (Eurocontrol), the European Coal and Steel Community, and the U.S.-Canadian auto agreement. Behind each of these arrangements is the principle of trading off some free-market efficiency for a more equitable sharing of benefits and burdens, taking into account not just the net positions of benefits and burdens, but the roles assigned in cooperation to each member country.

The Latin American auto industry could be restructured around the existing international companies, to form either an integrated unit within the Andean countries or a LAFTA-integrated industry. Alternatively, the industry could be meshed into the international automotive industry. Within the Andean Group, production could be divided among the several countries in order to produce some of the auto components in each (or a model in each). The components (or models) would then be exchanged among them. The volume of production would permit economic runs, and the production could be located so that each country would consider itself equally benefited, while protecting its balance-of-payments position. The resulting specialization would permit production of a less expensive auto than any produced under today's national orientations. Indeed, if the Andean countries are serious about integration, this approach would gain them the benefits of integration while also assuring that the benefits are spread equitably.

There would be a major concern with the mechanism of control. Would the arrangement be administered by the private companies, as under the U.S.-Canadian auto agreement? Would a high authority be required, as under the European Coal and Steel Community? Or would new control mechanisms be required, such as a Latin American multinational corporation—either public or private? Given the present structure of the auto industry, it seems likely that some new form of organization would be required in order to permit the combining of private supplier companies and international companies. But the interest of governments would also have to be represented, in order to give force and balance to the regional authority's decisions. This representation would also help remove these arrangements from being subject to U.S. antitrust laws.

Even greater economies of scale—to levels producing international competitiveness in autos—would be feasible if integration occurred over Latin America as a whole. Here, also, the international companies could be relied upon to bring about a pattern of specialization that would produce an acceptable sharing of production. If the larger markets of Mexico, Brazil, and Argentina were in the group, a higher degree of specialization could be obtained, and a larger number of existing companies would be permitted to survive. Between four and six international companies would be able to achieve levels of production competitive with international levels. Again, the problem of control is paramount, and a similar set of organizational alternatives is available—probably leading to a regional authority.

## INTEGRATION THROUGH THE MULTINATIONAL CORPORATION

Of course, if Latin American governments wished to take a still larger step toward reducing the costs of production, they could permit integration of productive facilities with those of the international companies throughout the world. This arrangement would give even greater power to the international companies, and it would be acceptable only if there were guarantees of equitable treatment for Latin American countries individually and as a whole. Such a move would require an international industrial agreement similar in intent to the international commodity agreements to set the location of production. The agreement would also have to provide for negotiation over prices of final products and components. Indeed, without such an agreement, the negotiated arrangement on sharing production and benefits might be seriously upset. However, the multinational corporations could effectively arrange and maintain such balances, while maintaining a competitive price for the final product. Of course, no one company could accept an agreement that made it uncompetitive. But there is at least one example that is worth citing: Different oil companies have accepted different agreements from the same governments and still remained competitive.

To what extent would governments set the rules for such an arrangement? The answer would depend on how much they think they would have to sacrifice efficiency in order to gain a more acceptable sharing of benefits and control. Efforts by governments to obtain all the benefits from national industry in automobiles have not produced internationally competitive companies. Nor have they substantially lowered the domestic costs of vehicles. Nevertheless, if the "efficiency" solutions are unacceptable to governments, they should seek "equity" solutions. Despite the admonitions of some economists, it is not evident that the cost of equity is always great in terms of efficiency (that is, in higher costs). There is a view that the market produces the only efficient (or "least-cost") solution. But this view depends on a large number of assumptions that cannot be made. On the contrary, because the significance of comparative advantage has been reduced, there are now many solutions that are of nearly equal efficiency, although they may vary substantially in equity terms.

There is at least one further problem with efficiency and equity. As a result of concern over the sharing of participation, some private enterprises are turning toward production and trade arrangements that provide company and host country with acceptable levels of both efficiency and equity. Compensation agreements have been reached in Europe, under which a company selling a complex abroad will agree to produce (or permit production of) some of the system in the purchaser's country. By these agreements, the location of production and patterns of trade are changed, so that more countries participate in a given industrial sector and specific companies are included. For example, if a company wishes to sell a single communications system to several national governments (or to large companies), its offer will sometimes be accepted only when it agrees to produce some of the system in the purchaser's country.

In Latin America, an effort has been made recently to meld the operations of several companies in a given sector—each of which was doing an inadequate volume of business—into a complex integrated across the region. This arrangement provides some specialization and achieves substantial economies of scale. In order to persuade the separate elements to combine, however, there had to be a careful balancing of the existing and future interests of the countries and companies. Each had to be persuaded that its share was equitable and would remain so. And guaranteeing the future of sharing arrangements even required a new organizational structure. Furthermore, private enterprise, once it has recognized the problem, will itself sometimes provide solutions to problems of both efficiency and equity.

## EQUITY AND THE ADVANCED COUNTRIES

This kind of solution cannot be applied to all commercial relations among countries. Many can still be conducted according to the idea of a free market. However, especially in areas where multinational corporations operate—such as markets with few sellers of high technology or of products requiring intensive marketing—it appears that equity solutions will be more in demand. Therefore, if the U.S. Government or a U.S. enterprise holds to the attitude that it has nothing to offer but support for unfettered private enterprise, it is unlikely to beat the opposition. Even if equity solutions seem too costly, it is worth trying to determine the real costs and the impact these solutions would have on other economic relations.

The advanced countries may gain benefits from moving toward equity solutions in some industrial sectors. For example, free trade will be quickly accepted in such circumstances. Once all the problems of sharing have been resolved, each country would tend to seek the least-cost operation and would not care to see others gain through the imposition of tariffs. Furthermore, there are implications for other aspects of foreign economic policy—such as changes in exchange rates. In this case, increasing stability in major industries would militate against a fluctuating rate system.

Finally, growing specialization in manufactured goods among

advanced and developing countries would produce a higher level of interdependence among countries in place of the present high dependence of the less advanced on the more highly industrialized. While countries below the Equator would like this result, it is not clear that the Northern Hemisphere is ready to share in this manner with its Southern neighbors. Yet, if this sharing does become acceptable, the multinational corporation could become an effective means for producing high levels both of efficiency and of equity. As a consequence, its present position in many countries of Latin America would be changed from that of stigmatized guest to that of welcome partner.

# 11

# Foreign Investment
# and Global Labor Adjustments

ROBERT D'A. SHAW

*For many years, organized labor in the United States stood firmly behind free trade—and other policies that could benefit poor nations. Recently, however, the attitude of labor has changed, as threats to U.S. jobs have emerged from "runaway mills." In labor's eyes, the culprit is the multinational corporation, which defends itself by saying that it brings added benefits to all. Meanwhile, poor countries have their own viewpoint on the problem. In this chapter, the author presents the arguments behind these contending views—and suggests that these differences are developing into major political conflicts in need of urgent resolution.—THE EDITORS*

We owe the word "sabotage" to Dutch workmen, who threw their sabots, or heavy wooden shoes, into the grinding gears of machinery introduced during the Industrial Revolution. This illustration is but one in the long history of conflict as workers are asked to adjust to the demands of new technologies. Yet,

This chapter is adapted from an article published in the *Columbia Journal of World Business,* July–August, 1971. Reprinted by permission. It was originally presented to the Development Issues Seminar, Overseas Development Council, on March 16, 1971.

despite local and often painful dislocations, the past quarter-century has shown that the industrial countries of the West are learning to cope with these conflicts. In recent years, however, a new technological challenge has been rising in the world; the so-called internationalization of production. This process describes the production of goods and services by combining the factors of production—capital, labor, skills, technology, and managerial know-how—from two or more countries. Essentially, capital and modern technology are being exported by the multinational corporations of the Western nations to other countries, where these factors can be mixed with unskilled labor and raw materials.

We can search in vain through the voluminous literature on the multinational corporations to find a good analysis of the effects that transfers of capital and technology have on workers in both the recipient and the exporting countries. And yet, these effects lie right at the heart of the rivalry between the multinational corporation and the nation-state. The strongest advocates of the corporations seem to dismiss the problem of labor, with the assumption that—as world production is rationalized—everybody will benefit. They feel that the objections of the nation-state to corporate activity are the last kicks of a dying but obstinate horse. Thus, Sidney Rolfe, in an article, "Updating Adam Smith," *Interplay*, November, 1968, can write:

> . . . there is increasing evidence that the conflict of our era is between ethnocentric nationalism and geocentric technology, between the cost of national pride and the benefit of organizing resources optimally in a spatially-expanded purview of the area within which resources can be organized.

Of course, the idea of "national pride" actually includes many legitimate social goals. Among the most important of these is the responsibility of the nation-state to strive for full employment and a decent standard of living for its work force. This responsibility has been embodied in the national philosophies of nearly every state. Yet, the pursuit of these goals is being challenged by many forces in today's world. At issue in this chapter, then, is whether the transfer of capital and technology across national boundaries is tending to harm or to benefit the interests of the world's workers.

## THE DOCTRINES OF COMPARATIVE
## ADVANTAGE AND FREE TRADE

For most economists, the solution to the problem of allocating resources between and within states lies in the doctrine of comparative advantage. Each country should produce the goods that are most suitable for its resource endowment: This means that a country like the United States should concentrate on high-productivity products, using advanced technology and large amounts of capital and skill; whereas Indonesia, for example, should focus on products using high levels of unskilled labor and natural resources. Under this theory, the welfare of the world would be enhanced if countries then traded the goods they produced most efficiently for those produced elsewhere with a minimum of barriers to that trade. And full employment should be created in each country. The strength of this doctrine's appeal is measured by a statement in *Quality of Life in the Americas*, the Rockefeller Report on Latin America:

> The division of labor is one of the tried and true economic principles that will be as valid in 1976 as it was in 1776 when it was first spelled out by Adam Smith. . . . All participants gain from the freest possible exchange of exports and imports, since that promotes an international division of labor. . . . Everyone gains in the process, just as they do in the division of labor within national boundaries.

The doctrines of comparative advantage and free trade have never fully applied to the actual patterns of the world economy's operations. This has been partly due to the problems of national balancing of exports and imports in the absence of a universal trading money. Another reason has been the need felt in many countries to protect workers in uncompetitive industries.

Nevertheless, the two doctrines represent an ideal for the trading of goods between countries. In its simple form, the theory of comparative advantage assumes that there is full employment in trading countries. It also assumes that factors of production are not transferred across national boundaries. But, in the last decade, the principal engine of international growth has not been trade, but rather the transfer of capital and technology across borders. In 1969, for example, some 3,400 U.S. firms had about $71 billion invested abroad, producing probably more than $200 billion worth of goods and services. American exports in the same year were about $48 billion. The rise of U.S. investment in affiliates overseas has been around 10 per cent a year over the last decade, despite government controls in the last few years; while the U.S. share of world exports has slipped slightly over the same period.

The central question in this chapter, then, is: What will this new force in the global economy mean for workers in both the United States and the developing countries? Specifically, are transfers of capital and technology a refinement of comparative advantage that will lead, with minor adjustments, to a more rational world production pattern? Or does the ease of transfers make comparative advantage obsolete? Combined with the revolution in the corporate mechanisms of communications and control, and the reduction of transport costs, do these transfers mean that the corporations might best pursue growth and profits by concentrating their production in low-wage countries while selling their product in high-wage ones? This, of course, is putting the question in an extreme and simplistic form. But is Herman Kahn, for example, right when he predicts that neither the United States nor Japan will be producing automobiles by 1985, because the production facilities will have been moved to cheap-wage areas like Southeast Asia? And if this nascent movement occurs on any large scale, what will happen to workers in both the United States and the poor countries?

This chapter can do no more than sketch the issues involved. It will not provide answers to the questions above, but merely serve as a basis for discussion. It will concentrate on the United States and the developing countries.

## THE GLOBAL LABOR SITUATION

The employment problem in the United States is well known. The unemployment figure is hovering around 6 per cent: It is more than 9 percent for people aged twenty to twenty-four; and around 14 per cent for blacks within that age group. Within the next five years, as many as 10 million workers could enter the civilian labor force, because of the high rate of population growth in the early 1950's, the reduction of military personnel, and the growing participation of women in the labor force.

All these people require decent jobs. To have "full" employment (actually, around 4 per cent unemployment) in 1976 will therefore require the creation of nearly 12 million additional jobs over the next four years. This need occurs at a time when the economy is facing a conversion problem for much defense-related production and employment into a civilian orientation. In this situation, it is perhaps not surprising that the unions are so concerned about what they see as the export by the multinational corporations of a large but uncounted number of jobs (one estimate has put a tentative figure of 400,000 on the number of jobs exported over the last two years, and this is seen as the beginning of an accelerating trend). The unions also feel that workers are being made to shoulder most of the burden of adjustment, which is particularly acute for elderly and black workers with few skills.

If we now turn our attention to the poor countries, we can see that the employment problem is even more serious there. One estimate has shown that perhaps 75 million people in the Third World are unemployed. But even this is only the tip of an iceberg. Under the pressure of the population explosion, at least 170 million additional workers will require jobs in the non-Communist poor countries in the 1970's: That is equivalent to providing jobs for the entire U.S. labor force *twice* over in the course of ten years.

Here again, the statistics can only scratch the surface of the problem. For the real tragedy in the poor countries is the poverty afflicting even most of those people who have jobs, because those jobs have such low productivity. The stark facts of that poverty dictate that few people can remain without jobs for long. In the Indian countryside, more than 200 million people exist on the equivalent of less than $5 per month. At these levels, there is simply no surplus to support workers without jobs. And the cushion of social security does not exist.

For most people in the poor countries, then, unemployment

is a disaster to be avoided at all costs. Often, the "jobs" these people take are of extremely low productivity. Some experts have estimated that, if these factors are taken into account, between one-quarter and one-third of the human resources in the poor countries are being totally wasted.

This problem, of course, has important political consequences. In a number of countries, the seriousness of the employment problem has become a key issue in extreme swings in governments, including, for example, Cuba, Chile, Peru, Ceylon, and Uganda. With growing frequency, these domestic political upheavals are likely to reverberate in the international arena. Such upheavals seem destined to affect the prospects for trade, investment, political alliances, and even travel. By the same token, the solution to the employment problem in the poor countries will depend, in part, on increased levels of trade, of development assistance, and of private investment from the rich nations.

## The Theory Behind the Multinational Corporation

The multinational corporations believe that their resources and their emphasis on the rationalization of global production can contribute to the solution of employment problems both in the United States and in the poor countries. They work across national boundaries in order to make the "best" use of the world's resources, including its labor forces. In doing so, they will also maximize their own growth rates and profits. Following this line of reasoning, U.S. investment in the poor countries has been growing rapidly, reaching a book value of $20 billion in 1969. And the requests for assistance from the Overseas Private Investment Corporation to corporations wanting to invest in developing countries are rising steadily.

With regard to the effects of this investment on U.S. labor, multinational corporations state that they are "updating Adam Smith," or bringing a sense of reality to comparative advantage in today's world. Arthur Watson of IBM said, "One can trade jobs internationally, which is what we have done through investment. We have not lost jobs." Mr. Watson succinctly summarized the view that the investment patterns of the large corporations, all under the control of a central headquarters, can bring about a rational international division of labor. National governments are often motivated to protect uncompetitive workers for political reasons or create inefficient industries for reasons of national pride or security. These all create barriers to the free movement of products and factors of production.

At the same time, however, multinational corporations are motivated principally by the dictates of the market place and the need for profits. They will therefore invest in the extraction of raw materials and the manufacture of labor-intensive components in the poor countries, where labor and raw materials are abundant. This, in turn, will add to the wealth of the United States through the repatriation of earnings. And the resources freed in the United States by this process, together with the earnings from abroad, can be invested in American jobs with high productivity and using sophisticated technologies.

The corporations also argue that low-productivity jobs in, for example, processing and assembly operations would in any case be lost to the United States as a result of competitive pressures from foreign firms. But, in this case, there would be no net benefit to the United States from earnings overseas and the creation of large, competitive organizations capable of treating the world as a single economic unit. In any case, they contend that the threat of "runaway plants" (the shipping abroad of labor-intensive production facilities) has been exaggerated. In 1968, the last year for which the Commerce Department has issued figures, only about $4.7 billion worth of the sales of U.S. foreign manufacturing affiliates were exported to the United States. This was only about 8 per cent of the total sales of the affiliates and about 10 per cent of U.S. imports. What is more, fully half of these sales were of Canadian automobiles and components under the special agreement with Canada. U.S. imports from manufacturing affiliates in the developing countries were a mere $405 million.

Turning to the employment problems of the developing countries, we can see that the multinational corporations have much to contribute. They provide direct investment to supplement the short domestic supplies of capital. They supply modern technology that can raise productivity to augment the process of economic growth, and that can enable the poor countries to compete in world markets. They train workers and managers, thus bringing the levels of human skills up to a higher level. They provide direct employment, and also a stimulus to the rest of the economy, through local suppliers and higher wages. And, finally, the corporations can sell their products in world markets, thus earning much needed foreign exchange to be used to create further employment. The exports of U.S. manufacturing affiliates in developing countries earned $1.4 billion in foreign exchange in 1968. This amounted to 10 per cent of the total aid, investment, and other financial flows from all the developed countries to the developing nations in the same year. If the exports of the petroleum and mining affiliates of U.S. corporations were included, the total foreign exchange earned would be several times higher.

So, from the corporations' point of view, workers in both the United States and the poor countries will benefit from their operations. Charles P. Kindleberger, in *International Economics,* has summarized this process:

A case can be made that the development of the large international corporation in the 20th century will prove in the long run to be a more effective device for equalizing wages, rents, and interest rates throughout the world than trade conducted in competitive markets by small merchants. The analogy is with the national corporations which in the United States after about 1890 helped to equalize wages, interest rates and rents within the country's borders by borrowing in the cheapest markets (New York) and investing where it was most productive in terms of costs and markets. The resultant movement of capital and shift in demand for labor was probably more effective in, say, raising wages in the South and lowering interest rates there than either trade by local companies or the limited direct movement of factors.

With such an array of advantages claimed for workers, it seems initially a little strange that workers in both the United States and the developing countries should be cautious in their attitudes toward multinational corporations. Yet, both groups, looking at more or less the same facts, present cogent arguments that the operations of the corporations are not benefiting workers as much as they should be.

## PROBLEMS FOR U.S. LABOR

The closing of plants in the United States and their reopening with cheaper labor in Europe, Asia, Mexico, and the Caribbean has brought home the impact of the new international economic forces to U.S. labor unions. In general, these unions have shifted in the last five years from support for free-trade policies toward an emphasis on the protection of workers' rights both in the United States and abroad. The unions are not so much worried about the present levels of imports and of overseas production as they are fearful of the trend that has started in the last few years. They note, for example, that U.S. investment in manufacturing in the developing countries has increased 200 per cent in the last decade. As we saw earlier, imports from U.S.-owned foreign affiliates amounted to only $4.7 billion in 1968, but this was up from $1.8 billion, or 4 per cent of total sales, in 1965. Imports from the developing countries under Section 807 of the Tariff Schedule (which confines tariffs to the value that is added abroad for components shipped from the United States and assembled in foreign plants) have been growing very rapidly, as the following figures show:

| Year | *Imports from Developing Countries under TSUS 807* *(in millions)* |
|------|------|
| 1966 | $ 60.5 |
| 1967 | 98.2 |
| 1968 | 215.9 |
| 1969 | 366.9 |

Nor is this phenomenon restricted to a few labor-intensive industries, such as shoes and textiles, that have hit the headlines. Products imported under TSUS 807 include such items as motor vehicles, aircraft, tractors, gas turbine engines, electronic memories, television and radio apparatus, air-conditioning machines, and even baseballs! In fact, what the multinational corporations see as a minor phenomenon—the imports from U.S. affiliates abroad—the unions see as a real menace for the future.

Thus, the unions claim that a large number of jobs in a wide spectrum of industries have been directly exported. At the same time, they hold the view that, for a number of reasons, the "trading up" of jobs is not occurring, so that the displaced workers are often not moving into higher-productivity employment. Partly, this is the result of imperfections in the labor market: It is simply very difficult to retrain and re-employ the black textile worker from South Carolina or the elderly Maine shoeworker. Another reason is the difficulty of converting the resources employed in the firms that cease production in the United States into more productive industries. The unions further claim that production in developing countries limits U.S. exports to those countries and to third countries.

But the more fundamental reasons for labor's concern center around the international transfers of capital and technology by multinational corporations. The transfer of the most modern technology can now be done with almost no time lag, so that a corporation can almost immediately send production facilities involving sophisticated technology abroad and train workers there to manufacture products with lower-unit labor costs. Philco-Ford, for example, developed a new series of minicircuits and began production in Taiwan. The unions fear that what begins as an assembly plant overseas can become a production facility as low-wage workers are trained. Bendix, for example, transferred the assembly of some aircraft components from Pennsylvania to Matamoros in Mexico: Recently, the Mexican plant has begun to machine the components as well.

All of this is taking place within the context of a wider transfer of technology between the industrialized countries. Thus, Europe and Japan are receiving the most sophisticated technology via U.S. affiliates, and their companies are buying licenses for U.S. technology or developing their own. The internationalization of automobile production by Ford is a good example of the first of these processes: Engines for the Pinto are produced in Britain; transmissions, in Germany.

Raymond Vernon, in *The Technology Factor in International Trade,* a recent study of the licensing, with government assistance, of aerospace technology to the Japanese firm Mitsubishi, concluded:

It is well known that the Japanese co-production programs required more man-hours than would have been required in the United States. It is also well known that certain parts and materials produced in Japan cost more than the U.S. counterparts. Furthermore, some investment and set-up costs were incurred that could have been avoided by purchasing from a "hot" production line. As a result, it has been commonly assumed that the Japanese planes cost anywhere from 20 to 100 per cent more than they would have in the United States. The actual cost data for the F-104J program confute these common notions, however. In fact, no premium was paid. The Japanese obtained the planes at a lower cost than they would have paid in the United States (actually about seven-eighths of the U.S. price). The high materials costs for the F-104J program appear to have been more than offset by the lower labor costs in Japan.

American labor, therefore, feels threatened by assaults from abroad on every type of industrial job. The doctrine of comparative advantage has been made irrelevant by the ability of the multinational corporation to ship capital and technology to other countries. There is simply no possibility, the unions claim, of shifting all the workers whose jobs may be affected into higher-productivity employment. The problem was summarized in *Business Week,* December 19, 1970:

Though they have injected $38 billion worth of repatriated profits into the U.S. economy over the past decade, the multinationals' rise has probably had an adverse affect on U.S. output and employment. Because companies have found it profitable to build plants abroad, foreign production has replaced exports. Not only has this meant fewer jobs and slower economic growth in the U.S., it has also generated balance-of-payments problems that are still far from being resolved.

The logical extension of this process is that more and more manufacturing jobs may be shipped to lower-wage countries, thus leaving an empty shell of a U.S. economy. Already, the transformation that has occurred in the economy has left only 26 per cent of the labor force in manufacturing, as compared to 35 per cent in Britain and 38 per cent in West Germany. Obviously, most of this transformation has occurred as the result of forces within the U.S. economy. But the question asked by the unions is: Will the internationalization of production accelerate the reduction in manufacturing jobs?

As seen by the unions, the core of the problem is that workers and their wage and labor standards are not being transferred internationally, whereas capital and technology are. The long-run equilibration that Professor Kindleberger mentioned is not even on the horizon, at least in part because of the abundance of labor in the poor countries. As we have seen, the supply of labor is growing faster than the number of jobs in these countries, so that real wages are unlikely to rise much in the next few years. Thus, while the productivity of foreign workers in U.S. affiliates can rise rapidly with new capital and technology, their wages are likely to remain only a fraction of those in the United States. The ratio of U.S. hourly earnings to those in foreign affiliates in 1969 for the assembly of office machines was as follows:

| | |
|---|---|
| United States to Mexico | 6.2 to 1 |
| United States to Taiwan | 9.8 to 1 |
| United States to Korea | 10.1 to 1 |
| United States to U.K. | 2.3 to 1 |

Yet, the productivity differential is far less. The benefits of these differentials may be reaped principally by the multinational corporations. They can produce with low labor costs and sell in the U.S. market at or near domestic prices, retaining the profits. And, with the creation of vast "international oligopolies" (markets with few sellers), there is little competition between firms. The unions note that earnings of U.S. foreign affiiliates rose 13 per cent in 1969, while the earnings of U.S. companies barely inched forward.

What can be done about this situation? The unions sympathize with the need to provide decent employment in other countries, and they have long been supporters of freer trade. But they see in the dynamic of the multinational corporation a threat to their own interests and a new force that is depriving workers of the gains of free trade. In fact, the unions are saying that what may have been true in 1776 is not true two centuries later. While the unions are hesitant to urge a more rigid trade policy as a means to protect jobs, they see little alternative until more is done to understand and control the operation of the big corporations. As a result of these fears, the AFL-CIO has been an active proponent of the Foreign Trade and Investment Act of 1972, introduced on September 28, 1971, by Senator Vance Hartke of Indiana and Representative James A. Burke of Massachusetts. This bill has enormous implications for the world economy and for the internationalization of production. Among its main provisions are the imposition of quotas on nearly all imports (with the quotas equal to the average imports during the period 1965–69); the restriction of the export of capital and technology (allowing only those exports that can be proved not to harm U.S. jobs); much harsher tax treatment of the multinational corporations; and the repeal of Section 807 of the Tariff Schedule.

U.S. unions are also seeking to cooperate with their counterparts abroad in order to raise wages and labor standards there. This cooperation may be either formal or informal. Theoretically, perhaps, the answer to control of multinational corporations lies, at least in part, in the creation of international unions. Yet, despite the growth of joint bargaining, there are insuperable cultural and legal barriers to the creation, at present, of effective international unions. The unions, therefore, feel that, for the time being, they must be protected through trade policy.

## What Happens in the Developing Countries?

While many developing countries still recognize the benefits they may derive from U.S. foreign investment, their attitudes toward the effects of such operations on their employment problem are tinged with dilemmas. Given the seriousness and the political importance of the lack of jobs, many countries are finding new urgency in their search for investment funds and foreign exchange, as well as for technical knowledge and access to world markets. The multinational corporation can supply these factors.

But the question is: Will their modes of operation provide employment only to a small number of workers, with no—or even adverse—effects on the rest of the labor force? There are three aspects of this question that cause special concern: the development of a "branch-plant mentality" in poor countries; the choice of technology, together with its effect on productivity and wages; and the lack of "spread effects" from some foreign investments into the rest of the economy—*i.e.*, the lack of new employment stimulated outside the industry in which investment takes place.

## Branch Plant Mentality

One feature of the international division of labor is that it requires greater national specialization in industry. Yet, the history of many poor countries has been dominated by what they feel is too large a measure of specialization. Robert Heilbronner, in "The Multinational Corporation and the Nation State," *New York Review of Books,* February 11, 1971, said that:

> Among the underdeveloped nations of the world a genuine specialization of labor did take place; accompanied by a more of less free importation of their products. But the emergence of banana-economies and coffee-economies and copper-economies did not bring with it the gradual convergence of living standards that was implicit in the theories of both Ricardo and Samuelson. Instead, the mono-economies discovered to their dismay that the ruling doctrine worked to widen rather than to narrow the disparity between themselves and their rich customers—a state of affairs for which standard theory had no explanation at all.

For this reason, many countries are anxious to diversify their economies and to reduce their reliance on the fluctuations of a small number of commodities in the world market. Yet, the operations of some corporations, in seeking sources of raw materials and cheap labor, tend to reassert specialization and consequently to make the host countries more dependent both on quite narrow world markets and on the needs of the corporation. At the same time, the loss of national control implicit in foreign ownership may allow the corporations to close down branch plants in one country and move them to another when it suits their investment plans. The electronics industry presents the most notable example: Whereas some companies began overseas assembly in Japan, much of this work has now been transferred to Taiwan in search of lower and more stable wages. Not only does this act directly affect the employees in the closed plant, it also breeds an atmosphere of competition between countries. Singapore, for example, is reported to have enacted restrictive labor legislation to keep union activity and wages down as an inducement to foreign investors.

Furthermore, since the locus of essential decision-making is in the United States, some branch plants do not provide much training and experience for local managers. And, in some cases, those professionals who do show their competence are moved to corporate headquarters, when they would otherwise have become valuable additions to the local entrepreneurial class.

## The Choice of Technology

The developing countries face their most difficult dilemmas over the set of fiscal and economic policies that are likely to influence the choice of technology used by foreign investors. Understandably, a foreign firm will tend to fall back on the technology that it has initially developed for use in its own country. Since the Western nations have relatively abundant supplies of capital and shortages of labor, these technologies are often more capital-intensive than the optimum for the poor countries with abundant labor and little capital. This problem has been aggravated in most developing countries by the policies designed to attract foreign capital. Overvalued exchange rates, low interest rates, tax holidays, and accelerated depreciation allowances have all helped to encourage the use of capital. This has often had harmful effects on the development of the over-all economy and society in the poor countries. In the first place, the ratio between capital and output in many industries has often been high. In part, this has been because of the frequent difficulty of using efficiently and maintaining the sophisticated Western machinery. And, in part, it has been because of often incredible underuse of capacity, resulting from lack of effective demand and the poor quality of many inputs.

At the same time, the use of capital-intensive plants has meant that a few workers in modern industry have benefited from very high productivity and relatively high wages, compared to the rest of the economy. In Colombia, for example, real wages for workers in modern industry doubled between 1955 and 1965, while the poorest half of the rural population has seen virtually no improvement in its position in the last forty years. This has caused a number of very severe social problems in the developing countries. For example, it has contributed to the inequality of income distribution that characterizes so many societies in the Third World. It has also been a major factor in encouraging migration to the cities. The populations of many capital cities in the developing countries is growing at 6 or 7 per cent a year—doubling in size every ten or twelve years. And this brings in its train staggering problems of slums, health, crime, and unemployment. Despite these problems, people continue to migrate, apparently in the hope of obtaining the magic opportunity of a job in modern industry, where wages are several times those prevailing in the countryside.

In regard to wage policies, the poor countries face an extremely difficult choice. On the one hand, they face pressures to raise wages and working standards for people already employed. On the other hand, they must create a vast number of new jobs as well as develop a competitive position in world markets. In the few countries that have worked to reduce distortions in the prices attached to factors of production (by increasing the price of capital and restraining wage increases), employment and exports have been growing very rapidly. These countries include Taiwan, Korea, and Singapore, where foreign investors have often found it worthwhile to adapt their Western-based technologies to suit the new situation. While this has created difficulties for U.S. labor in some industries, the salutary effect on the situation in these countries is very important to their futures. But, in most of the rest of the Third World, the effect of capital-intensive foreign investment has been much less pervasive, although a tiny elite of workers has received great benefits.

## The Spread Effect

For a number of reasons, the spread effect of much foreign investment has been rather limited. The "enclave" nature of many extractive industries is particularly striking. In Zambia, for instance, a semiskilled worker on the Copperbelt averages about $60 a week in pay—in a country where much of the population hardly earns that much a year. The difficulty is that these highly paid workers spend much of their income either on imported goods or on relatively capital-intensive, semiluxury goods, so that their earning power does not create much employment elsewhere in the economy. A number of capital-intensive manufacturing industries may have similar effects, though often muted, especially in the case of industries supplying capital or intermediate goods for use elsewhere in the economy.

For assembly plants, however, the effect on employment is somewhat different. These plants are labor-intensive in nature, so that directly they do provide a considerable number of jobs. However, a wide variety of ancillary activities that would ordinarily grow up with linkages to such operations are performed abroad.

Trying to maximize the number of jobs created through foreign investment thus poses a number of difficult choices for the industrial policies of the developing countries. Initially, of course, they have to decide what reliance they want to place on foreign resources. Second, they must forge policies affecting the prices of the factors of production, and hence the choice of technology and employment. Possible lines of approach in particular situations might include such devices as tax incentives based on increases in employment, a general wage subsidy, or a system that changes the investment incentives given to foreign investors according to changes in ratio of capital use to labor use. And foreign exchange and interest rates are crucial variables. Finally, with judicious safeguards, private enterprise may contribute to the growth of local entrepreneurship and employment through subcontracting and the encouragement of repair shops and other ancillary enterprises.

## Three Viewpoints Summarized

The multinational corporation is an enormously productive and flexible type of organization whose growth seems certain to continue. As the strength of its operations grows, it will entail changes throughout the world economy, just as growth and productivity shifts have altered patterns of investment and employment within national economies. But a question obviously looms in the minds of workers and governments around the world as to who will be the principal beneficiary of this new productive force, with its ability to transfer capital and technology across national borders. Is the untrammeled ideal of free movement for factors of production the best way to harness the multinational corporation in the interests of human needs?

With our present, rather feeble theoretical framework and our lack of knowledge about the ways in which multinational corporations work, we cannot give a definitive answer to this question. We simply do not know how many American jobs have been exported, and what proportion of these have been forced abroad by competition. Nor do we know what impact profits sent home have had on the growth of the U.S. economy. What we have learned, however, is that workers throughout the developed world are deeply concerned about maintaining their jobs in the face of new technological forces, at the very time when the need for new jobs and more foreign exchange is central to the survival and progress of the developing countries. As a consequence, the problem of global labor adjustments in response to the internationalization of production will be central to international relations in the coming decades.

From the brief discussion of three viewpoints set forward in this paper, we can get a glimpse of where the problem lies. In the first place, the poor countries have a desperate need for industrial jobs in order to help prevent the breakdown of their societies. But this requires, among other things, higher levels of manufactured exports. The multinational corporation, with its capital, technology, and managerial and marketing know-how, can be a most efficient vehicle for achieving these goals. In acting this way, however, the corporations are likely to create dislocations for particular groups of American workers. And, if the fear of American labor cannot be allayed to a reasonable degree, we will continue to face the prospect of growing demands for controls on foreign investment and imports that could seriously injure the developing countries.

## WHAT CAN BE DONE?

Merely to state the problem in this simple form is to raise a host of questions about what can be done. It is unlikely that the momentum of the multinational corporation can—or should—be stemmed entirely. That being the case, where, then, is the burden of adjustment to take place? Should there be tighter control of trade policies, in order to assure a pattern of trade development that is consistent with reasonable labor adjustments? And if so, is there a need for renovating and updating the General Agreement on Tariffs and Trade (GATT)? Or should the action be taken unilaterally by individual governments?

An alternative might be to work, as the unions suggest, for some more control over the operations of the multinational corporations. But this again raises the question of how it is to be done. One possibility might be through the institution of some form of international incorporation, either under the umbrella of a supranational organization or of an international agreement. The purpose of this would be to establish a set of ground rules and codes of conduct for both investors and host countries. This could directly or indirectly comprehend the problem of labor adjustment. (Senator Jacob Javits of New York, for example, has proposed the establishment of a sort of "GATT for International Investment.") Or the operations of the corporations might be supervised more closely by nation-states: The United States, for example, could extend its controls over direct investment and the transfer of technology; it could also broaden the coverage of bilateral tax treaties, so that they would apply to other operations of the multinational corporations.

There, are, of course, many difficulties with such arrangements. From the point of view of labor adjustments, the main, long-run problem concerns the ways in which technology is transferred, rather than the movement of capital itself. Although, in the case of the U.S. multinational corporation, technology transfer and direct investment have often gone hand in hand, it is possible for technology to be sold alone as a commodity. The Japanese, for example, tend to use long-term management contracts and the licensing of technology as a prime route of industrial involvement in Southeast Asia. Three-quarters of the licensing contracts made by Taiwan have been with Japanese firms. This process is hard to control, and its diminution would harm prospects for development in the Third World. Yet, it is this transfer of technology, even more than direct investment across national borders, that is threatening U.S. jobs. In other words, the internationalization of production, using many countries as sources for parts as well as for finished products, is a rapid trend; it does not necessarily require investment in supplier countries. Thus, it is clearly the internationalization of production, whether through the multinational corporations themselves or not, that is creating a major adjustment problem for workers.

Finally, the task of adjustment could be shouldered primarily by domestic firms and workers in industrialized countries, in response to competition from abroad—whether from trade or from the internationalization of production. In order for this policy to be acceptable, the levels and speed of government compensation would need to be raised. But it is also true that the adjustments made necessary by trade and the internationalization of production are part of a larger picture of growth and transformation within the U.S. economy. The solution, therefore, should really lie in an over-all, systematic man-power plan for the economy, which would be based on full employment and would allow for the gradual but continuous shift of workers from relatively less competitive industries into more competitive ones. At the same time, it is important that individual workers do not suffer loss in the process of transfer. In order to ease some of the hardship involved in this shift, an over-all man-power adjustment program may have to be combined with selective, short-term measures affecting trade and overseas investment.

The magnitude of the global employment problem and its serious implications for international relations make it essential that fresh thought be brought to the process of the internationalization of production. The problem must be incorporated into a global framework that comprehends the future of the relationships between nation-states. Needless to say, this is a tall order in a world beset by trends toward isolationism and neomercantilism.

# PART IV

# U.S. VIEWS

# 12

# The Politics of Aid Legislation

## DONALD M. FRASER

*Whether the United States makes a major contribution to de-
velopment assistance will depend as much upon practical politics
as upon the merits of the question. Representative Fraser of
Minnesota here presents his own view from Capitol Hill about
the role of the Congress, the President, and the political parties in
this process. He also indicates which rationale for foreign aid
makes the most sense, as he sees it. —THE EDITORS*

Foreign aid cannot be considered apart from the larger perspectives of foreign policy; and foreign policy, in turn, cannot be understood apart from the demands of internal American politics.
The American political system does not have highly developed
mechanisms for dealing with major questions of foreign policy.
The result has often been a cavalier point of view among foreign-
policy experts (both inside and outside government) toward Congress and the American public. "Manipulative" may be the kindest
word to describe many public explanations of official foreign-
policy decisions.

When evaluating the Senate action in defeating the foreign-aid
bill last year, we must take these realities into consideration. It is

This chapter is based on a paper presented to the Development Issues
Seminar, Overseas Development Council, May, 4, 1971.

impossible to analyze the Senate action accurately apart from the long history of congressional stalemates in the political struggles surrounding the Vietnam war. A rare opportunity was presented for liberals and conservatives to unite, for different reasons, and issue a severe blow to the executive in the area of foreign policy. The defeat of the aid bill in the Senate was rooted in the internal struggles of the American political system, rather than in any coherent or consistent critique of foreign-aid programs. Without economic-assistance programs, we do not have a very relevant foreign policy. However, there are completely contradictory ideas within Congress as to what our foreign policy should be, and, therefore, what our aid programs should be.

I do not subscribe to the theory that U.S. economic assistance to developing countries has lagged behind the programs of other nations because of lack of interest on the part of the American public. Rather, I blame the enormous pressures on the domestic budget, growing doubts among lawmakers concerning the political uses of aid, and fluctuations in party strength in Congress.

First, the Indochina war has led to a new concern about U.S. activities abroad. When a more conservative Congress met in early 1967, the dimensions of the Vietnam war were prompting new questions about U.S. foreign policy. Some House members, for example, began opposing the *entire* aid bill because of the uses of military aid. In the Senate, some members have become more skeptical of aid because of the possibilities that other involvements similar to that in Vietnam would flow out of economic assistance programs.

Second, recent congressional elections reduced the ranks of supporters of bilateral economic-aid programs. In recent years, congressional support for aid has come mostly from the Democrats. Republican support was greatest during the Eisenhower years and sagged after 1960. The 1966 elections, therefore, marked a turning point. That year, the Democrats lost 50 seats in the House. The result was the loss of a large number of aid supporters in Congress.

Third, new domestic programs in the areas of urban affairs, poverty, and education have added new demands on the U.S. Treasury. In the contest between military expenditures and social programs, aid tends to get lost. It is difficult to argue for more international aid when sufficient money is not available for housing, education, health, and other needs here at home.

While most members of Congress have not changed their votes on international development, the initiative has passed to the critics of aid. Their position has also been greatly fortified by the growing fiscal crisis.

## ATTITUDES IN CONGRESS TOWARD DEVELOPMENT AID

Skepticism about international development aid has persisted and is evident in the present Congress. For different reasons, friends and foes alike of development assistance find themselves critical of aid legislation. Visible returns from investing in development are uncertain. We no longer claim U.N. votes or friendship as objectives. The old anti-Communist rationale has lost appeal. And some senators and congressmen fear that economic-aid programs do, indeed, contain seeds of neo-imperialism —that we are helping countries for the wrong reasons.

The political effect of development aid in many countries also presents a mixed picture. Many recipient countries show little adherence to democratic practices; illegal transfers of power are still common; and individual rights are often violated.

Other complaints crop up repeatedly about mismanagement and poor administration of aid programs—although these criticisms are all out of proportion to the results that are actually achieved. Returned Peace Corps volunteers and academic consultants add their voices to the official reports of the General Accounting Office on the waste and inefficiency of some assistance programs. And the uncertain results of our own war on poverty has probably added to skepticism about the chances the developing nations have for making rapid economic progress.

All these doubts and questions arise in the midst of larger uncertainties about the foreign policy of the United States. We have become uncertain about which nations are important to our security. If we now believe that many areas of the world are not vital, the prospects for aid to those areas are not very good.

Wherever the United States has no vital interests—*i.e.*, interests worthy of a security treaty—our aid is likely to be very small. This is the case with African nations today. They have no U.S. security treaties and receive very little aid.

Those who feel that aid is important must therefore look for a more convincing rationale than the old one, in which commitments were perceived as means to assist countries important to national security. At the moment, the most persuasive argument for aid seems to be the moral imperative for the rich to help the poor. But the moral approach encounters the frustrating realities of national development. Instability, heavy-handed treatment of political opponents, social injustices—all these make it difficult to justify our aid efforts. The moral rationale wears progressively thinner as it is resurrected for each annual battle over aid bills.

## PROSPECTS IN CONGRESS

To this observer, at least, some of the actions taken by Congress are predicated on "acts of faith." That is, the decision whether to enact a new law or to create a new program depends more on one's *a priori* beliefs than upon new information. These beliefs may be the result of personal values or of a form of political ideology, or both. For example, many of us grew up in an era in which the notorious Smoot-Hawley tariffs of the 1930's were blamed for contributing significantly to the breakdown of world order. Since that time, our belief in the ideal of free trade has been unshakable. So, too, has been the belief in the validity of the cold war—until recently—in which economic and military aid to other countries played a key role. These beliefs formed an important *a priori* basis for supporting aid.

The degree of disillusionment among many congressmen and senators over the extension of the cold war into Vietnam is hard to overstate. The assumptions of the cold war have been shattered by Vietnam, but no new set of beliefs has taken their place.

It is doubtful that a new set of coherent beliefs will emerge from Congress itself. One of the most remarkable facts about Congress is the degree to which it is influenced by outside attitudes and pressures, and how little from its own internal processes. It is not generally understood that members of Congress themselves, when they want to change views *within* Congress, target their efforts to the outside world in the hope that Congress will be influenced in turn.

## THE ROLE OF POLITICAL PARTIES

Let us turn to an examination of the external influences that may operate on Congress. One of these influences—the most important one—is the President. This subject will be discussed separately. But a second influence, which is greatly neglected, is that of the political parties. In the United States, political parties are pragmatic rather than ideological; nevertheless, they significantly influence both the actions of the members of Congress and the actions of the President.

What U.S. political parties lack is extensive contact with, and involvement in, the international arena. Members of Congress and officials of the executive branch obviously have some involvement with other nations in an international context, but political leaders who do not hold elective office are largely denied the opportunity for communication with political movements and leaders across national boundaries.

Contrary to popular belief, we also lack a strong national political structure. National politics tend to be derivative of state politics. They are not carried on in their own right to the degree one finds in other countries. This means that national or international problems are not of great interest to substantial numbers of members in the Democratic or Republican parties. Thus, it is hard to get real political involvement in these areas.

Political parties could be a greater influence on congressional attitudes than they actually are. Influence is exerted not just by a party policy position affecting members of Congress, but also by the more subtle and long-term interactions between recruitment for party and public office and the party environment in which elections are held.

The objective here is not just to increase the political parties' potential to influence Congress along certain lines, but also to institutionalize the interdependence that exists in the world. The development of institutions implies that nations taking part share common interests, and that there is a need for each participant to gain wider understanding about the perspectives of the others.

Political communication among political activists plays a key role in this process. One member of a West European parliament, for example, has worked hard to create a European political movement to generate needed political control over transnational economic activities in the European Community. As yet, he has not succeeded, but the principle is sound: The growth of international institutions should be accompanied by the growth of political movements that can provide the necessary interaction between the institutions and the people affected by them.

The suggestion that a long-range solution to congressional actions on international aid lies in strenghtened roles for political parties may seem an unlikely path to pursue in the face of the low estate to which international aid has currently fallen. But its importance in the long run should be recognized and acted upon by those with some ability to influence change in our political parties. The Agency for International Development (AID) has some statutory authority to think about political skills and involvement, but it has been reluctant to explore any of these possibilities.

In the short run, the prospects for remedial action in Congress itself are very poor. With the authorization of a two-year extension of economic aid, any new initiatives will most likely await the outcome of the 1972 election. Individual members of Congress have strong opinions about new approaches to aid, but the possibility of pulling these opinions together into new aid legislation seems remote.

In the short run, then, aid supporters will be looking to the President for new leadership on this issue.

## THE ROLE OF THE PRESIDENT

The President can influence Congress more directly and effectively than anyone else. He can use his "bully pulpit" to influence public attitudes, which are then transmitted to Congress. His programs and proposals are generally given priority by the congressional committees. He has substantial political capital that he can expend in his relations with members of Congress in soliciting their support.

We have not had a major effort by a President in the aid field for the past half-dozen years. Members of Congress are relatively free to vote their own ideas about aid. Polls show that most voters are indifferent to the issue, and there is no documented case that any vote for or against aid caused any candidate serious trouble. On the other hand, if members thought the voters were taking more interest because of Presidential initiatives, this would undoubtedly encourage some of them to give more support to aid in their votes. A fresh effort by the President should be centered on a new rationale for aid, placed in the context of his vision of the world and the role that the United States must play in it.

## A New Rationale for Aid

A new awareness of international interdependence has been generated by events of recent years. In travel and communications, the planet has shrunk rapidly. Ventures into outer space have generated new images of the world as a limited place in which to live. There is also growing recognition of our interlocking ecological systems; awareness of the crisis in controlling the environment; and the sense that our planet provides fragile life-support systems contributes to the sense of interdependence.

It is this theme of interdependence that currently would have the greatest appeal to the American public. Along with all others on this planet, Americans share an interest in improving education, raising health standards, growing enough food, providing jobs, and creating workable political systems. The growth of international institutions depends upon the physical and mental health of the member states. The growth of institutional arrangements among states will lessen the likelihood of war and will offer the means to advance the welfare of all. Such arrangements will be essential to keep our ecological system in balance.

This new awareness of planetary interdependence has already been exemplified in new international undertakings. Treaties banning nuclear weapons in outer space and on the ocean floor, limitations on nuclear testing, agreements to contain airplane hijackings, oil spills on the high seas, and illicit opium traffic are but a few examples. The success of such international undertakings was hardly possible even a few years ago. As the international implications of environmental pollution are explored, the possibilities for international action expand significantly. The announcement, in late 1971, of an international institute of scientists from eight nations—the International Institute of Applied Systems Analysis, which includes the United States, the Soviet Union, and both East and West Germany—is a good example of an international response to a growing recognition of the gravity of problems common to all technological societies.

One of the most dramatic examples of a capacity to rise above national constraints is the European Community. One hopes not only that it will come to embrace other nations as well, but that it will also bring to fruition the very idea of West European political integration as envisioned in the Treaty of Rome. As a model of transnational institutional development, the European Community may well be one of the most promising developments of modern times.

## SHORT-TERM POSSIBILITIES FOR INCREASING DEVELOPMENT SUPPORT

While we await new Presidential initiatives, several other immediate possibilities should not be neglected to increase support for our development-assistance programs. These include new initiatives to ease trade restrictions, a greatly increased effort to reduce military spending in order to fund development efforts, a complete separation of military assistance from economic development, and a strategy to obtain multiyear authority for aid programs.

### Easing Trade Restrictions

For developing countries, free access to the markets of industrialized nations is an indispensable complement to development aid. The current pressures building in Congress for higher quotas, import limitations, and trade restrictions are alarming. If restrictive trade policies are enacted, the long-term effects on development programs could be extremely serious.

### Reducing Military Spending to Fund Increases in Development Programs

We should reduce the military budget and allocate the money saved to development aid. Twenty years from now, the United States will be far better off if it invests in the peaceful development of an ordered world than it will be if it spends the same dollars for military hardware and higher force levels. The United States can obtain all the military security that money can buy for $50–$60 billion a year.

Development and defense are related, because both deal with the kind of world we are in today and hope for tomorrow. A new rationale for development aid cannot develop without a simultaneous attempt to redefine the meaning of national security. The intercontinental ballistic missile (ICBM) and the nuclear warhead have made complete security for the nation-state impossible. In no country today can the army preserve an area of internal peace by pushing violence to the outskirts. Those people who strongly support aid *must*, therefore, join in the debate over national priorities. And, if they are successful, the shift in funding patterns will signal the beginning of a conscious political effort to determine where the real interests—and security—of our nation will lie in the next decades.

### Divorcing Economic Development Aid from Military Aid

Although U.S. military assistance is seriously criticized, the Nixon Administration has been committed to an increase in military aid. Separation of military aid from our development aid will help prevent the negative attitudes from spilling over to economic assistance.

In his April 21, 1971, foreign-aid message to Congress, President Nixon urged this separation. "This would enable us," he said, "to define our own objectives more clearly, fix responsibility for each program, and assess the progress of each in meeting its particular objectives." Indeed, military aid often has its own aims, which are not necessarily consistent with the goals of economic aid.

## Continuing Efforts to Win Multiyear Authorization for Aid

Finally, policies in other fields, such as trade, would be a shambles if legislation had to be extended every year, and thus be constantly open to revision, as is required of aid authorizations. Not only do yearly debates over aid have a debilitating effect in Congress, they also actively discourage long-term planning in the agencies that administer aid. Even a two-year authorization would be an improvement over the yearly bargaining process that aid must undergo.

## THE FUNDAMENTAL NEED

Increased public support for development aid is important; but, without a strong executive initiative, it is unlikely to develop. The fundamental need is to relate aid to the future organization of the world in a legitimate, durable, and convincing manner. The President must place his power behind this rationale for our development policy, and we—Congress and the people—must provide support through increased international development of our political parties. Perhaps then the United States will exercise its full potential to help build a peaceful world community.

# 13

# A Farewell to Foreign Aid

## FRANK CHURCH

*Whatever the merits of foreign aid, the U.S. bilateral effort has been in trouble for some time. Not only is there concern on the political right that the aid program is an "international give-away," but in recent years there has been growing opposition among liberals as well. In this chapter, Senator Church of Idaho presents his own reasons for opposing U.S. bilateral assistance.*—THE EDITORS

We stand this year at the end of one decade of disillusion, with no good reason to believe that we are not now embarked upon another. Ten years ago, the leaders of the United States—and, to a lesser degree, the American people—were filled with zeal about their global goals. With supreme confidence both in our power and in our capacity to make wise and effective use of it, we proclaimed the dawning of a new era, in which America would preserve world peace, stem communism, and lead the impoverished masses of mankind through the magic point of "takeoff" into a "decade of development." To bring these glories to pass—so

This extract from Senator Church's speech on the Senate floor of October 29, 1971, is reprinted from the Outlook Section of *The Washington Post,* November 7, 1971.

we allowed ourselves to believe—we had only to recognize the simple, central fact that Walt Rostow assured us would bring victory in Vietnam and success in all our other foreign enterprises, "the simple fact that we are the greatest power in the world—if we behave like it."

Looking back on the 1960's, no one can deny that we were indeed "the greatest power in the world," and that we surely did "behave like it"—if throwing our might and money around is the correct measure of "behaving like it." Nonetheless, we not only failed to accomplish what we set out to accomplish ten years ago; we have been thrown for losses across the board: In the name of preserving peace, we have waged an endless war; in the guise of serving as sentinel for the "free world," we have stood watch while free governments gave way to military dictatorship in country after country. Today, confidence in American leadership abroad is as gravely shaken as is confidence in the American dollar. As for the "decade of development," ten years of American foreign aid not only have failed to narrow the gap between rich nations and poor; the gap between the small, wealthy elites and the impoverished masses in most underdeveloped lands has also widened.

It seems important, if we are to learn something from these experiences, to consider why our aid programs have failed to achieve their objectives, and whether, indeed, those objectives were sound to begin with. The technicalities have been examined and re-examined; every few years a new commission conducts a new study, resulting in a new report and a new reorganization —and nothing else. Never yet have we considered in full measure the possibility that the failure of aid is not technical and administrative but conceptual and political, and that it can be understood only as an aspect of the larger failure of American foreign policy over the last decade. If that is the case, as I have come to believe, then it is futile to continue re-evaluating and reorganizing the aid program. Even the most efficient organization and the most competent management must fail if the program itself is rooted in obsolete conceptions of the national interest, and if the objectives meant to be achieved are unsound or unattainable, or both.

## THE PHANTOM OF IDEOLOGY

It is astonishing, in retrospect, how little we questioned the seeming verities of the cold war during the 1950's and 1960's. Conservatives railed against "international communism" and prescribed military aid; liberals, believing themselves more sophisticated, spoke of the "Sino-Soviet bloc" and the greater usefulness of economic aid. Neither questioned the premises of the cold war, or the purposes of aid. China and Russia alike were perceived as implacable enemies of the "free world"; if they differed, it was only on the most efficient means of "burying" us. Aid—both military and economic—was conceived primarily as an instrument of containment, a weapon in the cold war; and, if some Americans favored military assistance and others economic, that, too, was a matter of tactics, if not of how to "bury" the Communists, then, at least, of how to contain them.

Like most shibboleths, the trouble with containment was not that it was illusory in its original formulation, but that it was subsequently elevated to the status of a universal truth—which it is not—and applied in areas where it had no bearing. Vietnam is the principal case in point: We supported the French, then supplanted them, and finally plunged into a war in which we are now still engaged, because we had persuaded ourselves that Ho Chi Minh was the puppet of the Chinese, whom in turn—at least until the mid-1950's—we regarded as puppets of the Soviet Union.

These premises, however, were open to question from the outset. As early as January, 1945—so the Foreign Relations Committee was recently told by Allen Whiting, one of our leading China experts—Mao Tse-tung and Chou En-lai secretly informed President Roosevelt that they were willing to meet with him in Washington for exploratory talks as leaders of a Chinese political party. Soon thereafter—so reported an American foreign-service officer, John Stewart Service, at the time—Mao outlined a plan for postwar Chinese-American economic cooperation. "America," Mao told Service, "is not only the most suitable country to assist the economic development of China: She is also the only country fully able to participate. For all these reasons there must not

and cannot be any conflict, estrangement or misunderstanding between the Chinese people and America." Again, in 1946, Chou
En-lai made it clear to President Truman's special ambassador,
General George C. Marshall, that the Chinese Communists had no
wish to be totally dependent on Stalin. "Of course we will lean
to one side," he said. "But how far we lean depends upon you."

## THE HANOI APPEALS

It has also become apparent that the notion of "Asian communism with its headquarters in Peking" has been more myth than
reality. China had little or nothing to do with North Korea's
attack on South Korea in 1950 and entered the war, reluctantly,
only to counter General MacArthur's reckless thrust to the border
of Manchuria. China also had little to do with the Vietminh in-
surrection in Vietnam; indeed, the first Indochina war began
three years before the Chinese Communists won their own civil
war in China.

Just as China had no wish to rely exclusively on the Soviet
Union, Ho Chi Minh had no wish to be a satellite of China.
According to an article in the *Christian Science Monitor* of June
30, 1970, drawn from previously unpublished Pentagon papers,
the United States "ignored eight direct appeals for aid from
North Vietnamese Communist leader Ho Chi Minh in the first
five winter months following the end of World War II." Even
more astonishing, according to this account, "Ho also sent several
messages through secret channels even earlier, in August and
September of 1945, proposing that Vietnam be accorded the 'same
status as the Philippines'—an undetermined period of tutelage
preliminary to independence."

If there is any truth in this version of events—and the evidence
of much truth in it is overwhelming—we are forced to the conclusion that American foreign policy since World War II has
been based, in large part, on a false premise: the myth of the
Communist monolith. This is not to say that either of the great
Communist powers has been benign and friendly, but only that
they have not been consistent in their hostility, which, in part,
has been provoked by our own; that they have seldom acted in

concert; that both have influenced, but neither has ever really dominated, the Communist movements of Southeast Asia; and that both of the large Communist states and certain of the small ones —including Vietnam—have on certain occasions been willing and even eager to come to terms with the United States.

## A TALENT OF THE RUSSIANS

Even if the premise of a unified, aggressive "international communism" had been sound, the strategy for countering it with foreign aid was not. Experience has shown that, although military assistance can be a potent factor in counterinsurgency, it is by no means a reliable one; while American economic support has almost no influence whatever on whether a country "goes Communist," as Cuba and Chile have shown.

This is not for lack of skill or technical know-how on our part, but because of the irrelevance of the instrument to the objective. The countries of Asia and Africa—I must here exclude Latin America—that have remained non-Communist have done so not because the United States has succeeded in buying their allegiance or in launching them toward "takeoff" and self-sustaining economic growth, but because they have not wished to become Communist, regarding communism as an alien ideology, or because their populations have been too poor and illiterate to be interested in such sophistications as ideology or revolution.

Revealingly, the Russians have had no greater success in buying ideological converts with aid than we have had in trying to head them off. In one or two instances, small African countries have unceremoniously packed off their Russian aid technicians when their presence became too intrusive. Egypt, which has been the largest single recipient of Soviet foreign aid for the last fifteen years, has rigorously suppressed its internal Communists and repeatedly warned the Russians against meddling in internal Arab affairs. In July 1971, President Sadat responded to a Soviet appeal for Egyptian pressure against the crackdown on Communists in the Sudan with an angry address before the Arab Socialist Union, ·in which he declared that Egypt would never become Communist or recognize an Arab Communist government—although, President Sadat added, Egypt would remain friendly to the Soviet Union, even after a possible settlement with Israel. Occurrences such as this suggest the advisability of giving credit where it is due: When it comes to using aid for political purposes, the Russians have a greater talent for alienating people from communism than we do.

## AIDING DICTATORSHIPS

While experience has shown that our aid programs have little, if any, relevance either to the deterrence of communism or to the encouragement of democracy, they have been effective, in certain instances, in keeping unpopular regimes in power. They have certainly contributed to that end in the cases of the Greek colonels, the Pakistani generals, and the Brazilan junta. All of these regimes are dictatorships, but they are anti-Communist and therefore pass our eligibility test for membership in the "free world." A government may torture and terrorize its own population, but—from the standpoint of our policy-makers—as long as it remains anti-Communist, provides "stability," generally supports American foreign policy, and is hospitable to American investment, it qualifies, for purposes of aid, as a "free country."

"Stability" is an antiseptic word; it reveals nothing about how individual people live and die.

As the Tsars of Russia and the Sultans of Turkey understood very well, there is no better defense against radical revolution, no greater assurance of "stability," than an ignorant and inert population. Traveling in Latin America several years ago, Seth Tillman, a Senate staff member, noted repeatedly in his diary the gentleness, submissiveness, and conservatism of the *campesinos* in one country after another. "Like the peasants of northeastern Brazil," he noted, "the Indians in the barriadas of Lima are not revolutionary; they are too humble and ignorant and are therefore subrevolutionary or prerevolutionary. That, however, is not necessarily going to be the case with their prodigal offspring, many of whom are getting a little schooling and a little view of the world beyond the sierra and the barriada. Some of them are going to get ideas and it only takes a few who are smart and tough to make a revolution."

When revolution comes—as it likely will in many of the still "stable" countries of the Third World—it will bear no resemblance to the kind of benign, gradual "takeoff" into self-sustaining growth envisioned by American aid officials and private investors. The notion that a stable, nonrevolutionary social structure is the essential condition of economic development is a self-serving rationalization. It enables American policy-makers to believe that the interests of the United States, as they conceive them, are identical with the social and economic interests of the poor countries. "Stability," they insist, is not only essential for the exclusion of communism and the preservation of American influence; it is also in the best interests of the developing countries themselves, because—so the argument runs—revolution means violence, disruption, inefficient management, and the loss of investment capital, as well. In this way, we rationalize our support for regimes whose very existence is the principal barrier in their countries to real economic development and social justice.

## PSYCHOLOGY AND POLITICS

The conditions essential for development are not so much economic and technological as they are psychological and political. No infusion of capital and know-how from without can galvanize a society in which the rewards of development are grabbed up by a small, privileged caste while the majority of people are left hopeless, debilitated, and demoralized.

In countries long under the domination of corrupt oligarchies, nothing less than a radical redistribution of political power may be the essential precondition for economic development. If the bulk of the people are to make the concerted effort and accept the enormous sacrifices required for lifting a society out of chronic poverty, they have got to have some belief in the integrity of their leaders, in the commitment of those leaders to social justice, and in the equality of sacrifice required of the people. Reactionary regimes have neither the ability nor the interest to foster such a conception of social justice. They value aid from the United States as a means of maintaining, not of abolishing, inequalities of wealth and power. The lip service paid to reform is a crumb for their benefactors; it helps to make the Americans feel good, and it costs them nothing. In fact, American economic aid is commonly used to promote industrialization programs that generate a high level of consumption for the privileged, with little, if any, "trickle-down" benefit for the dispossessed.

At the same time, American military assistance, and such paramilitary programs as the training and equipping of a country's police force, help such regimes as those of Brazil, Greece, and Pakistan to suppress reformist movements. In this way, American aid is being used not to promote development but for the quite opposite purpose of supporting the rule of corrupt and stagnant —but vociferously anti-Communist—dictatorships.

## Servicing the *Status Quo*

Even if we should succeed in purging our minds of the anti-Communist obsession that has driven us into league with military dictatorships and oppressive oligarchies all over the globe, it would still be all but impossible for us to promote radical reform in the countries of the Third World. Even, indeed, if we were a revolutionary society ourselves and were committed to a revolutionary conception of development—as most assuredly we are not—there is still very little we could do to foster social revolution in alien societies.

The catalyst of radical change in any society must be an indigenous nationalism giving rise to a sense of community, commitment, and shared sacrifice. Can anyone seriously believe, for example, that the United States, through massive infusions of aid, could ever have persuaded, inspired, or cajoled the demoralized Chiang Kai-shek regime of the late 1940's into generating the kind of collective spirit that the Chinese Communists have generated?

I do not suggest that the United States prefers or admires the dictatorial regimes it subsidizes, but only that there is little we can do with our aid to change them, all the more since these regimes can blackmail us so easily with the threat of communism if they should fail. The Kennedy Administration did make an effort to encourage democratic and progressive policies in countries to which it extended aid, especially in Latin America; but that effort was a failure, and the reasons for that failure are instructive. We failed because we had neither the ability to impose reform from outside nor the will to pursue it from within. The one was simply impossible; the other went against the priority of our own interests as we conceived them. However much we may have wanted reform and development, we wanted "stability," anti-communism, and a favorable climate for investment more. The experience of twenty years of aid shows that we can neither bring about fundamental reform in tradition-encrusted societies nor prevent revolution in those countries where the tide of change runs deep and strong; all we can really do is to service the *status quo* in countries where it is not strongly challenged anyhow.

United States foreign aid certainly was unable to win us support at the time of the recent two votes at the United Nations relating to the admission of the People's Republic of China.

## PROFITABLE PHILANTHROPY

If our long-term loans, made in the name of nourishing development abroad, serve neither to deter communism nor to strengthen democratic government, and if they do so little to furnish the destitute with a broader measure of social justice wherever they may live, why do we persist in making them?

There is abundant evidence that our foreign-aid program is much less philanthropic than we have cared to portray. Indeed, the figures suggest that it is patently self-serving. Former AID Director William Gaud discloses that, as a result of tied loans, "93 per cent of AID funds are spent directly in the United States. . . . Just last year some 4,000 American firms in 50 states receieved $1.3 billion in AID funds for products supplied as part of the foreign aid program." Similarly, George D. Woods, former president of the World Bank, has observed that "bilateral programs of assistance have had as one of their primary objectives helping the high-income countries themselves; they have looked toward financing export sales, toward tactical support of diplomacy, toward holding military positions thought to be strategic."

In addition, our foreign aid, both economic and military, has encouraged relationships of sustained dependency on the United States. In many underdeveloped countries, repressive governments

draw reassurance from the arms we furnish and the military training we supply. As the source of money and weapons for the
armies and police forces, the U.S. Government acquires a certain
leverage over these regimes, while they last.

Surplus-food shipments under Public Law 480 (Food for Peace)
—on its face the most philanthropic of aid programs—in fact
have served to unload costly surpluses, "at virtually no economic
cost to the United States," according to economist Michael Hudson, a former balance-of-payments analyst for the Chase Man-
hattan Bank. At the same time, Hudson points out, the PL 480
program has put the aid-receiving countries in debt to us to the
extent of some $22 billion, "thereby tying them to the pursestrings
of the State Department and the U.S. Treasury for nearly 20
years to come."

## THE ALLIANCE FOR PROGRESS

Nowhere have we seen more clearly the ineffectiveness of aid
as a deterrent to revolutionary pressures and as an instrument
for the reconstruction of traditional societies than in Latin America. The Alliance for Progress represents the high-water mark of
our innocence in supposing that we could liberate traditional
societies from their centuries-long legacy of tyranny and stagnation
with a little bit of seed capital and some stirring rhetoric.

It is true that the per capita income of Latin American countries
has risen during the years of the Alliance for Progress, but it has
risen in so unbalanced and inequitable a way that the gains have
gone almost entirely to the 20 per cent of the population who live
within the modern economy. The benefits accruing to the lower
80 per cent have not even kept up with population growth, so that
they have become both relatively and absolutely poorer. Progress,
though visible, is illusory.

The distortions of public aid to Latin America are heightened
by the impact of private investment. Although U.S. direct investment in Latin America grew from $8 billion to $15 billion during
the 1960's and continues to grow at the rate of $1 billion a year,
according to Gary MacEoin in a 1970 article on Latin America,
U.S. companies withdraw $2 in dividends, royalties, and other

payments for every new dollar they invest. U.S. private companies exercise a "double negative impact": At the same time that they decapitalize Latin America by the withdrawal of profits, they plow back a part of their profits to gain increasing control of the mineral assets, industry, and production of Latin American countries.

Under this devastating North American onslaught, resentment of the United States has grown apace, and increasing numbers of Latin Americans have become convinced that they are the victims of a virulent new imperialism. As one Chilean political scientist commented on the experience of the 1960s': "If that is what one decade of development does for us, spare us from another. Foreign aid has been used, not to develop us, but to achieve the political purposes of the donors, to smother us in debt, to buy up our most dynamic productive assets."

## A SPREADING MONEY TREE

I can no longer cast my vote to prolong the bilateral aid program, as it is now administered. I could understand—though perhaps not condone—a foreign-aid program that is essentially self-serving. We live, after all, in a selfish world. But the present program is designed primarily to serve private business interests at the expense of the American people. In far too many countries, as in the case of Brazil, we poured in our aid money for one overriding purpose—the stabilization of the economy in order to furnish American capital with a "favorable climate for investment."

Moreover, the risk of loss due to political instability, riot, revolution, or expropriation, has been largely lifted from the investor and shifted to the U.S. Government. The Overseas Private Investment Corporation, backed by the Federal Government, readily insures American companies against risks abroad for which no comparable insurance is available at home. The multimillion-dollar losses incurred by American copper companies, resulting from the nationalization of their holdings by Allende's Marxist regime in Chile, are likely to be borne—not by the companies that eagerly invested there—but by the American taxpayer. Our foreign-aid program has become a spreading money tree under which the biggest American businesses find shelter when they invest abroad! Small wonder that the crumbling ghettoes in our cities, along with our declining rural communities, have to beg and scrounge for new capital!

I am not a foe of a genuine foreign-aid program, having long since acknowledged that any country as advantaged as ours should do what it can to help other people improve their lot. But no longer will I endorse with my vote a foreign-aid program that has been twisted into a parody and a farce.

Another major preoccupation of the present foreign-aid program is the massive disbursement of munitions, which we either give away or make available at bargain-basement prices. We ply half a hundred foreign governments with our weaponry. Most of the world has become a dumping ground for ships, tanks, and planes that we label as excess to our needs. Easy credit is available at interest rates well below the cost of money to the U.S. Government. The Military Assistance Program has become a preposterous scandal. It should be drastically curtailed, not enlarged.

## LIMITS OF OUR CAPACITY

As for our long-term bilateral loans made in the name of promoting economic development, it is long past time that this function were passed over entirely to the World Bank, the Asian Bank, the Inter-American Development Bank, and other multilateral lending agencies, which were set up for this purpose. I am prepared, now and in the future, to support substantial U.S. contributions to these agencies. In this manner, we could set a worthy example of international responsibility and beckon other rich nations to share the load with us.

I would confine our bilateral aid in the future to technical-assistance grants, administered, where feasible, by the Peace Corps. It was through technical assistance—the successor to Harry Truman's original Point 4 program of foreign aid for Europe—that the "Green Revolution" was achieved in Asia and the hand of famine stayed. This aspect of our foreign aid, involving outright grants, not loans, has constituted the worthiest part of the program. On account of it—and in hopes that the objectionable parts would be whittled down and ultimately displaced—I have tarried too long as a supporter and indulged in too much wishful thinking.

Finally, I would advocate, as an alternative to the palliative of aid, that we lend positive support to developing countries by entering into commercial arrangements that redress the terms of trade that are now rigged against them.

As with so many of the difficult questions that divide and agitate our society, the answer to the dilemma of aid lies not abroad, not in the slums of Calcutta or in the rural backlands of Brazil, but within ourselves. Essentially, the question is whether we are prepared to recognize the limits of our own capacity—the moral and political as well as the technical and economic limits—and allow nature to take what may well be an uncongenial course in many countries of the Third World. The question, to put it another way, is whether we can recognize that there are some things we simply cannot do—such as restructuring another country through our own efforts—and other things that we cannot permanently prevent—such as social revolution, where and when its time has come.

# 14

# In Defense of Foreign Aid:
# A Rebuttal

ROBERT E. HUNTER

*The author answers Senator Church's criticisms of the U.S. bilateral economic-aid program*—THE EDITORS

There is much wisdom in what Senator Frank Church writes about our bilateral foreign-aid program. He correctly places the blame for many failures on our attitudes of power that have made foreign aid serve policies of arrogance, omnipotence, and even exploitation. It is difficult to fault the senator's concern about the role of our military-aid policies, which have left the Nixon Doctrine with little that does not derive from the defense-support programs of the 1950's. But the senator reserves some of his harshest criticism for bilateral aid designed for economic development.

Senator Church bases his argument on the premise that development aid in the 1960's failed. It did not deter communism, strengthen democratic governments, gain influence, or furnish the destitute with a broader measure of social justice. In some instances, he is right. But this is largely a reflection of the inflated

This chapter is adapted from the *New Republic,* November 20, 1971. Reprinted by permission of the *New Republic* © 1971, Harrison-Blaine of New Jersey, Inc.

expectations for economic aid that various administrations have fostered. The senator himself is not entirely free of this—witness his ambivalence on aid's being unable to win us support in the U.N. vote on China.

Behind the rhetoric, there was only one real goal that was—and is—a practical one: to promote some economic development, whatever objectives may be achieved incidental to it. Senator Church's central case really rests, therefore, on a single proposition: that U.S. bilateral economic aid cannot contribute significantly to this one goal. I don't think he makes his case. Furthermore, he provides no workable design for the new, positive approach he rightly says is needed for development cooperation. Before wrecking the old structure, he should help construct a new one.

Even in arguing against bilateral economic aid, Senator Church is precise in his focus: Technical assistance, administered through the Peace Corps, should go on. But development loans must be curtailed; and we must cease U.S. Government insurance of private foreign investment. Both of these he sees as merely forms of export-creation and profit-generation, financed by the American people and benefiting only private industry.

## DEVELOPMENT LOANS

The issue of development loans, to begin with, is far more complicated than Senator Church makes it out. His litany of failures overlooks many positive successes, and the fact that, for whatever reason, developing countries *did* achieve the one target set during the 1960's—growth at 5 per cent per year. This was a spectacular achievement. It represented a greater sustained leap forward than the U.S. or Western Europe ever achieved in any ten-year period during the period of our development. It can hardly be disputed that aid did furnish some of the sinews of growth. Because of aid, people were trained, capital was put in place and is producing goods; and countries like India were able to double their wheat production. More than this could hardly be expected from the relatively minor amount of money that Congress committed to the effort. Like ending poverty at home, poverty abroad will not disappear under the pressure of good wishes and token payments. Of course, resources from outside are no substitute for local efforts; but, in many countries, they provide the extra help that spells the difference between success and failure, confidence and lassitude.

Senator Church questions whether development loans and credits for our agricultural commodities might not do more harm than good. He is concerned that this aid creates "relationships of dependency," beginning with a level of debt that is a burden on poor countries' future development. The answer, however, is simple: Don't kill the flow of resources that are needed for development, but rather increase the percentage of loans that is outright grant.

Similarly, if U.S. goods purchased with development loans are priced higher than in the world market, as the Senator indicates, why do poor countries accept these loans? Most often, they simply cannot buy on commercial terms, because they lack foreign exchange. Thus, even when the cost of U.S. goods is higher, the favorable credit terms of the aid loan often represent the difference between a country's being able to buy tractors, trucks, and wheat from us and its having none at all. Here, Senator Church implies that our aid is worth less than the Administration says it is. He is right. But this is an argument for doing more, not less—for lending more, lending on softer terms, and giving more aid as grants.

Senator Church is also concerned that our aid—economic as well as military—helps to prop up repressive regimes. It is no secret that some regimes that receive our aid are "repressive" although many are not, including India, which has been the chief beneficiary of our development loans over the years. This whole issue consistently begs the question of the role that U.S. foreign aid, in any form, can play in preserving any regime. Belief in American omnipotence is not limited to the political Right; it has just as firm a grip on the Left. The Left may make a different judgment of American actions (evil instead of good), but it shares a belief with the Right in our power to influence events. Yet, we need only to look at the extreme cases of trying to do so—economic sanctions against countries like Rhodesia and cutting off all aid to Ceylon for expropriating U.S. businesses—to realize how hollow this pretension is. Other than exceptional cases like Vietnam, our economic aid doesn't prop up regimes, and withdrawing it won't make them fall.

## AID AND POLITICAL CHANGE

Furthermore, there is a bold assumption underlying the belief in a hands-off policy for the United States. Senator Church thinks that withdrawing our support will not only help lead to the downfall of repressive regimes, but permit the springing forth of "radical revolutions" that are the "only real hope for development" in many countries. In some places, revolution may be required. But in how many is it the key? Can one simplistic theory be substituted for another? There have been too many revolutions in the world since our own for us to forget that many fruits of that tree have been bitter. Action in the name of the "people" is no guarantee that there will be a more equitable distribution of income. Nor should we Americans judge that a stagnant economy like Cuba's is better—however much "equality" it provides—than an authoritarian regime like Taiwan's, which has an impressive record of both growth and social justice. In some countries, there may be little "trickle-down" of aid while the economy grows. But is that worse than none at all? And how do we judge whether we are expecting too much social change too soon?

Senator Church states that U.S. aid merely widens the gap between the developing world and us—and between rich and poor in developing countries themselves. In the former case, however, the problem would be worse if there were no aid at all. And in the latter case, the senator has lumped together all development loan aid and condemned it wholesale. Yet, the bulk of it goes to educate childen; to buy better seeds and fertilizer for farmers; to provide birth-control information, clean drinking water, roads, bridges, generators, and food supplements. These things that aid buys can help to close the income gap, not widen it.

These are some of problems raised by Senator Church's critique. Some of these may be reduced—if not solved—by more modesty in our expectations, and some by thinking through again the reasons that we have an aid program at all. Not only is there the simple humanitarian motive of wanting to see poorer countries have a chance to do something for themselves; there is also our general interest in a worldwide trading and monetary system that can work only if developing countries can play a role in it based on a greater sense of equity than prevails at present. Already, we are beginning to need the help of developing countries in coping with problems of the environment and narcotics. Tomorrow, the degree of interdependence will be greater. And there are positive benefits in the sheer survival of countries in the developing world, with some hope for the future. Development can be the key to all of these in many poor countries. And development will suffer if we close our pocketbook.

India is a prime example. We cannot rule out the importance of India's economic survival to us and to others. Nor can we ignore the dilemmas that would be posed for us if that country, too, disintegrated as Pakistan has done. But aid to refugees in the two Bengals is insufficient: India's political future also turns on having enough outside economic assistance that there will be a chance for it to cope with massive problems of poverty, malnutrition, and unemployment. Of course, we don't know that development loans from the United States will spell the difference between success and failure for India; but it is worth an investment of a few hundred million dollars a year to find out, especially when the Indian Government itself makes the request. And the issue is an even larger one: India—like Indonesia—depends on our bilateral development loans as the basis of an international cooperative effort, led by the World Bank, that multilateral institutions cannot sustain on their own. If we reduce our help for India, other rich countries will probably do likewise, and international cooperation will become more difficult in a number of fields.

## A POSITIVE ROLE FOR ECONOMIC AID

Furthermore, India is a good example of how we can avoid the dilemmas feared by Senator Church: repressive regimes; a U.S. military venture following an initial commitment of economic resources; a growing gap between rich and poor; and domination by the United States. Indeed, because India is the chief recipient of our aid—and the most likely to be hurt by any cut—it must be the prime example in any analysis.

This example of a positive role in U.S. policy for bilateral economic aid is not an isolated one. It is repeated in other areas where the United States continues to have an interest in stable development. Some of the methods need to be changed, and our definition of "self-interest" needs to be broadened; but the goal is still valid.

A disdain for legitimate United States self-interest is particularly evident in Senator Church's criticism of the role of U.S. private investment and trade abroad. It is true that the Export-Import Bank acts primarily to promote U.S. trade, not to aid development. It is also true that the bulk of U.S. development loans provide a subsidy to American business, since they are largely tied to purchases in this country. And it is true that Food for Peace is a form of subsidy to the American farmer. But what of it? These subsidies still help the poor countries develop and, if curtailed, would be replaced by some other form of government support for business and agriculture. If the senator wants to end the subsidy to American business, he will support the President's efforts to get all rich countries to stop tying their aid to their exports. He doesn't need to kill our export and investment promotion programs.

Entirely different, however, is the question of whether U.S. investments in developing countries always help more than they hurt. Abuses are obvious and have been cited by Senator Church. We do face a dilemma in extracting ourselves from exploitative arrangements—as in the case of Chile. But some countries, notably Mexico and several in East Asia, have worked out mutually satisfactory arrangements for a U.S. business role in their development, including increased local participation, control, and progressive divestment of outside ownership. There is nothing inherent to prevent U.S. private investment from earning reasonable profits under equitable arrangements with developing countries.

To be fair to Senator Church, he is not against the transfer of resources to the developing world, as such. For example, he has called for improvements in the terms of trade for poor countries: the ratio of the prices that countries get for their exports to those they pay for imports. This is a worthy objective, but it will require major changes in U.S. policy that are not now apparent, and these will be fought by business interests all the way. In recent years, it has become harder, rather than easier, for poor countries' products to enter the United States. Let us hope Senator Church will take the lead in the Senate to reverse this trend.

## THE ROLE OF MULTILATERAL INSTITUTIONS

Furthermore, Senator Church wants to rely increasingly on international financial institutions like the World Bank. Many experts agree with him; the President has already embraced this concept, as part of the Peterson Report. Unfortunately, the United States is severely limited in the extent to which it can, at this time, channel increased resources through these institutions. As the system currently works—at the insistence of Congress—any major increase in our contributions must be matched by other countries, which they will do only gradually. Instead of simply killing bilateral aid, Senator Church might try persuading his congressional colleagues to let the United States make voluntary, unmatched contributions.

It must be admitted that there is a real danger this would increase our influence in the way loans are granted by the multilateral institutions, thus bringing in some of the dilemmas that the senator sees in bilateral assistance. The Inter-American Development Bank is a good illustration: Because of our overwhelming financial contribution, pressures have built up with Congress for the United States to dominate the Bank's operations.

It is certainly a good idea to "go multilateral." But wanting to do this quickly is really arguing that the United States should curtail drastically the total amount of resources it devotes to development loans. Moreover, many senators and representatives support a bilateral loan program and oppose a multilateral one, precisely because of the matter of U.S. control over how the money is used.

Senator Church may support larger contributions to the multilateral institutions, although he is also concerned with the sheer magnitude of the foreign-aid budget (in commentary following his Senate speech, he cites our balance-of-payments difficulties). Yet, he himself has taken pains to show how little real economic aid we give, and how almost all of it—93 per cent of bilateral aid— is spent in this country. He simply cannot have the argument both ways; nor can he expect to reduce the dilemmas of aid without cost.

He emphasizes the importance of reordering our national priorities—the need to use the money here at home. But it is difficult to argue that the United States—the richest country in the world—cannot afford its proportionate share of an international effort that may be of critical importance to countries that are so much worse off than we. No one will have much sympathy for a people who "poor mouth" with a trillion-dollar economy. It is no idle statistic that we now rank twelfth out of the sixteen wealthiest countries in percentage of GNP devoted to governmental economic aid.

## AMERICAN RESPONSIBILITIES

At heart, what we are deciding now is whether the United States will play its part in meeting international responsibilities toward poor countries. A careful formula for sharing the burden has been agreed upon by the rich countries—a formula on which our government is now seriously in default. We should design a foreign-aid program that has fewer dilemmas. But the question most developing countries ask us is not "How?" but "How much?" And the answer has been: "Very little." In the vote on foreign aid on October 29, 1971, many senators were primarily concerned to shock the Administration into making some major changes in the program—indeed, in its whole foreign policy. This is an honored technique in Washington, and it may work this time. At least, in the long term, there is real value in separating economic from military aid in the appropriations process—as the Senate Foreign Relations Committee wants and as the President has recommended. Even if this results in lower economic aid in the short term, it may be worth it if we can establish a better way of looking at the needs of poor countries. But, without a fundamental commitment to the objectives of economic aid, however these are redefined, this change will only prove another excuse to short-change the poor of the world.

# List of Contributors

ROBERT E. HUNTER is a senior fellow of the Overseas Development Council. He formerly served on the White House staff under President Johnson, taught international relations at the London School of Economics, and was a research associate at the International Institute for Strategic Studies. His publications include *Security in Europe* and *The Soviet Dilemma in the Middle East*.

JOHN E. RIELLY is Executive Director of the Chicago Council on Foreign Relations. Formerly with the Latin American Bureau, Agency for International Development, he was foreign policy assistant to Senator and later Vice-President Hubert H. Humphrey, a consultant in the Office of European and International Affairs of the Ford Foundation, and a senior fellow of the Overseas Development Council. He is the author of *A New Rationale for Development Assistance*.

WILLARD L. THORP is Professor Emeritus at Amherst College and former Director of the Merrill Center for Economics. He was formerly Assistant Secretary of State for Economic Affairs, Chairman of the Development Assistance Committee of the OECD, U.S. Representative to the U.N. Economic and Social Council, and Director of the National Bureau of Economic Research. His publications include *The Reality of Foreign Aid* and *The United States and the Far East* (editor).

SAMUEL P. HUNTINGTON is Frank G. Thomson Professor of Government at Harvard University and a member of the Executive Committee of the Harvard Center for International Affairs. He was a member of President Nixon's Task Force on International Development (the Peterson Committee). He is Editor of the quarterly journal *Foreign Policy*. His many publications include *Political Order in Changing Societies, The Soldier and the State, The Common Defense,* and *Authoritarian Politics in Modern Society.*

HEDLEY BULL is Professor of International Relations, Australian National University. He was formerly Reader in International Relations at the London School of Economics, Director of the Arms Control and Disarmament Research Unit in the Foreign Office (London), and Research Associate at the International Institute for Strategic Studies. His publications include *The Control of the Arms Race.*

JAMES P. GRANT is President of the Overseas Development Council. He was formerly Deputy Assistant Secretary of State for Near East and South Asian Affairs, Director of the AID programs in Turkey and Ceylon, and Assistant Administrator of the Agency for International Development. His publications include *Economic and Business Outlook for the Developing Countries.*

HARALD B. MALMGREN is Deputy Special Representative for Trade Negotiations, with the rank of Ambassador. He was formerly a senior fellow at the Overseas Development Council; he also served as Assistant Special Representative for Trade Negotiations under Presidents Johnson and Nixon, and was head of the Economics Group at the Institute for Defense Analyses. His latest publication is entitled *International Economic Peacekeeping in Phase II.*

LESTER R. BROWN is a senior fellow of the Overseas Development Council. He was formerly adviser on foreign agricultural development to Secretary of Agriculture Orville L. Freeman and administrator of the International Agricultural Development Service of the U.S. Department of Agriculture. His publications include *Man, Land and Food* and *Seeds of Change.*

PETER P. GABRIEL is Principal of McKinsey & Company, Inc., the management consultant firm. He was formerly general manager of the Industrial Consultants Organization, S.A. (Caracas). His publications include *The International Transfer of Corporate Skills.*

JACK N. BEHRMAN is Professor of International Business at the Graduate School of Business Administration, University of North Carolina. He was formerly Visiting Professor, Harvard Business School; Professor of Economics and Business Administration at the University of Delaware; and Assistant Secretary of Commerce for Domestic and International Business. His publications include *National Interests and the Multinational Enterprise* and *U.S. International Business and Governments.*

ROBERT D'A. SHAW is an economist with the International Bank for Reconstruction and Development. He was formerly Assistant Representative of the British Council in Dar-es-Salaam, as Administrator of the British Volunteer Programme, and a research fellow of the Overseas Development Council. His publications include *Jobs and Agricultural Development* and *Rethinking Economic Development.*

DONALD M. FRASER is U.S. Representative (Democratic-Farmer-Labor) from the Fifth District of Minnesota and a member of the House committees on the District of Columbia and Foreign Affairs (Chairman, Subcommittee on International Organizations and Movements). He was formerly chairman of the Democratic Study Group and was an attorney and state senator in Minnesota prior to his election to Congress in 1962. His views on foreign aid have appeared in many periodicals, and he is a principal author and interpreter of Title IX of the Foreign Assistance Act.

FRANK CHURCH is Senior U.S. Senator from Idaho and a member of the Senate committees on Interior and Insular Affairs and Foreign Relations (Chairman, Subcommittee on Western Hemi-

sphere Affairs). He is also Chairman of the Senate Special
Committee on Aging. Before his election to the Senate in 1956,
he was engaged in private law practice. He has written and
lectured widely on problems relating to the U.S. role in the
world today.

# Bibliography

ADLER, JOHN H. (ed.). *Capital Movements & Economic Development*. New York: St. Martin's Press, 1969.

ASHER, ROBERT E. *Development Assistance in the Seventies: Alternatives for the United States*. Washington, D.C.: The Brookings Institution, 1970.

BARNET, RICHARD J. *Can the United States Promote Foreign Development?* Washington, D.C.: Overseas Development Council, July, 1971.

———. *Intervention and Revolution*. New York: World, 1968.

BEHRMAN, JACK N. *National Interests and the Multinational Enterprise*. Englewood Cliffs, N.J.: Prentice-Hall, 1970.

———. *Some Patterns in the Rise of Multinational Enterprise*. Chapel Hill: University of North Carolina School of Business, 1969.

———. *U.S. International Business and Governments*. New York: McGraw-Hill, 1971.

BHAGWATI, JAGDISH N. *Amount and Sharing of Aid*. Washington, D.C.: Overseas Development Council, August, 1970.

———. *The Economics of Underdeveloped Countries*. New York: McGraw-Hill, 1966.

BLACK, CYRIL E. *The Dynamics of Modernization: A Study in Comparative History*. New York: Harper & Row, 1966.

BLAUSTEIN, ARTHUR I., and ROGER R. WOOCK (eds.). *Man Against Poverty: World War III*. New York: Random House, 1968.

BROWN, LESTER R. *Seeds of Change: The Green Revolution and Development in the 1970's*. New York: Praeger (for the Overseas Development Council), 1970.

———. "The Social Impact of the Green Revolution," *International Conciliation*. New York: Carnegie Endowment for International Peace, January, 1971.

BULL, HEDLEY. *The Control of the Arms Race*. New York: Praeger (for the Institute for Strategic Studies), 1961.

CAIRNECROSS, A. K. *Factors in Economic Development*. London: Allen & Unwin, 1962.

CASTEL, HELENE (ed.). *World Development: An Introductory Reader*, New York: Macmillan, 1971.

CHURCH, FRANK. "The U.N. at Twenty-one." Washington, D.C.: U.S. Government Printing Office, 1967.

CLARK, PAUL G. *American Aid for Development*. New York: Praeger (for the Council on Foreign Relations), 1972.

COFFIN, FRANK M. *Witness for Aid*. Boston: Houghton Mifflin, 1964.

COHEN, BENJAMIN J. (ed.). *American Foreign Economic Policy*. New York: Harper & Row, 1968.

DUMONT, RENE, and BERNARD ROSIER. *The Hungry Future*. Translated by R. Linell and R. B. Sutcliffe. New York: Praeger, 1969.

ELDRIDGE, P. J. *The Politics of Foreign Aid in India*. London: Weidenfeld & Nicolson, 1969.

ELLIOTT, CHARLES. *The Development Debate*. London: SCM Press, 1971.

FANON, FRANZ. *The Wretched of the Earth*. New York: Grove Press, 1965.

*Foreign Assistance for the Seventies*. (President Nixon's Message to Congress, September 15, 1970.) Washington, D.C.: Agency for International Development, 1970.

FRANK, CHARLES. *Debt and Terms of Aid*. Washington, D.C.: Overseas Development Council, March, 1970.

FRIEDMANN, W., G. KALMANOFF, and R. MEAGHER. *International Financial Aid*. New York: Columbia University Press, 1966.

GABRIEL, PETER. *The International Transfer of Corporate Skills*. Boston: Harvard Business School, Division of Research, 1967.

GARDNER, RICHARD N., and MAX F. MILLIKAN (eds.). *The Global Partnership: International Agencies and Economic Development*. New York: Praeger, 1968.

GEIGER, THEODORE. *The Conflicted Relationship: The West and the Transformation of Asia, Africa and Latin America*. New York: McGraw-Hill (for the Council on Foreign Relations), 1967.

GOULET, DENIS. *The Cruel Choice: A New Concept in the Theory of Development*. New York: Atheneum, 1971.

——— and MICHAEL HUDSON. *The Myth of Aid: The Hidden Agenda of the Development Reports*. Maryknoll, N.Y.: Orbis Books, 1971.

GRANT, JAMES P. *Economic and Business Outlook for the Developing Countries in the 1970's: Trends and Issues*. Washington, D.C.: Overseas Development Council, August, 1970.

———. "Marginal Men: The Global Unemployment Crisis," *Foreign Affairs*, October, 1971

HEILBRONER, ROBERT L. "The Multinational Corporation and the Nation-State," *The New York Review of Books*, February 11, 1971.

HIRSCHMAN, A. O. *Development Prospects Observed*. Washington, D.C.: The Brookings Institution.

Howe, James. *Distributing the Benefits of Special Drawing Rights Among Nations Rich and Poor.* Washington, D.C.: Overseas Development Council, March, 1972.

Hunter, Guy. *Modernizing Peasant Societies.* London: Oxford University Press, 1969.

Hunter, Robert. *Development Assistance: Why Bother?* Washington, D.C.: Overseas Development Council, December, 1970.

———. "In Defense of Foreign Aid," *The New Republic,* November 20, 1971.

———. *The Soviet Dilemma in the Middle East.* London: Institute for Strategic Studies, 1969.

Huntington, Samuel P. *The Common Defense.* New York: Columbia University Press, 1961.

———. *Political Order in Changing Societies.* New Haven, Conn.: Yale University Press, 1968.

*International Development: Foreign Policy for Canadians.* Ottawa: Queen's Printer for Canada (for the Ministry for External Affairs), 1970.

Jackson, Sarah. *Economically Appropriate Technologies for Developing Countries.* Washington, D.C.: Overseas Development Council, February, 1972.

Jacoby, Neil. *U.S. Aid to Taiwan: A Study of Foreign Aid.* New York: Praeger, 1967.

Jaguaribe, Helio. *Economic & Political Development.* Cambridge, Mass.: Harvard University Press, 1968.

Jalee, Pierre. *The Third World in World Economy.* Translated by Mary Klopper. New York: Monthly Review Press, 1969.

Jaster, Robert. "Foreign Aid and Economic Development: The Shifting Soviet View," *International Affairs,* July, 1969.

Johnson, Harry G. *Economic Policies Toward Less Developed Countries.* (A Brookings Institution Study.) New York: Praeger, 1967.

———. *Trade Strategy for Rich and Poor Nations.* Toronto: University of Toronto Press, 1971.

———. *U.S. Economic Policy Toward the Developing Countries.* Washington, D.C.: Brookings Institution, 1968.

Kaplan, Jacob J. *The Challenge of Foreign Aid.* New York: Praeger, 1967.

Kenen, Peter. *Giant Among Nations.* New York: Harcourt, Brace, 1960.

Kindleberger, Charles P. (ed.). *The International Corporation.* Cambridge, Mass.: MIT Press, 1970.

Lewis, W. A. *The Theory of Economic Growth.* Homewood, Ill.: Irwin, 1955.

LITTLE, I. M. O., and J. M. CLIFFORD. *International Aid.* Chicago: Aldine, 1966.

MACBEAN, ALASTAIR. *Export Instability & Economic Development.* Cambridge, Mass.: Harvard University Press, 1966.

MADDISON, ANGUS. *Economic Progress and Policy in Developing Countries.* London: George Allen & Unwin, 1970.

MALMGREN, HARALD. *International Economic Peacekeeping in Phase II.* New York: Quadrangle Books, 1972.

―――. *Trade for Development.* Washington, D.C.: Overseas Development Council, March, 1971.

MASON, EDWARD S. *Economic Development in India and Pakistan.* Cambridge, Mass.: Harvard University Center for International Affairs, September, 1966.

―――. *Foreign Aid and Foreign Policy.* New York: Harper & Row, 1964.

MICHANEK, ERNST. *The World Development Plan: A Swedish Perspective.* Stockholm: Almquist & Wicksell, 1971.

MIKESELL, RAYMOND. *The Economics of Foreign Aid.* Chicago: Aldine, 1968.

MILLER, J. D. B. *The Politics of the Third World.* New York: Oxford University Press, issued under the auspices of the Royal Institute of International Affairs, 1966.

MILLIKAN, MAX F. *American Foreign Aid: Strategy for the 1970's.* New York: Foreign Policy Association (Headline Series No. 196), August, 1969.

MONTGOMERY, JOHN. *Foreign Aid in International Politics.* Englewood Cliffs, N.J.: Prentice-Hall, 1967.

MORGAN, THEODORE, and GEORGE W. BETZ *Economic Development: Readings in Theory and Practice.* Belmont, Calif.: Wadsworth, 1970.

MORGENTHAU, HANS. "A Political Theory of Foreign Aid," *American Political Science Review,* LVI (June, 1962).

MYRDAL, GUNNAR. *The Challenge of World Poverty: A World Anti-Poverty Program in Outline.* New York: Random House, 1970.

NELSON, JOAN M. *Aid, Influence and Foreign Policy.* New York: Macmillan, 1968.

NOVACK, DAVID E., and ROBERT LEKACHMAN (eds.). *Development and Society: The Dynamics of Economic Change.* New York: St. Martin's Press, 1964.

OWEN, WILFRED. *Distance and Development.* Washington, D.C.: The Brookings Institution, 1968.

OWENS, EDGAR, and ROBERT SHAW. *Development Reconsidered.* Lexington, Mass.: Heath, 1972.

*Partners in Development: Report of the Commission on International Development.* Lester B. Pearson, Chairman. New York: Praeger, 1969.

PETRAS, JAMES. *Politics and Social Forces in Chilean Development.* Berkeley: University of California Press, 1969.

———— and MAURICE ZEITLIN (eds.). *Latin America: Reform or Revolution.* New York: Fawcett World Library, 1968.

PINCUS, JOHN. *Trade, Aid and Development.* New York: McGraw-Hill, 1967.

PREBISCH, RAUL. *Change and Development: Latin America's Great Task.* Washington, D.C.: Inter-American Development Bank, 1970.

RHODES, ROBERT I. (ed.). *Imperialism and Underdevelopment: A Reader.* New York: Monthly Review Press, 1970.

RIELLY, JOHN, and ROBERT HUNTER. "The Development Policy of the Nixon Administration." Washington, D.C.: Overseas Development Council, February, 1971.

————. "A New Rationale for Development Assistance," *World Affairs Quarterly*, Summer, 1971.

ROLFE, SIDNEY, and WALTER DAMM (eds.). *The Multinational Corporation in the World Economy.* New York: Praeger, 1970.

SHAW, ROBERT. *Jobs and Agricultural Development.* Washington, D.C.: Overseas Development Council, November, 1970.

————. *Rethinking Economic Development.* New York: Foreign Policy Association (Headline Series No. 208), December, 1971.

SUFRIN, SIDNEY L. *Technical Assistance: Theory and Guidelines.* Syracuse, N.Y.: Syracuse University Press, 1966.

THORP, WILLARD L. *The New Inflation.* New York: McGraw-Hill, 1959.

————. *The Reality of Foreign Aid.* New York: Praeger (for the Council on Foreign Relations), 1971.

————. *The United States and the Far East.* Englewood Cliffs, N.J.: Prentice-Hall, 1961.

*U.S. Foreign Assistance in the 1970's: A New Approach.* (Report to the President from the Task Force on International Development, March 4, 1970.) Washington, D.C.: Superintendent of Documents, 1970.

VERBIT, GILBERT P. *Trade Agreements for Developing Countries.* New York: Columbia University Press, 1969.

VERNON, RAYMOND. *Sovereignty at Bay: The Multinational Spread of U.S. Enterprises.* New York: Basic Books, 1971.

WARD, BARBARA. *The Lopsided World.* New York: Norton, 1968.

————. *The Rich Nations and the Poor Nations.* New York: Norton, 1962.

————, LENORE D'ANJOU, and J. D. RUNNALS. *The Widening Gap: Development in the 1970's.* New York: Columbia University Press, 1971.

# Index